I ACCUSE DE GAULLE

I ACCUSE
DE GAULLE

I
ACCUSE
DE GAULLE

HENRI DE KERILLIS

TRANSLATED FROM THE FRENCH BY HAROLD ROSENBERG

HARCOURT, BRACE AND COMPANY, NEW YORK

Contents

Note to the American Reader

American readers ought to bear in mind that this book was written primarily for Frenchmen. Many of its details are peculiar to French life, to French history and tradition, to French sensibility— it seemed to me that these should be retained. So many Americans are eager to have a better grasp of the contents of the French mind. So many American soldiers were startled and disturbed witnesses, both in Africa and in France itself, of the birth and first movements of De Gaullism. In order better to understand what they have seen, they need a familiarity with the inner workings of the French attitude.

Besides, De Gaullism is connected with a whole complex of international phenomena; it has already had its international repercussions and will have others in the future, and it ought to be known in its essence and its specific design. The French text has therefore been followed to the letter in the translation.

Preface

"And ye shall know the truth, and the truth shall make you free."

GOSPEL OF ST. JOHN, VIII, 32.

THE author of this book is an exile, weak and isolated, grief-stricken, with nothing left him but his conscience and the certainty that he is fighting for the truth.

The man he is attacking has raised himself by means of the political swirls of the war to the pinnacle of honor, fame and power: he is the undisputed master of France. He has enthusiastic supporters in countries other than his own. He has at his command overwhelming resources, the whole apparatus of a great State, with which to beat down those who dare stand in his way.

Why then have I written this book?

For one reason, strange and paradoxical though it may seem, to defend myself against an accusation. Certain French newspapers have denounced me as a traitor. A member of the French government has taken up this accusation on his own account. He was misled by an odious and diabolical propaganda. In this horrible war, men, like nations, have often been turned thus from their true friends and hurled against one another. The havoc wrought by lies, calumnies, psychological poisons, has backed up the work of tanks, guns, and firing squads.

I continued throughout the entire occupation writing incessantly for a French newspaper in New York, proclaiming the sufferings and the martyrdom of France defiled by the Germans, denouncing those French traitors who were collaborating with them, and hailing the heroism of those who went on fighting.

I had belonged to the vanguard of the French Resistance at a time when there was only a handful of us in France to fight against German ideas and the spies and traitors in the pay of Germany, and to denounce Hitlerite lusts, preparations, and plans. It was precisely because I belonged to the first wave of anti-German and anti-Hitler fighters that I was forced to leave France with the first wave of exiles. I was the only one out of 525 non-Communist deputies to vote in the Chamber of Deputies against the French capitulation at Munich in 1938; the only one to denounce, from the tribune of the Chamber and every day in my Paris newspaper, the work of the Abetzes, the Brinons, the Déats, and the Doriots; the only one to name Marshal Pétain in the middle of the war, six months before the capitulation, as the man who would be chosen to negotiate with Germany. On October 22, 1939, I wrote in *L'Epoque:*

An effort is being made to persuade Marshal Pétain that he ought to resign himself to accepting the leadership of a cabinet which would include the most notorious defeatists. According to the conspirators, the old marshal would then play a role similar to that of Hindenburg opening the door to Hitler in a moment of discouragement. Such an idea, needless to say, could never have sprung from a French mind.

It was these activities that led General de Gaulle to cable me in December, 1941:

You are a loyal Frenchman. You were right, you are still right.

And to write me in January, 1942:

Why doesn't a man like you—with such gifts, attainments and reputation, and who has seen so clearly in so many matters—play a more prominent part? I had hoped to see you start a French newspaper in the United States which would help me. Is that out of the question?

I had been obliged to flee from France at the time of the armistice just as the French police, acting upon orders from the Gestapo, was about to lay hands on me. Driven from my country as the mortal enemy of the Germans and of those who made common cause with them, deprived of my French citizenship by Marshal Pétain, of my Legion of Honor and other decorations won on the battlefields of 1914-1918, stripped of my possessions—am I a traitor to be called to account along with men like Déat and Laval?

I was a passionate, enthusiastic De Gaullist in June, 1940.

I called for unity under this French general who had sworn to continue the war to the end at the side of the Allies and to purge in battle a spirit corrupted by politics.

In January, 1942, I was one of the founders of the French De Gaullist newspaper, *Pour la Victoire,* published in New York. The articles I wrote for it aroused considerable interest, and General de Gaulle was moved to cable me from London in December of that year:

I have read your splendid articles. You are filling the role I had imagined for you. I have always thought you would be the Maurice Barrès and the De Mun of this war.

Despite distance and obstacles, my fervent appeals in behalf of General de Gaulle, during the time I was a De Gaullist, were heard and understood in France. My own son responded to them. At great risk, he managed to escape from occupied Paris and joined General de Gaulle in November, 1942. He became a lieutenant in a parachutist group, and was dropped into France. Wounded, he was betrayed by the Vichy militia and fell into the hands of the Germans. The Gestapo tortured and murdered him.

Does the French Minister of Foreign Affairs accuse me of having been the enemy of my only son, who was a hero and martyr of the French Resistance?

I can only quote for him one of the last letters my son wrote to me before he went to his death:

Father, I thank you for what you have done. I thank you for being a De Gaullist before De Gaulle, with De Gaulle, after De Gaulle.

Yes, I was a De Gaullist even before De Gaulle in my prewar struggles. And I was a De Gaullist with De Gaulle until March, 1943. Then I renounced De Gaullism.

For five months General de Gaulle had been refusing to go to Tunisia and fight beside General Giraud against the German armies of Von Arnim at a time when those armies were endangering all of French North Africa and threatening to push the Allies into the sea. I had seen De Gaulle's representatives in New York, in carrying out his orders, under circumstances to be described later, attempt to induce the crew of the *Richelieu* to desert, just as that magnificent battleship was about to leave for action in the Atlantic—and they did succeed in removing the gunners from a merchantman which, as a result, was sunk by the Germans. I realized then that all De Gaulle's acts were directed not toward war, but toward politics and the seizure of power for his own purposes.

And I was a De Gaullist after De Gaulle.

Yes, for I wanted to remain faithful to the ideal of June, 1940, even after De Gaulle had abandoned that ideal—faithful to the principle of war to the end rather than of politics to the end—faithful to a single thought, the liberation of France, and indifferent to personal political aspirations which had nothing whatsoever to do with that liberation. I wished to remain faithful to the mandate given me by the French people; faithful to their legal institutions until they could change themselves in the established way. I refused to join in the division of honors and jobs, perquisites and portfolios, distributed among upstarts of the defeat while forty million Frenchmen suffered and bled under the heel of the oppressor.

A De Gaullist after De Gaulle?

Yes, when I saw that both a tragic fatality and a ruthless logic were compelling him to behave no longer as an ally, but often as an enemy of the liberators of France.

In exile I watched America's prodigious war effort. I saw the miracle of its production: the power of its organizing and creative ability; its military genius adapting itself simultaneously to the different wars of the air, the sea, and the land, and far surpassing the achievements of the old military castes of Europe; the proofs of its unselfishness, generosity, and heroism. . . . And from the letters which General de Gaulle wrote me, from the propaganda in his newspapers, from actions performed during months and years, I realized that conflict between America and De Gaulle was inevitable. While America was giving lavishly of her blood and her money for the great democratic ideal of human liberty, General de Gaulle was inclining more and more toward a neo-fascism that was the very thing America had set out to destroy.

Only the United States could liberate and save France. But General de Gaulle was unwilling to admit this. Even on D-Day when the Americans landed on the Normandy beaches, he refused in his radio "Appeal to the French People" to acknowledge their sacrifice and heroism.

France, in the future, cannot recover her ruined material strength without the help of America. Nor can she renew her moral strength except in an atmosphere of morality composed of love and gratitude toward her Allies, particularly toward America, which set her free. And this, too, General de Gaulle has denied. In London, in Algiers, in Paris, wherever he has gone, he has left behind him a trail of mistrust, ingratitude, and hostility toward America.

This book attacks not only a man, but a legend. It assails mighty powers—namely, the weighty forces of hope, illusion, phantasy, romanticism, fanaticism, propaganda, mystification, and lies. It declares war on that almost divine realm through which pass one after the other the false demigods—those symbolic men who rise to prominence in the apotheosis of beguiled and misled souls only to vanish afterward in catastrophes and maledictions.

This is a truthful book: the texts quoted, the deeds recorded, the facts related—all are true. It was written in the belief that by truth alone must the future be built and history set on its course. Even if at first it sometimes produces bitter disappointment and bewilderment, in the end truth always triumphs, because it is the great light without which the poor intelligence of mankind would only go adrift.

A civilization, a decadent world, is going down in pain, convulsions and death. A new civilization, a new world, is about to be born. In the pangs of death are intermingled the pangs of childbirth. Compared with the magnitude of such events, this book is a small thing; but it concerns the life and destiny of a great country. If France deceives herself too long she will drag other countries down with her into the night of error. Though he pay dearly for it and suffer much, it is necessary that this witness should speak.

I ACCUSE
DE GAULLE

1. A Good Beginning

War is less onerous than slavery.

VAUVENARGUES

To the degree that man's judgment can anticipate that of history, we can be sure that France's armistice with the Germans was a mistake that worked against both the honor and the best interests of France. Against its honor—because France had asked for and received from Britain a formal agreement according to which both countries pledged themselves never to make peace without the consent of the other. Against the interests of France—because the armistice was an obvious trap set by the Germans to neutralize the undefeated and practically invincible French fleet while the Germans attacked England; also to prevent the French generals from mobilizing in North Africa, with the aid of Britain, an imperial army of 500,000 to a million men.

The armistice was contrary to the honor and interests of France because if Germany granted an armistice at all it was only for the reason that it found it of value to its armed forces, its ambitions, and its conquests; and it was therefore the duty of the French government to resist to the end—to the bitter end, to the last limit of human endurance—the plans of its mortal and implacable enemy. There is now absolutely no doubt that if Germany had not foreseen these advantages it would never have halted its armies on the roads of Toulouse, Perpignan, Marseilles, and Toulon. Was it from pity or from love that it built at Vichy a tiny artificial France in order to create in the French mind and in the whole world an illusion of independence?

It was contrary to the honor and the interests of France, because the armistice was not, despite all appearances, merely a military event. It meant the definite acceptance, without appeal, of the law of the conqueror who was waging war in the name of a revolutionary ideology and of a barbaric philosophy of enslaving the defeated. The signers of the armistice thus accepted in advance the disappearance of France.

It has been maintained that if the armistice had been refused the German armies would have pursued the French armies as far as North Africa, that they would easily have defeated them, and that the Mediterranean would then also have been lost for the British and, later, for the Americans. It is therefore concluded that the armistice preserved an essential pledge of future victory.

What a paradoxical and inconsistent argument! Firstly, the Germans did not have a chance in June, 1940, of crossing the Mediterranean patrolled by the British and French fleets, any more than they had a chance of crossing the English Channel. They had no ships, no landing equipment. They had no large groups of parachutists. The point of North Africa closest to them was Gibraltar, and four years of war proved that they did not want to and were unable to attack Gibraltar. They were not able to and did not want to venture toward the south, toward Africa, into remote and savage territory, when their whole strategy rested on lightning attacks to the north and to the east, against England and Russia.

And besides, even if it were true that, owing to changes in the situation, unforeseeable in June, 1940, the armistice had indirectly provided some advantages to the Allied cause, these advantages could not be credited to the signers of the armistice because they did not enter into their calculations. On the contrary, they justified their surrender by the conviction that England would fall in the next few weeks and that Germany had already won the war. This belief is in fact the only excuse they can offer posterity; for if at the supreme and decisive moment they had withdrawn from England the help of the fleet and the help of the North African army without being certain of British defeat, what excuse could they have?

Everyone knows their main arguments: "The African army," they say, "had neither guns nor ammunition."

That's true. But in England the British Army, too, was without guns or ammunition. In both cases supremacy at sea protected the disabled armies and guaranteed the time they needed to equip themselves with the aid of British and American industry.

"We have," they also say, "spared France a good deal of suffering."

That is not true. The armistice brought with it a train of humiliations and nameless misfortunes, and finally helped along the execution of the conqueror's slave program. The tragic fate of France can be compared to that of Belgium, Holland, Czechoslovakia, or Poland. In what way did it differ from theirs? In none. All the conquered countries found themselves in the end in the same frightful position. The delays, the temporizings, or the hesitations of the conqueror, depended on opportunist considerations or cynical calculations. The armistice did not spare France a grain of misery. On the contrary, it deprived her of the only consolation which might have comforted, sustained, and united her in her adversity: that of adding a new glorious page to her history, of having fallen while preserving her honor.

Marshal Pétain and General Weygand are the men chiefly responsible for the armistice. Too old to recognize the ruthless character of an apocalyptic revolutionary war, they judged the military situation according to the historical precedents of 1815 and 1870. Overwhelmed by their defeat, they could not conceive that it would not sweep England away also. They saw only its "contemptible little army," as the German generals did in 1914. Besides, General Weygand was obsessed by the fear of a social revolution—without realizing that such a revolution could not break out under the bellies of German tanks—and he wanted to retain a part of the Army to prevent another Paris Commune. As for Marshal Pétain, he was sunk in the absurd illusion that the Germans respected and esteemed him, that his presence alone would assuage their terrible hunger, that the armistice would give him a chance to become the shield and protector of prostrate France.

Neither of these men had the slightest notion of the incalculable effects of their capitulation. Senile representatives of a superannuated military caste, whose imagination was grounded on the plan of the Maginot Line—that is, on the thousand-year-old conception of the Great Wall of China—typical representatives of the tired, worn out and decadent bourgeois, unwilling to make sacrifices or a supreme effort, they chose the solution that seemed easiest and most logical, without an inkling of the dreadful mechanism into which they were thrusting France. They did not even surmise that by a fatal gravitation the armistice would lead to collaboration and, consequently, to the rapid moral, political, and social decay of the country. Still more surprising, they did not even grasp that to conclude an armistice with the Germans meant to sign one also with all the Frenchmen who had joined forces with the Germans. Marshal Pétain condemned himself automatically not only to shake hands with Hitler but also with the traitor Brinon, the traitor Déat, the traitor Doriot, the miserable Laval, and to bestow honors on all of them. He condemned himself to throw the prison gates open to scoundrels and to shut them upon virtuous men, upon the best sons of France who rose up against the conqueror.

Here we touch on one of the most poignant aspects of the drama of the armistice. For even if collaboration had been necessary or justified in order to "fool the Germans" or to "gain time," it was not necessary that a Marshal of France, symbol of the defense of Verdun, symbol of desperate heroism, guardian of the reputation of the Army, should put himself in a position to perform political acts which would confuse and shock people's conscience. If all was lost, there was still honor to be saved. Marshal Pétain put himself in the position of compromising and losing it.

The rebellion of General de Gaulle in June, 1940, must be 'seen within this context. The honor of France demanded that a soldier—and soldiers—should refuse to respond to the call of the armistice. It was necessary that there be taken up somewhere, as on the battlefield of Bazeilles, the famous "last stand" where the final survivors fight to the death. And, indubitably, such is the original image that Frenchmen have of General de Gaulle; a simple, fine, and pure image which affected them profoundly, cleansing them of an indelible stain and relieving their horrible burden of shame. This image showed itself later to be a false one; but it explains, all the same, a great upsurge of the French soul.

Beyond question, therefore, General de Gaulle was correct in condemning the disastrous armistice negotiated by Marshal Pétain. But even if Pétain had not been wrong in arranging this armistice, even if we accept his supporters' argument of "the inevitable act," even if we grant the absurd theory that he saved France from suffering, that does not detract from the admirable gesture of De Gaulle. France needed a general who would rise up in the midst of total disaster, announce his faith in victory, and take the leadership of the resistance movement—and France was fortunate in having such a general.

General de Gaulle's merits have been discussed from the point of view of the ease with which he could "play the hero on the radio without personal risk." It is true that the British definitely made matters easier for him. General Spears, whom Churchill sent to Paris as "observer and personal ambassador," had promised General de Gaulle that he would be responsible for the safety of his wife and four children, and had guaranteed him, come what may, the pay and retirement pension of a British brigadier general, as well as the privilege of British citizenship should he be unable to return to France. The same offers were quickly extended to all De Gaulle volunteers by a clause in the agreement between Churchill and De Gaulle, dated July 1, 1940:

The volunteers will receive pay on a basis to be settled separately by agreement between General de Gaulle and the Departments concerned.

The volunteers and their dependents will be granted pensions and other benefits in respect of the disablement or death of the volunteers on a basis to be settled by separate agreement between General de Gaulle and the Departments concerned.

His Majesty's Government are willing to afford special facilities to such volunteers to acquire British nationality. . . .

It is therefore true that General de Gaulle obtained exceptional advantages and guarantees for himself and his family and for his comrades and their families. But that detracts little from the value of his action.

To estimate the amount of credit which, in all fairness, is due De Gaulle, we might best consider the problem from another point of view: would any other French general, placed in similar circumstances, in as close touch with the British and subjected to their offers and their pressure, have acted as vigorously, swiftly, and decisively? But let us remember, though, that for years De Gaulle had been in open revolt against the theories of the General Staff, that he professed ideas which his superior officers considered revolutionary, and that he was, consequently, particularly predisposed to an act of insubordination—not to say overt rebellion—which would have been impossible to most of the other generals.

De Gaulle's act had immediate consequences. His words may not have been heard or understood by the great majority of Frenchmen, but their effect was far-reaching. He spoke a language vibrant with faith in the destiny of France: it urged revolt not only against Germany, but against the weak, the timid, the cowards, the would-be intellectuals, the decadents and the pontiffs of a dying age, who were preparing consciously to become the accomplices of the enemy. He brought a surge of hope. He sowed in the hearts of men the seeds of a future rich harvest of heroism. De Gaulle's very name, so like that of ancient Gaul, out of which France sprang, suggested an element of predestination, which added to the symbolism of his magnificent, romantic gesture. The fact that his face, his bearing, his personality were unknown to the French and that his voice alone came to them over the air waves, lent to his speeches a heavenly quality and surrounded them with mystery. History will note that the De Gaulle legend was largely a creation of radio—perhaps the first great political achievement of radio in the history of the world.

In any event, it is undeniable that the name of General de Gaulle, his action, and his words formed a rallying point in French consciousness in the midst of terrible trials; and this of itself entitles him to historical recognition.

Unfortunately, the familiar mental phenomena, which, in all periods agitate uprooted exiles, have exaggerated, distorted, and exalted General de Gaulle's role out of all reality.

In this tragic war, the most appalling and cruel of all wars, which has shed torrents of blood and, above all, oceans of tears, a general whose big achievement was produced in London, on the radio, out of danger, surrounded by his family, in comfort, in an armchair, suddenly became a colossus of glory, a demigod before whom all must bow down or else be accused of treason. To say that General de Gaulle has experienced none of the material or spiritual sufferings by which forty million Frenchmen have been tortured is not to disparage him; on the contrary, it is merely to state the fact that to him alone, among millions, defeat brought only an easy personal success, the caress of enormous fame. It is also true that although he never set foot on a battlefield, never incurred the responsibilities of military leadership, he has been depicted as the incarnation of all sorrow, all agony, all the desperate heroism of other men. He himself was swiftly caught up in that strange state of being; like an actor who is carried away by the part he was playing, or a self-hypnotized mystic, he turned into an unpredictable and disconcerting personage. On his desk in London he placed a vase containing some of the soil of France, and would show it to his friends as the source of his inspiration. Framed between portraits of Joan of Arc and Napoleon, he would receive visitors from every part of the world, men like Wendell Willkie, and during the course of the interview he would slowly turn his eyes on these pictures, absorbing them in contemplation, as if a sort of mystical communion existed between him and them.

In short, General de Gaulle overlooked no move that might excite and impress his followers, that might create about him a kind of supernatural atmosphere, until it was impossible for one to miss the orchestrations of a stirring and frenzied propaganda campaign, designed to place over his head the halo of a divinity and surround him with enthusiasm, adoration, fanaticism, and madness.

A British Member of Parliament told me that one day De Gaulle had a particularly lively conversation with Churchill in the course of which the Prime Minister criticized sharply certain of the general's attitudes and phrases which seemed to place him on a superhuman plane and prevented calm discussion of diplomatic and military affairs.

"You tend to forget," De Gaulle replied, his eyes blazing with anger, "that when you talk to me, you are talking to France!"

The old Englishman drew himself up, took his cigar out of his mouth, looked at De Gaulle and flung at him harshly:

"General, you are a Frenchman and you may represent certain other Frenchmen. But you are not the whole of France."

De Gaulle got up and, without a word, walked out.

2. A Bad Course

The mask drops, the man remains. And the hero vanishes.
                                                        J. B. ROUSSEAU

GENERAL DE GAULLE'S magnificent appeal to the French nation on June 18, 1940, was the appeal of a soldier. Both in letter and in spirit it meant:

"I am a military leader who remains on the battlefield which the others have deserted. I appeal to Frenchmen everywhere in the world to join me in a fight to the finish. I myself will lead them into battle. If it be my good fortune, alone or with the help of our Allies, to liberate portions of French territory, I shall establish a military regime there until the liberation of France and the restoration of a civil government. Under all circumstances, therefore, I shall behave strictly as a soldier, and to this effect I take my oath before the flag."

That, beyond doubt, is the sense in which all Frenchmen understood De Gaulle's appeal, both those who responded to it and those who shrugged it aside or even condemned it. And at once a handful of men who were to be the vanguard of the great French revolt against defeat and dishonor hastened from all corners of the earth to the London refuge where the torch and the soul of immortal France had miraculously reappeared. For all Frenchmen, then, as for the world at large, the beginning of "De Gaullism" was military in character, and nothing but military, its stark beauty unmarred by the slightest blemish of politics. And De Gaulle himself did everything in his power to confirm, emphasize, and hail this purely military character of his movement.

On June 17, 1940, in London, he said to me:

"I shall form a committee to widen the idea of resistance, to spread the idea of a fight to the finish to the entire French population, so that old men, women, children, intellectuals, workingmen, and peasants shall realize that it is their duty to get into the fight. Politics, which divides people, must be kept out, and the hatred of Germany unite us. I reject politics so that the fight may go on. . . ."

A few days later De Gaulle replied to letters filled with anxious questions that were pouring in from all parts of the world. Here is one he wrote to Baron de Benoist, President of the French National Committee in Egypt:

London, July 24, 1940

Mr. President:

I am sending you herewith an official letter covering the task I am asking you to perform in furthering our country's cause. But besides, I wish to tell you personally how much I appreciate your attitude and your action.

Make sure to tell everyone that our movement is above and beyond all politics and politicians. Those who expect something different must be either ignorant, malicious, or self-interested.

Our morale is excellent. Let us close ranks, keep firmly united, and go forward together.

With sincere regards,

Charles de Gaulle

To this letter was attached an official message to the National Committee in Egypt. Here the general again affirmed:

I wish to make it clear that my sole aim is the liberation of French territory, the defense of the Empire and the re-establishment of national freedom.

The military force I am organizing is not concerned with politics. Under my command are officers, soldiers, technicians, industrialists. They have but one thought—to free France.

On July 1, 1940, General de Gaulle and Prime Minister Churchill signed an agreement which constitutes the official charter of the

Free French movement. This agreement stipulates that General de Gaulle shall receive supreme command "of a French army composed of volunteers." On August 7 De Gaulle wrote Churchill acknowledging receipt of a memorandum concerning that French army.

> 4 Carlton Gardens
> London, S. W. 1
> August 7, 1940

My dear Prime Minister:

You have been good enough to send me a memorandum dealing with the organization, employment and conditions of service of the forces of French volunteers which is at present being constituted under my command.

In the capacity in which I have been recognized by His Majesty's Government in the United Kingdom as leader of all Frenchmen wherever they may be, who rally to me in support of the Allied cause, I hereby inform you that I accept this memorandum. It will be considered as constituting an agreement concluded between us in regard to these conditions.

I am glad that on this occasion His Majesty's Government have taken an opportunity to state that they are determined, when victory has been gained by the Allied arms, to secure the full restoration of the independence and greatness of France.

For my part, I confirm to you that the French force now in process of constitution is intended to take part in operations against the common enemy—Germany, Italy or any other hostile foreign power—including the defence of French territories and territories under French mandate, and the defence of British territories and communications and territories under British mandate.

> Yours sincerely,
>
> C. de Gaulle

This is an extremely interesting letter.

In the first place General de Gaulle notes that the British Government is "determined to secure the full restoration of the independence and greatness of France." This realistic acknowledgment can mean but one thing: that it is henceforth up to England, the only country still fighting, to restore the former greatness of France. A handful of Frenchmen rallying around a brigadier general in revolt are compelled to rely on British loyalty, British promises, British honor—a position at once painful and magnificent. For that handful of Frenchmen and that general know that alone they can accomplish nothing except to go on fighting and, if need be, die. Why then should they bother about politics? Politics can be forgotten so long as France is captive. Time enough to talk of politics when England and her future Allies have liberated France and restored her to her former position.

De Gaulle also "confirms" that the French force being organized will take part, *under his command,* in operations against the enemy and in the defense of such French or British territories as are not yet in German hands.

Now, what happened during the last two weeks of August and the first ten days of September, 1940? It is plain that some of those who had gathered around De Gaulle presented a line of argument that strongly influenced him and quickly brought about profound changes in his point of view. They pointed out that France's downfall had been accompanied by the collapse of the institutions of the Third Republic; they compared the situation to that of September, 1870, when the French Empire disintegrated after the surrender at Sedan. France was now, consequently, in a state of "political vacuum"—the constitution was suspended. Hence, if he, General de Gaulle were only clever enough, and sufficiently daring and ambitious, he could fill that vacuum, regenerate French politics, and become one of the great architects of history, marked by Destiny.

This sort of talk troubled the general, but it also excited and attracted him, for it fitted in with his own dreams. He did not know the people who were promoting these views. He was not aware that the most intense and eloquent of them, a certain Captain Passy, now a colonel whose real name is De Wavrain, had been before the war a member of the Cagoulards.* He had no notion that these young revolutionaries—consciously or unconsciously— were supporters of antidemocratic doctrines current long before the

* See Chapter 3.

collapse of France; or that all of them, even those who were sincerely anti-German, had long been steeped in the troubled atmosphere in which Nazi ideas flourished.

And very quickly, almost without transition, De Gaulle changed his tone, his language, his thoughts, his goal, without anyone about him suspecting it, save that small group of young and eloquent tempters—naturally, it would not have occurred to those Frenchmen who had come to join him from across the seas.

And thus General de Gaulle formed his "National Committee" in September, 1940, and took advantage of the occasion, amid silence and mystery, to demand that the British recognize it as "the political power" representing France.

The Foreign Office was much perturbed and did not reply.

On October 27, 1940, De Gaulle issued from Brazzaville a "manifesto" whose language sounds the new note:

> No French Government now exists. The organization at Vichy which uses this name is unconstitutional and under orders of the invader. A new power must assume responsibility for the direction of the French war effort. I shall exercise my powers in the name of France and solely for its defense.
>
> C. de Gaulle

What did De Gaulle mean by this? Actually, there was still a French government. One might hate that government, one might despise it, one might insist that it ruled only with the consent of the enemy, one might rebel against it, but one could not deny its existence. In the first place, that government had received its authority from the National Assembly. Also, it controlled the administration of France and what was left of the Army, the Navy, and the Air Corps. It retained full authority over the Empire. Moreover, that government was still recognized by all neutral governments. Soviet Russia, the United States, China, Brazil—all had their ambassadors at Vichy. And though Great Britain had withdrawn her own ambassador, she had requested Canada to keep her envoy M. Pierre Dupuy there. Undoubtedly, therefore, a French government did exist—and to assert that it did not and to create a "New Power" was to rush headlong into political adventuring.

It was on October 27, 1940, that General de Gaulle performed the first public and official act that completely altered the exclusively military direction of his movement. This took place four months after the magnificent order of the day of June 18, 1940, three months after his repeated promises that he "would never play politics" and two months after the Churchill-De Gaulle memorandum concerning the organization of a French military force in London under the command of General de Gaulle. From now on actual military command of the Fighting French was permanently abandoned in favor of winning the New Power.

De Gaulle renewed forthwith his demand that the British government recognize the New Power he had created. His manner was at once pleading, insistent, and almost threatening. The British Minister for Foreign Affairs flatly turned him down with the following reply:

His Majesty's Government are prepared to regard the Free French National Committee as representing all Frenchmen, wherever they may be, who rally to the Free French movement in support of the Allied cause and to treat with the Committee on all questions involving their collaboration with the Free French movement and with overseas territories which place themselves under the Free French. In making this communication, I should make it clear that His Majesty's Government are not to be regarded as expressing any views as to the various constitutional and juridical questions involved. In particular, while His Majesty's Government would be happy to maintain their representation with the Free French, they could not accredit a diplomatic representative to you or receive a diplomatic representative accredited by you, since this would involve your recognition as a sovereign state.

Thus Lord Halifax, British Minister for Foreign Affairs, was clear, formal, and explicit. He was quite willing to recognize the existence of a Free French movement outside of subjugated France. But he refused to accede to the extravagant demands of a French brigadier general who claimed to represent France and desired to exchange ambassadors with His Majesty, the King of Great Britain.

This was the beginning of a bitter conflict which was to continue throughout the war—a conflict which was to bring General de Gaulle into violent opposition first to England, then to America, and was constantly to disturb the harmony between England and the United States.

From that time onward De Gaulle ceased to be a soldier. He lost interest in his "armed forces" and neglected his command. He gave up the actual fight for liberation. He was dominated by a single idea, a piercing, obsessive and stormy idea, the idea of the New Power whose leader he would be. The problem of liberation became confused in his mind with the problem of setting up the New Power and little by little, slipped into the background. And the idea of the New Power itself underwent changes, constantly being altered and amplified, until at last De Gaulle suddenly uttered the words, "the Fourth Republic," and announced that he would be its president. The military undertaking of an obscure brigadier general in exile in London seemed to him childish and insignificant compared with the great political adventure shaping itself on the horizon. A usurper, a pretender, stood revealed. Thus politics, banished from the military movement, returned with a rush. It returned muddled by the personal equation and by human ambition, and unadorned by any great ideology.

Our entire history, all our political traditions and especially our patriotic intuitions teach us that in France a soldier may never become a politician—much less a statesman. This is an almost immutable law of French national life. No country has produced greater generals than France, but none of those generals has ever been called either by a monarchy or a republic to play a dominant role outside of military affairs. French governments have chosen their leaders among financiers and cardinals, aristocrats and commoners, tax collectors and comptrollers, famous lawmakers and orators, never among soldiers. The outstanding exception to this rule was the Napoleonic adventure—but Napoleon in particular was a usurper, who maintained his position only by producing in France an extraordinary delirium of heroism and glory, and who finally went down all the same in catastrophic collapse. Another example is General de Cavaignac, hero for a day of barricades and tragedy. The French people cast him aside in a most significant plebiscite. Then there was Marshal MacMahon, mounting to power on the ruins of a great defeat; once again the people rejected such leadership. After the famous challenge hurled at him from the depths of the popular mind: "Submit or resign," he handed in his resignation. And finally, there was Marshal Pétain. . . .

The Third Republic went so far in its deliberate determination to prevent soldiers—even the most famous—from entering political life, as to refuse them their right to exercise citizenship privileges. A military man 'could not vote. Marshal Foch died without ever casting a vote or expressing his opinion regarding the terms of the peace won by his genius.

There is nothing more stirring than the oath the young Saint-Cyrien makes to himself * the day he puts on the blue shako and enters upon his office: "My country, you give me a sword and I thank you. I swear to draw it only to protect and defend you. As long as I wear it, I shall abstain from the turmoil of public life. While in uniform I shall never enter a place where affairs of State are debated. I shall never go to the polls where your fate is decided. My country, I shall be worthy of your trust to my last breath. I shall never abuse the power which you entrust to me. I ask of life no greater glory than to die for you, and I want none of the public honors others may claim of you. . . ."

De Gaulle, too, took such an oath.

The attitude it expresses toward the role of military men in politics is of the very essence of democratic doctrine. England, as everyone knows, carefully separates civil and military authority; she actually goes farther than France in this respect. Even in time of war an English general never becomes Secretary of War, an admiral Secretary of the Navy, any soldier—even a Marshal—head of the government. Wellington is the only exception.

* St. Cyr is the French Military Academy.

The same practice and the same instinctive reactions prevail in the United States. In April, 1944, when the presidential election campaign got under way, the Republicans considered for a moment nominating Genéral MacArthur, the man who saved Australia, a legendary hero in the eyes of the American people. At once public opinion protested with surprising vehemence. On April 15 the New York *Herald Tribune,* a leading conservative Republican organ, published a significant article:

To invest any general now commanding American armies anywhere in the world with the qualifications for the Presidency requires an act of sheer faith—or, to put it more bluntly, wishful thinking. It is a dangerous form of phantasy because it introduces political complications where they may be most fatal—on the battlefront, because it might exchange a useful officer for a bad President, because it might create in this country that friction between military and civil authorities which has been the bane of many European and South American countries, because it shows a tendency to think in terms of personalities and symbols instead of the usual hard-headed American insistence on concrete issues. Quite apart from General MacArthur's unknown views on domestic and foreign affairs or on the prospect of his candidacy, those who are promoting that candidacy are doing a disservice to him and to the country.

Yet in the possibility foreseen by the *Herald Tribune*—and so vigorously rejected—the general in question would have taken office by legal means. MacArthur would have run for the Presidency on the same strictly constitutional basis as General de Cavaignac when he sought the votes of the French people, and Marshal MacMahon when he invoked the "16th of May." *

The case of General de Gaulle, on the other hand, is that of a general taking advantage of a state of war and of his country's misfortunes to embark upon an illegal seizure of political power. Obviously, Marshal Pétain had created a precedent. But at least Pétain was no longer on active duty. A retired officer, a former ambassador, an ex-cabinet minister, his military status was of secondary importance. Even so it was enough to trouble the conscience of the

---

* Date of abortive *coup d'état,* 1877.

French Army and to do further harm to France. Moreover, Pétain had been installed in office by the National Assembly, whereas De Gaulle was a soldier and on active duty, a soldier who had voluntarily taken his place on the battlefield for a fight to the finish and had rallied other soldiers there; yet he abandoned that battlefield, deserted those soldiers, to grasp at a New Power. The effect could only be to deepen the confusion of conscience and do further harm to France. . . .

This will be made plain in this book, but what will not be visible are the effects which the "De Gaulle case" will have on the future development of French life. The day when a general took advantage of events and of his military power and prestige to usurp a political role, a dangerous precedent was set. Modern France has engaged in three cruel wars—1870, 1914, 1939—full of confidence in her army and without ever imagining that she might have to fear unhealthy ambitions in her generals. That confidence has now been destroyed, that sense of security is lost. From now on the French people will no longer suffer the torments of war without wondering anxiously whether the men to whom they have entrusted the sword may not draw it against them to further their own ambitions.

In the course of his extended adventure, of his long victorious struggle for power, has De Gaulle sometimes felt a twinge of doubt, anxiety, remorse? Perhaps— We shall see that on one occasion he promised that if General Weygand, commander of the Army in Africa, re-entered the war "he would place himself under his orders." When General Giraud escaped from Germany and arrived in Vichy, the same promise was made to him. Again in Algiers, where De Gaulle spent long days contemplating one of the world's most beautiful landscapes from the heights of the Villa des Oliviers, he had the following conversation with a correspondent of the *New York Sun*:

"Is it true that you are thinking of becoming President of the Fourth French Republic?"

"I have never given it a thought. You are the first to mention it to me. . . . Why, no! I am not a professional politician. The moment France is freed of the last German, I shall retire from politics."

This reply, reminiscent of a great Roman, Cincinnatus, was apparently only a propaganda trick intended to dissipate the doubts of oversensitive observers. For two days later, on October 26, 1943, M. de Menthon, Minister of Justice of the Committee of Liberation, broadcast from Algiers to France that General de Gaulle would be the first President of the Fourth French Republic. For De Gaulle to be thinking of his illusive political career while France was still under the yoke was enough to shock many Frenchmen. The general was quick to realize this, and he made a slight correction—very slight:

"Menthon spoke without my knowledge. But I see clearly that I cannot act differently without failing in the mission which history has assigned to me."

De Gaulle actually believes that history has chosen him for a mission—the mission to seize the New Power. He has heard the call of Destiny. He has heard the voices of Joan of Arc. Unfortunately, as we have said, those voices are not those heard by Joan of Arc—they are the voices of the Cagoulards. And that explains everything that follows.

3. The Entourage

Each sought to compete in vice with whoever succeeded in prostituting his loyalty at the highest price.

RICHELIEU

Around the Pretender were men whom France either knew too well or had not known at all till now, men without honor, rank or position; the type of men who, in every age, are accomplices in violent overthrows; men to whom may be applied what Sallust said in speaking of the rabble about Cataline, what Caesar himself said in describing his confederates: "The eternal dregs of abnormal societies."

GAMBETTA (THE BAUDIN TRIAL)

DIFFICULT as it is to believe, De Gaulle's circle in London was from the very beginning of the movement infiltrated by the Cagoulards—the notorious Cagoulards. They came there by two different paths.

Some sincerely responded to his call of June 18, 1940. There can be no doubt that many Cagoulards were good patriots who had stupidly become involved in what they took to be simply an anti-Communist organization, never dreaming that it was inspired, backed, armed, and controlled by the Germans and Italians. They had no idea that the Cagoulards would one day become the shock brigade of French nazism—just as the Falange was that of Spanish nazism, the Iron Guard of Roumanian nazism, and Mosley's Black Shirts of British nazism. Attracted by the mystery of a secret so-

22

ciety, by the possibility of satisfying their taste for direct action, by the brutality of its ferociously antidemocratic and anti-Semitic doctrine, they had yet reacted violently against the downfall and humiliation of France. And they were ready to divert their spirit of adventure to the fight to the finish against the Germans.

However, another Cagoulard current had swept down upon London—strong-arm men, less naïve and better trained for the part they were expected to play. They were determined to serve Germany within the French forces being organized in exile. The speed with which the Germans sent French traitors whom they could trust to Marshal Pétain, then to General de Gaulle, was a masterpiece of Nazi strategy. While some flocked to Vichy and worked their way into every branch of the state administration, in order to carry on their spying, sabotage and betrayal, others slipped across to England with the aid and blessing of the Gestapo. They turned up at De Gaulle's headquarters, filled with tales of their "escape," and they shouted "Long live De Gaulle!" with wilder enthusiasm than any of the other refugees. Naturally, they were received with open arms.

De Gaulle fell headlong into the Cagoulard trap. He did not know of the documents concerning the Fifth Column, he knew little of its ramifications in French life, he had not the slightest knowledge or experience of politics, and he easily became the tool of men skilled in conspiracy and treason. He could not distinguish the existence of the two Cagoulard currents which have already been mentioned, for the Cagoulards themselves were often misled by these separate trends. Those of good faith believed in the good faith of the others. The traitors thought that all the others were traitors too. How could anyone find his way through such a maze? The only solution would have been to give each man a gun and send him out to fight the Germans. This method, however, was not to De Gaulle's liking. He was not looking for soldiers but for politicians.

There is no doubt that eventually De Gaulle discovered proof of pro-German treason among his closest supporters. But by then it was too late to untangle the threads and clean house. The same tragic psychological mechanisms that had concealed and protected the activities of the Nazis in France before the war now shielded the activities of the Cagoulards in London. The dupes who in perfect good faith had attended Abetz's luncheons in Paris at the time of Munich had later become his most ardent defenders, for they could not admit, without endangering their political careers or social positions, that they had accepted invitations and favors from an enemy spy. De Gaulle, who through ignorance had admitted Cagoulards into his innermost circle, could not acknowledge that fact at the time of Dakar without dealing his own prestige a crushing blow. Thus he became first the defender, then the protector, and finally the prisoner of this group. In this fashion the Cagoulards gained a powerful hold over the newborn De Gaullism; and their influence explains why the movement developed such unexpected states of mind and adopted such strange methods.

The Cagoulard Passy—who was to become General de Gaulle's evil genius throughout the four years of exile—appeared in London in July, 1940, just when French troops were returning to France from Norway, and joined the De Gaullists. He probably belonged to the category of patriotic, anti-German Cagoulards mentioned above. It would have been a good thing to have given him a chance to fight, allowing people to forget how readily he had become before the war a member of an organization set up by the Germans. Unfortunately, however, instead of letting him redeem himself, General de Gaulle made him his confidant and adviser, then the founder, recruiter, and head of the De Gaullist police—which was to become the prop of the new regime and the principal instrument of the revolution. Passy was made the all-powerful head of the De Gaullist Gestapo.

Colonel Passy is said to have shown genuine personal courage on his secret missions in France, but not enough is known in New York to allow me either to confirm or deny this. However, even if he did do risky things that were of great value, these ought to be weighed against the incredibly mad and tragic deeds for which his police have been responsible.

Quite naturally, Passy selected his henchmen from among his old

classmates at the *Ecole Polytechnique* and among the more daring
Cagoulards. For reasons of security, and in keeping with the prac-
tices of many secret societies, these men adopted false names and
identities. Two of them deserve special mention: Captain Collins
and M. Meiffre, known respectively as Howard and Treize. Both
were to play an important role in one of the most serious and
extraordinary episodes that revealed the methods of De Gaullism in
London—the case of Admiral Muselier.

Admiral Muselier was the first naval officer to join De Gaulle
after July, 1940. I cannot undertake to delineate the actual personality
of a man who has so many friends and so many enemies. Before
the war he had been openly at odds with Admiral Darlan, who had
cracked down and retired him. As a result Darlan's many friends
in the Navy became Muselier's bitter enemies—all of which makes
impartial judgment difficult. However, even his enemies recognized
that he was a man of remarkable intelligence, unbounded energy,
and tremendous courage.

De Gaulle promptly took a dislike to Vice-Admiral Muselier, his
superior in rank—three stars against two—because in 1940 the vice-
admiral was in command of French aviation and of the French
fleet in British ports (a hundred-odd small fighting craft and merchantmen), whereas De Gaulle's own command consisted of only
1,800 men, more or less, of the land forces. De Gaulle made up his
mind to get rid of this potentially dangerous rival. The prime interest of the "Muselier affair" lies in the fact that it follows the same
psychological pattern—in certain respects even the same technique—
as the "Giraud affair" and that it ends in a similar triumph for
General de Gaulle.

The plot hatched by the "De Gaullist Cagoulards" may be told
in a few words. On January 1, 1941, the British police broke into
Admiral Muselier's home and arrested him for high treason. They
had found a letter in which Muselier acknowledged receipt of 2,000
pounds sterling in payment for information supplied to Vichy
about the plan of the British attack on Dakar.

The repercussions of this scandal can be easily imagined. Was

General de Gaulle's highest ranking associate a traitor responsible for the Anglo-French disaster at Dakar?

The accusation was short-lived. It was proved that the admiral was the victim of a Cagoulard frame-up arranged by Howard and Treize, men high in the confidence of Colonel Passy and General de Gaulle. Howard and Treize had invented the story of the 2,000 pounds sterling, forged the letter—and made sure that it would fall into the hands of the British police. Howard and Treize were promptly arrested and sent to prison on the Isle of Man, while the British Foreign Secretary sent the following letter to Admiral Muselier:

Dear Admiral Muselier,

I have been charged to convey to you an expression of the deep regret of His Majesty's Government that you should have been detained by the British authorities on suspicions which have now been proved to be unsubstantiated.

His Majesty's Government have satisfied themselves that the documents, which at first appeared to cast suspicions on you, are spurious. As soon as this conclusion was reached, instructions were given for your immediate release.

His Majesty's Government look forward to continuing their collaboration with yourself and with the Free French Naval Forces under your command, which are rendering such signal services to the Allied cause.

I would beg at the same time to convey the regrets of His Majesty's Government to Lieutenant Villers.

With renewed and deep regrets, believe me,

Yours sincerely,
Anthony Eden

(Lieutenant Villers, who had been arrested at the same time as the admiral, had also attracted attention because of his violent quarrels with the Cagoulards in London.)

Admiral Muselier emerged unscathed from this attack. But in General de Gaulle's mind his fate had been decided. It was simply necessary to find means more subtle than the crude police methods of the Cagoulards—these were to become available a year later at the time of the occupation of the islands of Saint-Pierre and Miquelon.

Meanwhile the British were becoming more and more alarmed at Cagoulard activities among the De Gaullists. Among other things, the De Gaullist police insisted upon being informed about the movements, not only of Frenchmen in London, but even of French agents working in France for the British Intelligence Service. This threatened the structure and the secrecy of the Intelligence Service itself and gave rise to a number of dramatic incidents.

A Frenchman who had escaped from France was "questioned" by the De Gaullist police and refused to divulge the names of other Frenchmen working for England. He was arrested, thrown into prison and, apparently, died there.

On the same order is the story of one Dufour, who brought suit in the British courts against De Gaulle and his Cagoulard collaborators. The following are the principal extracts of the accusation made by M. Dufour before the High Court of Justice in London.

1943......D......No. 465

In the High Court of Justice
    King's Bench Division
Folios 23.

Writ issued the 6th day of August, 1943

Between......

Maurice Henri Dufour	—Plaintiff
.... and	
General Charles de Gaulle	
Lieutenant-Colonel André Passy	
Captain Roger Wybot	
Captain François Girard	
Colonel Louis Renouard	
Commandant de Person	
Commandant Etienne Cauchois and	
Commandant Pierre Simon	Defendants

. . . On 23rd June, 1940 he (M. Dufour) was severely wounded in the region of the kidneys and taken prisoner by the Germans.

On 13th March, 1941 the Plaintiff was released by the Germans on account of his wound and was sent to a hospital in France from which he was discharged on 7th June, 1941. He was then employed by the Vichy Government at an internment camp in what was then unoccupied France. While so employed he came into contact with the British Secret Service, by which he was employed in certain activities, and it became necessary for the Plaintiff to escape from France. He left France on 15th February, 1942 and arrived in England on 28th March 1942.

On 18th May 1942 the Plaintiff was requested to proceed to 10 Duke Street, Manchester Square, M.1, which is the headquarters of the Bureau Central Renseignements Affaires Militaires [Central Bureau of Military Intelligence] of the Free French Forces. The Defendant Lt. Col. Passy is or was at all material times the officer in command of the said Bureau and the Defendants Capt. Wybot and Capt. Girard served under the Defendant Lt. Col. Passy in the said Bureau. On or after 18th May 1942 the said three Defendants wrongfully conspired together to procure from the Plaintiff information to which they were not entitled concerning his said activities with the British Secret Service, and for this purpose to assault, beat, imprison and otherwise maltreat and injure the Plaintiff. Each of the acts hereinafter alleged as being done by the Defendants Capt. Wybot and Capt. Girard was an overt act in the said conspiracy. The Defendant Lt. Col. Passy was at all material times well aware of the commission of the said acts and caused and permitted the same to be done.

The Plaintiff arrived at the said Bureau at 2:45 p.m. on 18th May 1942. From 3:00 p.m. until 6:30 p.m. on the said day the Plaintiff was interrogated by the Defendant Capt. Wybot about his activities. There-after, after an interval of about 2 hours, during which he was kept in the custody of 2 French soldiers and given no food, he was again inter-rogated from 8:30 p.m. until about 10:30 p.m. by the Defendants Capt. Wybot and Capt. Girard and other officers in the Free French Forces, whose names the Plaintiff does not know; during this interrogation the Plaintiff was kept under a bright light. At about 10:30 p.m. the Plaintiff was directed to strip to the waist, which he did. The Defendants Capt. Wybot and Capt. Girard then struck the Plaintiff with their fists re-peatedly in the face and beat him across the small of his back with a steel rod bound in leather, striking him particularly in the place where he had been wounded as aforesaid thus causing him severe pain and suffering. They threatened to kill him and threatened also that a girl with whom he was friendly and who was then serving in the British F.A.N.Y. Service would be raped, saying, "We have arrested Mlle Borrel and we shall make her speak by whatever means are necessary even if we must rape her one after the other." They continued to treat the

Plaintiff in this manner until about 3:00 a.m. on 19th May, when he was taken down to a cellar in the basement of the premises at 10 Duke Street aforesaid.

The Plaintiff was confined in the said cellar from 19th to 29th May 1942 inclusive. The said cellar was about three meters in length and two-and-a-half in width. It had no furniture, no light and little ventilation. It was so low that the Plaintiff could only just stand up at one end. During this period the Plaintiff was brought up nearly every night, and interrogated, beaten and maltreated by the Defendants Capt. Wybot and Capt. Girard in the manner hereinbefore described.

The Plaintiff was then sent to the Free French Forces camp at Old Dean Park, Camberley, where, except for an interval from 17th July until 17th August 1942, during which he escaped and was at large, he was imprisoned from 23rd May until early in December 1942. His imprisonment as aforesaid was effected by the Defendant Commandant de Person, the officer in command of the said camp, pursuant (*inter alia*) to an order given by the Defendant, Col. Renouard, the officer in command of the Free French Land Forces in Britain, in or about the beginning of June 1942 and to a *mandat de dépôt* dated 10th July 1942 signed by the Defendant Commandant Simon.

In the beginning of December 1942 the Plaintiff escaped for the second time from the said camp and is now residing in London. . . .

This lawsuit brought to light two astonishing accusations. Firstly, that the De Gaullist Cagoulards dared to apply in the heart of London the methods of interrogation and torture practiced in the German death camps. And secondly, that they did not use them on Frenchmen suspected of collaborating with the Nazis, but on those collaborating with the British.

The case made a considerable stir in both the British and the American press. The United Press gave it world-wide publicity in a dispatch dated September 18, 1943.

There is no doubt that the documents relating to the Dufour case were in the file which Mr. Churchill took with him on one of his visits to America. The outcome of the whole affair has never been made public. According to certain American observers, the British induced Dufour to withdraw his complaint at the time they decided to change their policy toward De Gaulle, and Dufour is said to have received 50,000 pounds sterling for withdrawing the suit.

Still more serious occurrences can be traced to the activity of the Cagoulards. The British setback at Dakar in 1940, for example, must be attributed to pro-German espionage in London De Gaullist circles. Berlin and Vichy were informed of the preparations for the attack. The Cagoulards accused Admiral Muselier of high treason not only in the hope of ruining him, but to cover the work of their own agents. The British Intelligence Service was so convinced of this that it arrested two members of the clique closest to General de Gaulle.

The death of Captain d'Estiennes d'Orves is another Cagoulard crime. This unfortunate officer arrived in London from France and was sent back by the general on a mission to Brest, in occupied territory. Betrayed by the radio operator who had been assigned to him in London, Captain d'Estiennes d'Orves was captured by the Germans, tortured and shot.

A similar tragedy, laid to the same sources by the British, was the death of M. Jean Moulin. He had come to London from France, under the pseudonym of Monsieur X., to receive orders concerning the organization of Resistance groups in France. General de Gaulle made Monsieur X. a member of the French National Committee, introduced him to the highest British authorities, and took advantage of his presence in the British capital to press home the point that he, De Gaulle, was the recognized leader of the Resistance movement. He then ordered Monsieur X. back to France. The Germans, mysteriously tipped off, promptly arrested Jean Moulin, tortured and executed him.

The De Gaullist police had no sooner moved from London to Algiers when the French in North Africa discovered how similar were its methods to those of the German police: endless investigations, espionage, a whole system of bargaining and informing, the use of *agents provocateurs;* arrests, kidnappings, illegal imprisonments and torture. To mention but one episode, the mysterious disappearance of the famous author and flyer, De Saint-Exupéry, an implacable adversary of De Gaulle, was immediately blamed on the De Gaullist Cagoulards. Some reports say that he was shot down while on a mission by the plane sent along to protect him. According to others, a time bomb was set in his plane which exploded while he was in the air.

Other incidents of a different character are no less revealing.

In 1941, Professor Pierre Tissier, Master of Petitions in the Council of State and head of the financial section of Free France, a man very prominent at that time in the De Gaullist hierarchy, published in London a book called *The Vichy Government,* which purported to be a critical study of Vichy policy and a statement of the De Gaullist position. This book, one of the few which De Gaullism, so poor in general ideas, has produced, aroused considerable interest. The manner in which certain problems were stated and doctrines formulated clearly identified the Cagoulard and even Nazi influences with which the Free French movement was saturated at the time of its political inception. Particularly significant, for instance, is Professor Tissier's treatment of the Jewish question and his theories of racial selection:

Even France has her Jewish problem. This is an incontrovertible fact and no realistic policy can ignore it. . . .

The Jewish problem, while not exactly the same as that of other aliens, must be attacked by the same methods. First of all, aliens and Jews must be cut off from all ties with the homeland. So far as possible they must be scattered about the country. . . .

A policy covering birth and the physical and moral improvement of the population must accompany the policy of assimilation. . . .

There remains also the more delicate question of the selection in child-bearing. Here, too, it would be foolish to close our eyes to the facts. France must not breed children indiscriminately. We must have recourse to eugenics and—why mince words?—to the practical control of sterilization. . . .

Sterilization should be performed officially wherever it is apparent that a person is suffering from a disease or an incurable infirmity that might be passed on to his children; this being carried out chiefly during army medical examinations and regular compulsory medical check-ups. . . .

If, in the course of pregnancy, there appears the danger that the child may not be born sound and healthy, an abortion must be performed under legal supervision. . . .

These theories deeply stirred the Catholics and Jews in exile. De Gaulle ordered the book withdrawn from circulation and, if I am not mistaken, a new expurgated edition was printed. The original anti-Semitic tendency of De Gaullism was soon forgotten. Even the semblance of it vanished when Jews in London and New York, inspired by the sufferings of their people, joined the De Gaullist organization and took a preponderant place in it. However, anti-Semitism persisted and still persists in the depths of the movement, like an indelible mark left by the Cagoulards.

Side by side with the Cagoulard influence there was also that of the France-Germany Committee.

In 1941 I learned that M. Jules Romains, the well-known author, was one of the members of the Board of Directors of the De Gaullist society "France Forever" in New York. The choice could not have been more unfortunate, for Romains had been the principal author and signatory—with the Hitlerites Fabre-Luce and Paul Marion—of the famous "plan of the 9th of July" (1937) to which all the prewar fascist groups adhered. He had called for a "government of fact" which would be "charged with the task of defining, under its own authority, an economic and social organization." Between this plan and the general purposes for which the France-Germany Society was founded in 1932 by Herr Otto Abetz there existed a remarkable parallel. This society was an agency of German propaganda, and it is worth noting that Romains' name appeared on the inside cover of its publication along with the names of other directors of the France-Germany Committee, and that his name continued to be so listed until 1939. Moreover, Romains has actively and personally defended the purposes of that strange super-German society in a book called *Le Couple France-Allemagne* (The French-German Couple). In it he wrote:

Delcassé's * ghost must be pleased. We are beginning again—or at least so it looks—to encircle Germany, while our ambassador, to gain

* Delcassé was the French Foreign Minister of the early twentieth century who was mainly responsible for the *Entente Cordiale*.

time, pays lip service to the leader of the German people. Soon the picture will be complete—the Russian alliance included. . . . (p. 41)

We fail to perceive that there is in reality a German good faith. It is
of a personal kind. It is not like ours, which is legalistic in nature. . . .
The German good faith is, so to speak, feudal. It is a tie linking man
to man: a personal loyalty. . . ." (p. 52)

Some people have sworn to prevent any sort of reconciliation between
these two nations which is another way of saying that they have sworn
. . . to make conflict inevitable between these two nations at a more or
less distant date. (p. 123)

It would take me too long to enumerate them. I wish to point out,
however, the influences, not concrete, perhaps, but diffused, of Jewish
opinion. (p. 75)

I am confident that everywhere—I was sure of it yesterday in Germany—what youth wants and is working for is not war. (p. 126)

Yes, this is another thing Herr Rosenberg said to me the other day.
"When I saw M. Barthou rushing around Europe, don't you think that
I felt encircled?" (p. 91)

Oh, to be sure, Barthou's method was brilliant. It was better perhaps
than no method at all. But it was dangerous. . . . It is a little too soon
to judge the new cabinet setup. It has one great advantage over the
preceding one. It is headed by young men. . . . M. Laval, in particular,
seems to me to be a very level-headed man. . . . (p. 132)

All the major themes of Abetz and De Brinon are repeated in
these lines: hatred of the Russian Alliance; German good faith;
Germany does not want war; references to Jewish responsibility;
the encirclement of Germany and the name of Laval. . . .

Of course, I do not mean to suggest that Romains was a traitor
like one or more of the other directors of France-Germany. I maintain, however, that he was a dupe and the unwitting victim of Nazi
agents and Nazi ideas. Hence to make room for Romains inside
De Gaullism, particularly a De Gaullism turned political, was highly
unwise. The least one could ask of a former member of the France-
Germany Committee in exile was that he keep silent, repent, and
remain in the background.

Accordingly, I sent General de Gaulle a report on the case of Jules
Romains and the other members of the France-Germany Committee
who had strayed into De Gaullism. I reminded him that I was well

acquainted with the workings of that organization, that I had been the one to denounce Abetz and De Brinon—so effectively, indeed, that the German Ambassador in Paris had tried to compel the Daladier government to hail me into court because of my attacks against Abetz—and that at the outbreak of the war, M. de Brinon had sued me in the Court of Summary Jurisdiction of the Seine for a million francs because of my accusations against the France-Germany Committee. I also reminded him that Georges Mandel had several times demanded the arrest of the entire board of directors and of the principal members of the France-Germany Committee.

But the only result I obtained was that Romains became a prominent contributor to *La Marseillaise,* De Gaulle's official organ. His articles appeared in big type under banner headlines. Obviously, the France-Germany Committee and Jules Romains had supporters among the people close to De Gaulle.

M. Pleven, a financier, was attached to De Gaulle from the first as confidential advisor. His influence was, to say the least, unfortunate. When he came to Washington, I pointed out to him the potential menace of the inner circle in London, with its Cagoulards, its ex-members of the France-Germany Committee, its former adherents of the *Action Française,* and other adventurers from all parties. He listened to me, but that impromptu minister thought he was hearing a detective story. In the end he laughed and asked me to talk about serious matters.

In all sincerity, we must admit that the Free French movement, born in defeat and in exile, could not altogether escape being penetrated by the terrible apparatus of German treachery. But the creation of a political party instead of an army of liberation, coupled with De Gaulle's lack of experience, increased the hazards. In political De Gaullism the healthy elements could not counterbalance the dangerous influences. The real heroes who fled the shores of Brittany and risked their lives to cross the Channel in fishing boats were not anxious to be transformed into political agents. They had gone to London to enlist in the French Army and to fight. With

very few exceptions only the adventurers jumped at the opportunity
to play politics. They quickly formed a large and powerful clique
around General de Gaulle, a maffia that attached less importance to
the liberation of France than to the opening offered them to reshape
their careers and share in the spoils of an era of political piracy. The
De Gaullist coterie in London became a center for upstarts of the
defeat. Greedy or servile men with unsavory pasts and false identities
elbowed and jostled one another, pressing De Gaulle to accentuate
the adventuresome character of the movement. They had nothing
to gain by a return to normal conditions, which would put them
back in their old places and rob them of their jobs as police officers,
propagandists, ministers, and ambassadors at salaries which were
sometimes fantastic. They dreamt of a praetorian *coup d'état* that
would hand over a France liberated by the Allies to their leader and
protect their sinecures.

The fixed idea of this group was, obviously, to isolate De Gaulle
from anyone who might acquaint him with their real background
or who, through reputation and experience, might some day sup-
plant him politically. In this their aims coincided with the general's
own inclinations and his unbridled ambition. And therein lies the
explanation of their complete success. Any outstanding officer or
civilian became automatically the sworn enemy of the political conspirators.

I first became aware of this state of affairs when I suggested to
De Gaulle that an attempt be made to rescue the political prisoners
whom Marshal Pétain was holding in Vichy prisons by order of the
Gestapo. In December, 1940, I sent the general one of the most
important reports to come out of France—it is still too early for
me to give further details about it. This report suggested that there
was a good chance to rescue Paul Reynaud, Georges Mandel,
Daladier, Blum, and General Gamelin. I received no reply.

Several weeks later I offered to turn over to De Gaulle certain
funds which I had saved from German confiscation and to which
I had complete legal title. Those who recall my prewar political
activities know that certain admirers of my patriotic efforts placed

at my disposal large sums of money, some for use in connection with my Propaganda Center, others for any purpose I might choose. The latter sums were entirely my property. I had intended to use them for postwar political activities but they were a care and a responsibility to me.

After some hesitation I decided to write to De Gaulle in London and offer him at least a part of these funds. I handed a letter to M. de Sieyès, the general's representative in New York. In a little while I received De Gaulle's reply, dated March 12, 1941:

In case you have no other suggestion, I should like to propose a most proper and valuable way of utilizing these funds. We are planning to build a powerful radio station, either at Brazzaville or perhaps at Algiers, if events turn out favorably. The cost of this undertaking is estimated at $200,000, $60,000 of which we already have.

We intend to obtain the remainder from Frenchmen living in the United States. To this end we plan to start a subscription campaign.

I believe that if you subscribed at the head of the list as "a group of anonymous Frenchmen" for the sum of $20,000, this gesture would fulfill the wish you mention in your letter, have a considerable moral effect and undoubtedly influence many of our fellow countrymen to make substantial contributions. And this radio station would remain in every way a French undertaking.

I found this letter satisfactory, but with certain reservations, which I made very clear in my reply:

Agreed. I shall be glad to send you $20,000 to start off the subscription you are about to open in America for the Brazzaville radio station. I am delighted to be of use in your noble cause and I beg you to send me word when I may make the first payment.

Please let me know as soon as possible, since there are a few problems to be solved. A small part of the money is in Canada; the rest is in the United States. However, as you know, the Americans have frozen all foreign accounts and the Canadians being at war have closed their borders against the withdrawal of money as strictly as the British. I shall therefore have to comply with certain regulations in both countries. On the American side these will perhaps be somewhat more complicated than I had foreseen, to judge from a conversation I had yesterday with Mr. Chambers, an American lawyer, who will do what he can for me with the Federal Reserve Bank. In any event I wish to carry out the transaction in full compliance with American laws and procedures.

At your request I shall make the contribution anonymously, but I should like to obtain a receipt in my name from your representative in New York. Though I am the legal owner of the funds and free to dispose of them as I see fit, for ethical reasons which you will understand I should like to have some record of these transactions.

With that settled, let me say frankly that, as regards further contributions of money, I should prefer to apply them to more personal objectives, if I may say so, than radio Brazzaville. It seems to me that you should not have much difficulty in enlisting the aid of the British government for such a project. A radio station is as much a part of your war equipment as guns and tanks. Why devote to it private funds which, compared to the vast amount of public funds at your disposal, are a drop in the bucket?

There is one use to which I should much prefer to see this money put, for both sentimental and political reasons which I am sure you will understand. Please refer to my last report on the possibility of rescuing Paul Reynaud, Gamelin, Mandel, Daladier, and Blum. These men are prisoners of Pétain and the Germans, and we must try to free them. I know that you don't particularly like all of them. I recall your comments about several. But personal considerations should not enter into this. What prestige could be won by Free France through showing solidarity and, at the same time, her spirit of initiative and daring in organizing the escape of these political prisoners, who may, I'm afraid, become martyrs! Now, as I said before, it is quite easy to rescue them. It could be done by a small force with the help of one of your ships or an English ship. According to my information there would not even be a fight. It is a cannon shot of several million francs fired at you know whom. That is all. The doors of the prison will open of their own accord. How happy I should be to furnish that money for freedom and revenge!

Considering the extreme moral and material disorder of occupied France, it would have been child's play for De Gaulle with the aid of the English to organize the rescue of the political prisoners. The gates of the darkest fortresses had opened to General Giraud,* as

* General Giraud was gotten out of Koenigstein by Colonel de Linarès of the Secret Services, at that time stationed in Lyons. He spent less than 10,000 francs on the escape.

well as to General Dalattre de Tassigny and many others. Men had been freed who were held in the center of Germany, in the very dens of the Gestapo. And the Germans have also carried out amazing rescues, the most spectacular of which was that of Mussolini.

In addition to political reasons, De Gaulle should have had personal reasons, sentimental reasons even greater than mine, for rescuing Paul Reynaud. As Premier, Reynaud had lifted De Gaulle out of obscurity and appointed him Under-Secretary of State—thus furnishing the springboard for his spectacular career. Therefore I expected that my proposal would be approved by De Gaulle, and I looked forward to a prompt and enthusiastic acceptance.

I was wrong. Not only did De Gaulle not reply to my letter but he forthwith dropped his plan for a public subscription in America—in order to conceal the fact that he was accepting my money for certain purposes and rejecting it for others.

I knew that the British harbored a stubborn hostility—partly justified—against both Reynaud and Daladier, and at first I thought that the suggestion to rescue the Vichy prisoners had been vetoed by them. A good deal later, however, I wrote to a friend of mine, a person who belonged to De Gaulle's coterie in London, asking for an explanation. I received the following reply:

Your proposal made a very bad impression on several people who have influence with the boss. The prospect of having three ex-Premiers, a former Minister and the former Generalissimo show up in London struck them as catastrophic for the General's future. These important figures would have promptly become the outstanding representatives of France and would have been qualified to speak in her name here. . . . This, you understand, was not a pleasant thought. It was better to quash your plan. I have heard it said that you are quite insufferable with your eccentric ideas.

In what way was my idea eccentric? Not only was I proposing that innocent victims be snatched from the Germans but was in effect trying to form an impressive group of French representatives in exile. Greatly as I admired De Gaulle in the beginning, he was in my view only a brigadier general, without sufficient stature for the great military and, above all, the great moral role demanded of the French in exile.

From New York I was still unable to grasp clearly the changes taking place in London and the new trend of De Gaullism toward the Fascist idea of the man-symbol, the man-savior, the Man of Destiny. But instinctively I sensed what was going on. I had seen only too well the contagious effect of German and Italian ideas on ill-starred movements like the prewar leagues not to fear a rebirth and growth of those unhealthy forces in the midst of war.

Of all the political figures in the previous government Georges Mandel was, in my opinion, the man who had shown the most courage, foresight, and discernment. It seemed to me that his influence among the exiles could be tremendous, and I was therefore very anxious for the De Gaullists to rescue him. Today, with the passage of time, I am more than ever convinced that the mere presence of Mandel in London would have forced De Gaulle to abandon all or part of his political activities, would have confined him to his military role, and would have saved France from the questionable adventure into which she has been dragged.

But Mandel was the one man whom the Cagoulards in London feared above all. This former Minister of the Interior in the Reynaud cabinet knew too much about their organization, their affiliations, their personalities, and their past. Had Mandel appeared in London those strange gentlemen with the names of subway stations, and their accomplices, would not have remained very long in their key positions in the De Gaullist movement. The Cagoulards were therefore violently opposed to my rescue plan and saw to it that it fell through. Later, they were to scuttle another project of no less importance.

In June, 1942, the American government, which was becoming more and more uneasy at the turn De Gaullism was taking, considered an undertaking of great political dimensions. It involved getting Herriot and Jeanneney, Presidents of the Chamber of Deputies and of the Senate, respectively, out of France and of bringing them to Washington. The American government felt that the presidents of both houses of the French legislature, men respected for their patriotism and their anti-German sentiments, and undeniable representatives of republican legitimacy, were best qualified to crystallize the republican spirit of the exiles scattered throughout the world, to counteract General de Gaulle's dictatorial ambitions and to strengthen the determination of the French at home to fight to the bitter end. Unfortunately, the Americans encountered numerous difficulties and the matter dragged on for more than a year. The chief complications were caused by Herriot himself, who for a long time mistakenly thought that he could be of more use in France than in exile and that his place was at his presidential post among the members of Parliament.

In any case the American plans leaked out and very much worried De Gaulle. De Gaullist groups in exile immediately started a whispering campaign of extreme violence against Jeanneney and Herriot. They were accused of "Pétainism," of conciliating the enemy, denounced as "old fossils" and referred to with hatred. Instructions along these lines were sent to De Gaullist agents and the De Gaullist press everywhere.

The most typical example of this explosion of violence was described on August 30, 1942, in *La Marseillaise,* under the name of François Quilici. The pretext was Laval's suppression of the two French Chambers on order of the Germans. Far from blaming Laval and the Germans, Quilici loudly seconded them.

The President of the Senate and the President of the Chamber of Deputies are now out of a job—they have joined the ranks of the unemployed. I confess that their hard luck leaves me cold. . . . The republican in me, inherited from a long line of peasants and a father who was a postal clerk, is undisturbed by the faint crash made by the fall of one of the last vestiges of the rotten regime which Jeanneney and Herriot deserted on July 10, 1940. . . .

Those two men knew the terms of the armistice. . . . They did not speak up. . . .

High-ranking dignitaries, they knew that the Republic was being overthrown from within. They did not speak up. . . .

Neither of them grasped that opportunity to castigate the traitors.

Neither of them demanded an accounting. Neither of them tried to put fresh life into the opposition in order to bolster up at the final poll a minority of 80. Neither of them has vowed revenge. . . . Neither of them has uttered the protest on which a humiliated nation pins its pride.

Here we must recall the magnificent, courageous protest which Jeanneney and Herriot sent to Laval upon the dissolution of the two Chambers at the very moment when the above article was being written, a protest involving much more difficulty and danger than the one voiced by De Gaulle and Quilici—at a safe distance from the Germans:

I realize that not everyone can derail a train or throw a bomb—but what have these gentlemen (Jeanneney and Herriot) done? . . . Like Candide, they have cultivated their garden.

Because the anonymous masses from which we spring are resisting, a queer myth has been created concerning the meaning of "resistance." If men prominent in public life abstain from doing harm, if they simply keep out of sight, it is said that they are resisting. All that is required of these leaders is the immobility of an oyster clinging to its rock.

It is said, furthermore, that Laval gave that order because he was afraid of some action, a meeting of the Chambers on the day the Allies land on French soil. Well, it may be that we shall see those important people with their presumptuous tripe come forth to meet our volunteers —although for months, fear has kept them shuddering in the dark. Perhaps new France, seeking in pain for its new form, may, in the chaos of suddenly regained freedom, place her trust temporarily in certain men who have served her badly. But what does that matter? The future, the great future stability, lies elsewhere. . . .

Both the British and the Americans, who, rightly, considered Quilici the "mouthpiece of General de Gaulle," were shocked by this language—to the extent that the United States Secretary of State took occasion at his press conference to say a few words in praise of Herriot. And the upshot was that a month later De Gaulle himself, learning of the first arrest of the President of the Chamber, made some slightly corrective remarks.

He refused to yield, however, on the basic issue. He had no more

wish to see Herriot and Jeanneney in London than he had to rescue
Georges Mandel and the imprisoned ex-ministers.

Did Herriot know how the general felt towards him? Quite
likely! For it is reported in Allied official circles that when Herriot
was urged for the third time to come to America, he finally replied:

"All right, I shall go into exile, but only if my presence there
makes for unity, not dissension. I shall go if the Americans, the
British, and General de Gaulle really want me to."

He never went.

- The Gestapo was aware of what was being said among London
exiles. Perhaps they received confirmation through the wretched
chatter of a refugee in New York. And we know what happened
to the unfortunate ex-Premier.

Thus, neither he nor Mandel (who was murdered in Paris) was
in London to hinder De Gaulle's progress towards seizure of the
New Power. The plan succeeded perfectly. All dangerous competition, all republican authority, had been eliminated before the triumphal entry into liberated Paris. In the Allied trucks that carried
De Gaulle rode men the public had never heard of, men who had
risen through the petty intrigues of life in exile, the aristocrats of
De Gaullism—an Adrien Tixier, a Pleven, a Diethelm, one or two
of the most obscure and least esteemed survivors of the Third Republic and, tucked away in the background, hiding their heads
under their hoods, Colonel Passy and his police.

They passed beneath the Arc de Triomphe and took over the
salaries, the honors, and the power. . . .

4. The De Gaullist Press

The press is not intended to enlighten the people but to blind them.   GOEBBELS

WE have already mentioned *La Marseillaise,* the official organ of De Gaullism. The New York *Herald Tribune* had announced the founding of that newspaper in a dispatch from its London correspondent, dated June 5, 1942:

> *La Marseillaise* will reflect directly and officially the views, policies and interests of the Free French movement, it was revealed, and will be edited from Carlton Gardens, General Charles de Gaulle's headquarters in London. Theoretically it will be designed exclusively for the fighting forces of France and in this sense it will be a French counterpart of the *Stars and Stripes* published for the American forces in Great Britain.
> It will, however, be distributed without charge, part of the agreement with British authorities being that it will not be put on sale.
> Of the daily newspapers supporting the Allied cause, the most important is *France* which, it was explained today in connection with the forthcoming appearance of *La Marseillaise,* in no way officially represents the De Gaullist government.

Theoretically, the line of *La Marseillaise* on foreign policy should have been easy to define. All that was needed was to take a position diametrically opposed to the propaganda campaigns, theories and ideas of the prewar pro-German press and of the French-language press in Paris and Vichy. Hence *La Marseillaise* should have been consistently pro-British, pro-Russian, and pro-American. It was clear that France's only hope of salvation lay with the British, the Rus-

sians, and the Americans. It was all very well to have declared in a
romantic and glorious order of the day: "France has not lost a war.
She has only lost a battle." But alas, that was not true. France had
lost her war. And only her allies could win another that would
save her. Political realism therefore required that French patriots
cling to the Allies, in complete confidence, in perfect friendship, inspired by gratitude and hope. This outlines the policy that should
have been adopted by a De Gaullist newspaper faced with the task
of repairing the psychological damage which the enemies of France
had wrought on the French mind.

This war was, moreover, the war of democracy. French independence was not the only thing involved. A great human principle, a great philosophy, a concept of civilization, was also at stake.
To restore to the French spirit the democratic ideal sapped by fascism
and nazism, it was necessary to forge a genuine ideological front
with the Anglo-Saxon countries which were champions of that ideal.
Failure to do so would inevitably create dangerous political confusion. It also meant that France might participate symbolically
in a military victory over Germany, without that victory being also
a victory over nazism.

Besides, it was obvious to all intelligent observers, to all informed
statesmen, that America was the chief hope of France. The day
America threw into the balance the colossal weight of her industrial
power, her human reserves and her creative genius, it was clear that
she would become the decisive factor in the victory. In the ominous
darkness of the storm devastating the world, an experienced pilot
could see that America would one day be the best guarantee of
French independence, her strongest protector, and, in any event,
her most disinterested friend. America asked nothing of France
and claimed nothing.

Over and above these practical considerations was a sentimental
and moral factor. France, wounded, humiliated, besmirched, and
on her knees, had need of a noble and tender sentiment to sustain
her, lift her to her feet, and nurse her back to health. And fortu-
nately, she had received from history and tradition the heritage of

Lafayette and of Rochambeau, preserved and piously cherished through the ages by both Frenchmen and Americans. What this heritage represented in the way of comfort, purity, and, under the circumstances, the providential, should have been made use of and glorified.

Everyone knew that one day, toward the end of the war or after the war, difficulties would inevitably arise between the French and the Allies—even between the French and the Americans. But those difficulties, so easily foreseen, should have been thrust back in time and space and been driven from the mind, in order to beautify and strengthen the regenerative powers that in the midst of disaster were forming themselves within the depths of the conscience. A French general, leading a small French army into battle at the side of the British, Americans, and Russians, did not have to look beyond the battlefield where the salvation of France was to be decided and where the Allies were to mingle their blood. All he had to do was to wave his sword and leap forward to the attack, shoulder to shoulder with the saviors of his country.

That is why the policy of *La Marseillaise* should have been so simple to define, so simple to formulate, so simple to present:

"Frenchmen, you have been fooled and tricked, you have been led into a bottomless pit of calamity through abominable and shameful lies. You have been made to believe that your friends, your allies, your liberators, were your worst enemies—and they are now trying to make you accept your conquerors as your protectors. We, De Gaullists, tear aside the veil of treachery. We, De Gaullists, cry aloud the saving truth: Hate Germany, love England, love Russia, most of all, love America, your friend for one hundred and fifty years!"

But what did *La Marseillaise* do?

Exactly the opposite. Published in London and therefore not in a position to attack England too violently, *La Marseillaise* picked up the anti-American campaigns of prewar days, using almost the same terms and the same forms featured by the *Action Française, Le Matin, Je Suis Partout, Gringoire.* It echoed the anti-American

fury of Vichy and Paris, often surpassing them in violence. This
may be difficult to believe, but it is so. Here are the facts and the
texts.

Shortly after our newspaper *Pour la Victoire* appeared in New
York, *La Marseillaise* made us a curious offer. They asked us to
carry a two-page insert each week in *Pour la Victoire* under their
name. Since we were De Gaullists, though completely independent
and much more moderate than *La Marseillaise,* we accepted. Soon
our newspaper in New York carried reprints of leading articles
appearing in *La Marseillaise* in London.

In the beginning all went well. Soon, however, we began to feel
alarmed by the vehemence, the frenzy, the fanaticism, of the articles
written in London. We were interested in a military De Gaullism,
in a general who was raising a French Army to aid in the liberation
of France. *La Marseillaise* took the angry tone of a revolutionary
faction. Conspicuous in this line were the contributions of its editor,
Quilici. At the time we were not aware that this obscure writer had
won the full confidence of De Gaulle, whom he overwhelmed week
after week with dithyrambic and semimystical encomiums, composed in an involved, heavy, and pretentious style.

We were soon forced to realize—with some uneasiness—that, not
content with extolling the semidivinity of De Gaulle, *La Marseillaise* had set out to teach Mr. Roosevelt a few political lessons and
to compel *Pour la Victoire* to publish them in New York. Roosevelt's
mistake, according to Quilici, was to keep an ambassador at Vichy
instead of dispatching him . . . to General de Gaulle in London.

Incidentally, in recognizing the Vichy government, the United
States was recognizing the actual state of affairs. Besides, America
wanted to be present in the real France, France captive and martyred, with her forty million people. Lastly, there was absolutely
no reason why America should send an ambassador to a French
brigadier general in London whose sole avowed purpose was to
raise a little army to help liberate France. America's presence at
Vichy permitted her to establish useful political contacts, to lay the
foundations for her Intelligence Service, and—a factor of prime

importance—to keep a closer watch on Germany. The quarrel between De Gaulle and Roosevelt on this point—a quarrel that greatly
worsened De Gaulle's relations with America—showed that in a
disconcerting degree he lacked political acumen and an understanding of French and of American interests.

Pour la Victoire was supposed to publish De Gaulle's bitter attacks on Roosevelt. We found that impossible. Without a moment's
hesitation we cut from the material *La Marseillaise* cabled us everything we considered discourteous to President Roosevelt and to
America.

There is no point in reproducing here the endless exchange of
communications that resulted between *La Marseillaise* and *Pour la
Victoire*. However, as a sample, here is Quilici's cable of September
22, 1942:

POUR LA VICTOIRE, 535 Fifth Avenue, New York

CANNOT ACCEPT RESERVATION REGARDING ARTICLES CONCERNING AMERICA
STOP ISSUING NEW YORK EDITION SOLELY FOR PURPOSE OF EXPRESSING OUR
OPINION THERE STOP WE RESUME TRANSMISSION TO SAVE TIME BUT YOU
WILL RECEIVE EDITORIAL WITH OUR PERMISSION TO PRINT ONLY DEPENDING
ON YOUR EARLY REPLY STOP

We replied the same day, in a friendly tone:

QUILICI MARSELIB LONDON

DESIRE EXPLAIN RESERVATION RE AMERICA STOP NO QUESTION OF PREVENT-
ING MARSEILLAISE EXPRESSING OPINION STOP BUT IMPOSSIBLE IGNORE IN
MARSEILLAISE PAGES GENERAL STATUS FOREIGN PRESS UNITED STATES STOP
AMERICA GRANTS WIDE LATITUDE EXILED PRESS ON CONDITION NO ATTACKS
ON GOVERNMENT AND STRICT OBSERVANCE LAWS OF COUNTRY STOP YOU CAN
APPRECIATE ON READING VICTOIRE GENEROSITY AMERICAN AUTHORITIES PAR-
TICULARLY TOWARDS FIGHTING FRENCH STOP AMERICAN EDITION MARSEIL-
LAISE WILL BENEFIT SAME STATUS VICTOIRE BUT MUST OBSERVE SAME RULES
STOP CONVINCED THERE WILL BE NO DIFFICULTY STOP IN EVENT DIFFICULTY
WE ARE SURE EVERYTHING CAN BE ARRANGED EASILY FRIENDLY SPIRIT OF
COLLABORATION STOP AWAIT NEXT EDITORIAL COPY STOP

The interest of these two documents lies in the date—September
22, 1942.

The violent antipathy shown by De Gaulle, his press, and his party, toward America and toward Roosevelt throughout the war does not date, as is generally believed, from the American landing in North Africa. Two months before that event, De Gaullist propaganda had already begun attacking the President, even presuming to fight him in America. This can only be explained by taking into account the violently anti-American Cagoulard influences prevailing in De Gaullist circles in London and De Gaulle's own antidemocratic attitude.

After November 8, 1942, when the Americans went ashore in North Africa, the anti-American tone of *La Marseillaise* reached the pitch of exasperation.

I shall describe later on the circumstances under which the expedition was carried out, the perfectly sound reasons why the Americans did not ask De Gaulle's aid—chief among these being his failures at Dakar and in Syria—and why they signed the agreement with Admiral Darlan at a moment when they were faced with the dangerous possibility of having to fight the French regular Army. (They themselves are the first to admit that in detail they sometimes make mistakes and blunders.) They were suddenly confronted with the European Revolution, with a portion of the French Empire deformed and corrupted by German and Vichy propaganda. They had to navigate in the midst of seas whipped up by passions which they could not understand.

Had De Gaullism been a union of Frenchmen with the sole purpose of liberating France, it would have placed itself at the disposal of the Americans to be of whatever aid it could and to guide them, if needed, in the formidable task before them. De Gaullism did just the opposite. To complicate the work of the Americans it sided with the Vichyites. And *La Marseillaise* began sending *Pour la Victoire* articles openly insulting to President Roosevelt, General Eisenhower, and the American Army.

On one occasion they cabled a so-called interview with a sailor of the *Jean-Bart,* the French battleship sunk by American guns at Casablanca. To the question "What were your impressions when you first saw the American fleet?" the French sailor replied: "My comrades and I had a single reaction: 'The dirty swine!'"

On November 27 *La Marseillaise* sent us an article which contained the following:

No matter how much we are assured that Algeria, Tunisia and Morocco will be restored to us intact, that the Senate will not nullify Roosevelt's promises as it did Wilson's in 1918, and that the *Jean-Bart* will be replaced with a brand-new ship, we are nevertheless convinced that France has suffered a grave injury. Viewed in the light not of our passing generation but of History, the occupation by our American friends of a land that has cost us so much blood is actually a more serious blow to our country than Nazi occupation of French departments, because it is a blow to our honor.

This text, a monument of ingratitude towards America, staggered us. Under the signature of a Frenchman—influenced by De Gaullist fanaticism as he had been for a long time by the fanaticism of Maurras—we recognized the language of German propagandists in Paris. We could not think of publishing the article in New York.

Besides, the Americans, who, naturally, scrutinized the cables between *La Marseillaise* and *Pour la Victoire,* could not fail to be extremely annoyed by the tenor of such articles. The *Pour la Victoire-La Marseillaise* quarrel therefore assumed a serious meaning beyond the level of the two newspapers. We appealed persistently, to Adrien Tixier, De Gaulle's representative in Washington, probably the most subservient and mediocre personality in the De Gaullist movement. The latter cabled the general, but the replies from London were explicit: Quilici had the full confidence of the general, who approved entirely of his actions and his anti-American articles. Hence the general demanded that *Pour la Victoire* comply and publish the articles.

Pour la Victoire did not comply. On January 13, 1943, Quilici notified us by cable that he was terminating all collaboration:

UNDERSTAND MY EDITORIALS SEVERELY CUT STOP CONSIDER USELESS CONTINUE COLLABORATION STOP MARSEILLAISE ACCEPTS BREAK YOU HAVE MADE

INEVITABLE STOP GIVING ORDERS FOR IMMEDIATE PAYMENT MONEY DUE
YOU STOP

This break brought down upon us furious attacks by De Gaullists
in New York and London. They spread the rumor that *Pour la
Victoire* had been bought out by President Roosevelt and the State
Department, and that the order to suspend publication of *La Marseillaise's* articles in New York had come from the White House. We
were denounced as traitors guilty of trying to stifle the great voice
of General de Gaulle.

However, the scandal did not end there. *La Marseillaise* continued its campaign in London. The British government watched it
with the keenest anxiety and displeasure.

Churchill and Eden sent for De Gaulle and protested. Not only
was it deplorable, they asserted, that the official organ of the Free
French should attack President Roosevelt and America, but, what
was worse, the Americans might believe that the attacks were inspired by the British. The British ministers complained that De
Gaulle was creating disharmony between England and the United
States, and requested him to put an end to these activities. De Gaulle
protested haughtily and invoked his famous argument about French
sovereign rights—as usual confusing De Gaullist sovereignty with
French sovereignty.

It is impossible to reprint here all headlines, news items and
articles of *La Marseillaise* which deserve notice in this respect. In
its anti-American, and sometimes also anti-British, propaganda the
De Gaullist paper made use of rare imagination and all the tricks
of the journalistic trade. A favorite device was to have articles hostile
to Roosevelt published in London and New York under the by-
lines of British and American journalists converted to De Gaullism
—and sometimes paid out of the De Gaullist propaganda budget.
These pieces were then reprinted with inflammatory headlines and
comments. The British censor could not intervene, since the French
newspaper was merely reprinting material that had already appeared
in British or American papers.

Quilici and other editors of *La Marseillaise* were never at a loss for anti-American themes. On December 13, 1942, in a "Letter from a Volunteer," M. Pompei wrote insolently:

I fear that Europeans who, as a whole, have not had the privilege of studying philosophy in the movies, may have retained deplorably old-fashioned notions with respect to the freedom of peoples to live as they like.

A charming way to greet Americans who were dying on the battlefields of North Africa by the side of French soldiers!

On December 27, one Brilhac wrote, in a "Letter to My Friend Sam":

We who belong to these bloodstained lands declare that the new slavery must be abolished and the slave drivers, no matter how star-spangled, must be sent to the electric chair.

Brilhac is supposedly speaking of the new European slavery, of German slavery. But how can one miss the implication that this equivocal language is aimed at the Americans when he refers to the "star-spangled" slave drivers and calls for the electric chair.

On January 17 Quilici accused the Americans of stirring up anarchy in North Africa by refusing to adopt "the natural solution"; in other words, by refusing to hand over North Africa to the dictatorship of De Gaulle:

Because they turned down the natural solution which even our enemies looked for, they have anarchy instead. They are now trying to blame this anarchy on the French. They accuse us of being unable to agree among ourselves when we have never been more united. But we are united against Vichy, and Vichy is what they are trying to impose upon us. I have even read that if the French do not yield, a friendly government will take over the administration of our territories. I cannot believe that an ally of my people would consent to barter its status of ally for that of an occupation force and so humiliate a great nation fighting so desperately against the common enemy.

Let us note in passing the accusation which was to become one of the slogans of the De Gaullist whispering campaign throughout the world: not only do the Americans intend to take over the administration of France, but they want to "impose" Vichy on liberated France. President Roosevelt is therefore a Fascist. And America is not called a "liberating power" but an "occupation force."

On January 24, in huge type covering eight columns, *La Marseillaise* published so-called reports of De Gaulle's partisans in Algiers on American activity in North Africa. There, these strange De Gaullists already express regret at having helped the Allies to land:

> There have been many deaths in our ranks. Our men thought they were giving their lives for OUR idea. I greatly fear they died for prunes,* as they say in France.

It is clear that the De Gaullists thought they were fighting for *their* idea—in other words, for De Gaulle. The moment De Gaulle did not stand to gain by the Algiers coup, they felt they had "died for prunes."

They forgot France.

And here is the incredible attack on Mr. Murphy, President Roosevelt's representative in Algiers:

> Mr. Murphy, who is in the habit of associating only with the big Pétainist planters, shuts his door to republicans. . . . In a pinch, he reprimands his subordinates when they show an inopportune zeal in denouncing the activities of the Fifth Column.

Mr. Murphy, a representative of the State Department, is denounced to the French in exile as the friend of the big pro-German planters, and he is openly accused of protecting the Fifth Column; in other words, French traitors working for Hitler.

Such examples, remarkable for their crudeness and their violence, give but an incomplete impression of the technique used by *La Marseillaise*. By omitting comment upon certain events, by insinuations, nuances in headlines, subtitles, captions and cartoons, De Gaulle's newspaper constantly distilled hostility to America, and, from time to time, to Great Britain, too. It excelled in the art of arousing in the French distrust, fear, and, sometimes, even hatred

* A colloquial expression meaning "for nothing."

of their liberators. In short, it operated in exactly the same way as the Vichy press.

Pompei also wrote:

> Like many people I believe that liberating a country meant throwing out the foreign enemy and jailing our own scum.* I thought liberating a country meant saying to its people: you are free in the country of your creation. Get to work, liquidate, build, increase and multiply—and send us word when you have the housewarming. But apparently these statesmen who play at being military strategists, these strategists turned diplomats, these financiers and government officials who dabble in business, have found something else.
>
> Too bad. . . .

So then, the Americans were not liberating France but were doing "something else."

Quilici and his friends delighted in repeating that the Americans were "occupying" North Africa and that they wished to "occupy" France—this put them, in the mind of the French public, on the same plane with the German occupiers. And along with the word "occupy," the words "place under guardianship" occurred again and again. On March 14 Quilici wrote:

> Recently Cardinal Suhard . . . went to Rome. There he requested that Washington be informed of his great desire for American troops to occupy France on conclusion of the peace in order to prevent "Bolshevism."
>
> Now, one thing is certain! The French will never accept guardianship, however friendly.

Once again we must ask the French in France who read these lines: Did Vichy do better? Did they do better in Paris?

And the same Quilici wrote again, on May 23:

> Like the sandwich men of Vichy, the proconsuls are still at their posts. To keep them there, to uphold the law of the Marshal, and justify their strange shifts, they have for some time been using the excuse of "military necessity." The fall of Tunis put an end to those necessities which common sense had already condemned. Now suddenly new necessities

* French: *"Foutre l'ennemi dehors et les salopards dedans."*

turn up: "general strategic necessities arising from the Italian situation." A magnificent bubble, yet very transparent, in which we can see the astonishing perspectives for Europe adopted by certain people without Europe's consent.

According to De Gaulle's official newspaper, America is going to create a "magnificent bubble" in Europe. And she is planning to remake Europe against its will.

During the spring of 1943 *La Marseillaise* sharpened its weekly stabs-in-the-back of France's allies. On June 26 under the heading "A Moral Crisis," Quilici wrote:

The North African crisis is neither organic nor French. It is a moral and an external crisis. It is a crisis of international morality, and I am not the only one to be alarmed by it. It is easy to condemn the quarrels which apparently divide the French. To tell the truth, our troubles have been and are caused by a secret but firm determination to rule out the natural solution, the one all Frenchmen desire.

So the Americans had brought about a "moral crisis." They were also to blame for the crisis in North Africa that was tearing apart its political fabric and the French Army and Navy—and which was, alas, in large part the result of De Gaullist propaganda.

External pressures led to the co-presidency. External pressures are bringing about the co-command (reference to the Giraud-De Gaulle civil and military regimes). Let them not plead military necessity. The unity of the French Army is a French affair and it could be solved now were it not for outside interference.

Perhaps the meaning of this war is changing. . . . At first, it was a war for existence. Perhaps it is becoming more than a war for existence. We shall wage it with even greater enthusiasm to safeguard the rights of France that are being threatened.

What is the meaning of this ambiguous language? Which war are they referring to? Did they want to declare war on America for threatening the rights of France?

This time the British became thoroughly incensed. Churchill and Eden held a long conference. They decided to ban the publication of De Gaulle's paper in London. A brief telephone call informed the general's office that the license issued to *La Marseillaise* by His Majesty's Government had been revoked. The paper was no longer to appear in British territory.

What was De Gaulle's reaction?

He replied, in substance:

French sovereign rights are involved. If I wish to insult Roosevelt and the Anglo-Saxons I have the right to do so: I am master in my own house. I shall take my Quilici and my *Marseillaise* to Algiers, where we shall continue to quote to you your four freedoms in the teeth of your bayonets.

And actually *the* Quilici and *La Marseillaise*, banned in London, left by plane for Algiers—and started in all over again. It would take a volume to list the anti-American material put out by the De Gaullist paper. Historians of the De Gaullist political epic will find it all in the newspaper files of the Algerian library. The refrain "France under guardianship," invented by Goebbels and De Brinon, was repeated like a litany. On May 13, 1944, Quilici wrote:

The only power that can be established in France is the French Committee of National Liberation. However, the United States and England both refuse to recognize it as the provisional government of France. By this refusal, by this formal and arbitrary denial of a recognized and undisputable fact operating in daily life, France is left without a government. By this legalistic maneuver French power is subordinated to the Allied Command, in other words, France has been placed under guardianship.

And now—note this date: June 17, 1944.

On June 6 the Americans had invaded the shores of Normandy. The battle was still raging. General Eisenhower had taken Bayeux, but was held up at Carentan, Saint-Lô, and Caen. French beaches were littered with the bodies of dead GIs.

And all Quilici could find to say was:

The French must not be made to feel that the arrival among them of their welcomed comrades-in-arms means merely changing the forces of occupation.

He then goes on to accuse Cordell Hull, Churchill, and Eden of
not keeping their promises to De Gaulle, accuses Roosevelt of im-
posing on the French an American administration (the AMG)
and of considering the installation of Chautemps in Paris:

So much undeserved humiliation [with regard to the currency] . . .
a situation so distressing for the French and prejudicial to the Allies in
the eyes of the French and decent people everywhere, must have important motives behind it. Especially since Mr. Cordell Hull's promises,
reticent as they were, and the more definite promises of Mr. Churchill
and Mr. Eden, have not been fulfilled. Mr. Roosevelt's hostility to General de Gaulle has been mentioned. That may exist—though we should
like to know the reasons for it. However, the leader of a great country,
a man like the President of the United States, who is said to be diabol-
ically clever, does not build power politics on his personal feelings. In any
event, he does not persist in doing so after suffering a defeat like that
first one in North Africa. Mr. Roosevelt, it appears, has his own ideas
on the organization of French power. How much weight does he
imagine those ideas will have with the French, who invented the saying, "Every coal miner is master in his own house." * Mr. Roosevelt is
properly scrupulous and does not wish to force the issue. That is why
he imposes on us the AMG.

And, at the end, the usual trick: an American pro-De Gaulle newspaperman, a pal of the French De Gaullists, chose this moment—
when the guns were thundering in Normandy, when Eisenhower
was launching the attack to free France—to accuse President Roosevelt of seeking to take over French colonies. Quilici seized on that
article:

This Wednesday I came across another extraordinary article, a clipping
from the *United States News* of April 14, 1944. It is important to note
that this article is now being distributed among Allied soldiers in North
Africa. It explains America's policy of acquiring strategic bases throughout the world. The *Digest* prints the following résumé of it:
"Mr. Roosevelt and his advisers do not forget that the French, without a fight, turned over to Japan the big French naval base at Saigon,
Indo-China, thereby enabling Japan to outflank Singapore, and to cut
U. S. access to rubber and tin. The President remembers that, when the

* French: *Charbonnier est maître chez lui.*

United States was hardest pressed by German submarines, the French island of Martinique served as a hostile dagger aimed at the vitals of our Caribbean defenses. He has said definitely that French Dakar cannot be left under a control that will threaten the approaches to this hemisphere.

"The President is thinking also," the article goes on to say, "of Madagascar, New Caledonia, French Guiana, the islands of Miquelon and Saint-Pierre. He is unwilling to see the whole French empire restored intact, without guarantees that will protect U. S. security. General de Gaulle, on the other hand, insists on the restoration of France as a sovereign world power. He adamantly claims full rights to all French possessions. The unyielding attitude of General de Gaulle regarding these possessions is said to be the real explanation for Mr. Roosevelt's reluctance to give him complete recognition."

So the Americans covet Guiana, Martinique, Caledonia, Madagascar. And what else? Truly, the anti-American propaganda of *La Marseillaise* drew its inspiration from the slogans and themes of the Germans.

Exactly one month later, Roosevelt and Churchill partially recognized General de Gaulle; the former against his will, for he considered "the De Gaulle adventure" to be extremely dangerous for France, and doomed in advance to lead to a dictatorship; the latter equally against his will, but with the idea that Great Britain ought to play the De Gaullist card against the Communist card. The general was therefore able to return to France in Allied motor-trucks and set up an administration. It might have been expected that after this move the De Gaullist newspaper would give up its anti-Americanism. Not at all. On August 14, 1944, Quilici bitterly criticized General Eisenhower and accused him of trying to choose a French government:

I leave it to my colleagues in the United States and in England to judge if military men are fit for this political task, whether military authorities are qualified to recognize a government.

The observation has a certain piquancy: a general accusing military authorities of fundamental political incompetence!

But Quilici went on:

In every way, France will reject being placed under the guardianship of authorities—even French authorities—chosen by an outsider, though he be an ally and a friend.

"France which brought freedom to the world," declared General de Gaulle amid the applause of the Advisory Assembly. "France does not need advice from outside her borders in order to decide how to re-establish freedom in her own land."

France, I may add, would not permit Frenchmen to lend themselves to this game. We have had enough trouble setting up a State again in the midst of suffering. He who attacks French unity, he who attacks the security of the State, deserves the punishment of a traitor.

In passing let us underscore those last few words which, in the reader's mind, will acquire a fresh significance when we come to study General de Gaulle's attitude at the time of the Normandy landing: the Frenchmen who help American troops will be said to deserve the *punishment of traitors*.

Here is what the war record of *La Marseillaise* adds up to:

—It was eliminated from New York by *Pour la Victoire* on account of its anti-Americanism;

—Mr. Churchill banned it from London on account of its anti-Americanism and the difficulty it was causing in Anglo-American relations;

—In most of the major occurrences of the war, and notably at the time of the occupation of North Africa, it operated in a manner that differed very little from the techniques of the Vichy press;

—It greeted the entrance of the American liberators into Normandy by playing up that event as a "change of occupancy" and by threatening French "traitors" who helped the Americans establish order behind the front;

—It employed as a leading contributor Jules Romains, listed as a member of the board of directors of the France-Germany Committee, and featured his articles.

That is the way General de Gaulle's official newspaper in exile fought German propaganda throughout the entire tragedy of the occupation of France.

Historians, however, will not judge the role of the De Gaulle press in the war solely on the basis of *La Marseillaise*. Since it was an official organ and its articles were practically edited in De Gaulle's office, to which François Quilici had access at all times, and since it was published under the eye of the Anglo-American authorities, the newspaper was compelled to maintain a certain restraint. None whatsoever was shown by the newspapers of Brazzaville, Beirut, Madagascar, Nouméa, and other places, which were also financed by the general. The most outrageous, the most vulgar of all, *France Nouvelle*, was circulated in South America and particularly in Buenos Aires, which was throughout the war the most active center in the world of pro-Nazi and anti-Anglo-Saxon intrigue. *France Nouvelle* made wonderful use of the anti-Allied political atmosphere in which it appeared. Its most violent articles, aimed at General Giraud, always pointed past him to the State Department in Washington and the White House. "General Henri Giraud, American, General of Wall Street and the London Stock Exchange," the title of one of them, conveys the tone. I quote from it:

Anglo-Saxon newspapermen in Algiers [it begins] must have had some good horse-laughs the beginning of this week. . . .

We owe those Anglo-Saxon colleagues of ours a debt of gratitude for letting the cat out of the bag [the American plan to place General Giraud in command of the army above General de Gaulle] and giving us a chance to estimate the extent of the new and final injury which two "friendly" governments have just inflicted on the people of France.

What "final injury" had America inflicted on France? Why, its liberation!

An example of the good taste of *France Nouvelle* (Mr. Goebbels must have appreciated it) is a cartoon portraying Giraud as a grotesque dummy seated on the knee of a ventriloquist—the Dollar.

And·during the battle of Normandy, when the American soldiers were fighting on the beaches, *France Nouvelle* (June 24, 1944) printed the following reply to a foreign anti-De Gaullist newspaperman:

We are fully aware of the value of the dollar. We also know that
we will get the bill and that it will be a stiff one. But we don't give
a damn. . . .

You also add that American soldiers were the first to shed their blood
in Normandy. . . . But the prophets in Washington have no right to
use the blood of the dead and wounded as a means of forcing their
point of view on us.

The editor of this paper, a certain Guérin, was awarded the "Cross
of Liberation" for his articles, General de Gaulle himself making
the presentation. He was appointed "Deputy of the Resistance in
South America" to attend the Consultative Assembly in Algiers.
Honors were heaped upon him. Had he exercised his talents in
Paris or in Vichy and written exactly the same things, he would
probably have received the Iron Cross. Between the propaganda
of Nazi Pétainism and that of De Gaullism there was only a difference of geographical location. The traitors Suarès, Béraud, Brasil-
lach, Maurras, Lauzanne wrote nothing more violent against the
Allies than the De Gaulle journalists. Some of these authors have
been accused of taking German money. But the De Gaulle journalists insulted Great Britain and America with the money those
countries themselves furnished for the De Gaulle cause. This ag-
gravating circumstance did not prevent them, the moment they
arrived in Paris, from clamoring for—and in some cases obtaining
—the death of Pétainist writers. . . .

5. Vicissitudes of the Empire

I have never thought one should count that maxim wise which holds that the art of ruling lies in causing dissension and disorder on all sides.

LOUIS XIV

In those periods when order reigned in Rome, the Empire was bathed in grandeur. But when debauchery and corruption appeared, unrest and revolt at once spread everywhere.

TAINE

PRIOR to the liberation of France the De Gaullist experiment found expression throughout the French Empire in a depressing series of mishaps, dissensions, scandals, and in the case of Syria, complete catastrophe.

New York was a poor observation post for the events that were taking place in the Congo and in French West Africa. There were no good American correspondents at Brazzaville or Dahomey or in the Sudan, and Frenchmen traveling from the colonies to London, the headquarters of De Gaullism, did not pass through the United States. Remote rumors, too indirect to be worth recording, apprised us of the mistakes being made by the De Gaullist administration in those territories.

One important personage did come to New York from Brazzaville during the war, in April, 1942—Surgeon General Sicé, a first-rate officer and scientist, noted for his discoveries in tropical diseases. He was one of the first high-ranking officials to give active support to De Gaullism, and was one of the rallying points of the French in Equatorial Africa after the setback at Dakar. The Americans welcomed him cordially to the United States and provided him with liberal means to carry on his scientific researches and to improve sanitation in Brazzaville. He made an excellent impression here and left for London promising to return with full authority to confirm arrangements made verbally. The Americans never saw him again. Scarcely had Surgeon General Sicé reached De Gaulle when he was made a virtual prisoner. He was given an official post in the Department of Health in London—a soldier snatched from the battlefield, a scientist kept from his research laboratory. Later it was learned that he had been the victim of a vicious conspiracy that had originated in Brazzaville and in De Gaulle's staff headquarters. The name of a De Gaullist commissioner was mentioned; and there was also a matter of a business deal in which private interests were involved. For the rest, the Brazzaville radio and a few excerpts from the Brazzaville newspapers that reached America gave an incomplete but clear idea of the state of demoralization and fanaticism that prevailed in what was for a long time the "capital of the De Gaullist Empire." The story of the Sicé affair will have to be written later, after the necessary investigations have been made.

Another distant theater of De Gaullist operations was easier to keep an eye on—New Caledonia. There, the Americans sent their Marines, their soldiers, their officials, and their newspapermen; for New Caledonia was one of the vital strategic positions of the war of the Pacific, commanding the communication lines with Australia. Moreover, French officials and fighting men of Oceania on their way back to London had to pass through the United States, thus bringing in news. Everyone soon knew that De Gaullism was behaving badly there, causing personal quarrels, ceaseless administrative scandals and chronic fighting among Frenchmen, among De Gaullists themselves, and between local and American authorities. The latter were uneasy, and really took alarm when the Japanese advance threatened the island. Admiral Stark finally had to consider taking over complete charge of New Caledonia to put an end to the dangerous confusion.

We must, in justice, admit that De Gaulle did make an effort to bring order into the situation. But how could he have succeeded? He was directly responsible for the vast unrest sweeping over the French colonies. A general who had remained on the battlefield, dominating by his courage and selflessness the great drama of conscience set in motion by the French tragedy, would quickly have established moral unity among the bewildered and desperate French colonials cut off from the metropolis. But a general deserting the battleground of the fight to the finish, to which he had summoned Frenchmen from every corner of the world, in order to leap into a great adventure out of which he hoped to build his own political fortune, flaunting his greed before everyone and attracting as his accomplices the worst adventurers, could only provoke moral unrest and political upheavals.

On May 20, 1942, the Washington correspondent of the New York *Times* commented on an item issued by the State Department:

A conflict between two Free French Governors in New Caledonia has produced such a state of administrative demoralization that the United States has appealed to General Charles de Gaulle, leader of the Free French movement, to straighten out affairs in the interest of the common cause. Great Britain is understood to be supporting the plea.

The situation is most acute in New Caledonia but is duplicated to an extent in other Free French regions, such as Syria, where the Free French are reported to be in controversy with the British, and in French Equatorial Africa.

In the face of these conditions the United States is urging General de Gaulle to co-ordinate his forces and achieve unity of administration and purpose in order that the Free French will be able to oppose efficiently the common enemy rather than dissipate their strength by internal dissension.

The reference to the two governors touches on a matter typical of De Gaullist methods. Lacking precise information about the officials who rallied to his cause, and, above all, wishing to hand out positions on the basis of personal loyalty to himself, De Gaulle frequently appointed several people to the same post. The result was confusion of authority and immediate disputes. When M. Pleven arrived in New York to replace the delegate of Free France, M. de Sieyès, a former classmate of De Gaulle's who had fallen from grace, he appointed four delegates at the same time: M.M. Aglion, Boegner, Tixier, and De Roussy de Sales. At once intrigues and innumerable complications arose. The saying went around Washington that "Great Britain has only one ambassador, Lord Halifax, but De Gaulle has four!" Finally M. Adrien Tixier was chosen because he was a good yes-man—and the three other "delegates" vanished from the scene.

At Nouméa, De Gaulle had appointed two governors, Admiral d'Argenlieu and M. Sautot, and their noisy quarrels in the Australian and New Zealand press shocked our allies. Bertrand Hulen cabled:

The two Governors became so violently opposed to each other that an armed clash was narrowly averted. The populace sided with M. Sautot, but Admiral d'Argenlieu had the guns of his warships trained on Nouméa. Under these circumstances, M. Sautot fled to New Zealand.

The populace was so aroused, however, that Admiral d'Argenlieu found it convenient to leave for some undisclosed island in the Pacific. For the present, therefore, New Caledonia is without a Governor.

As a matter of fact, the De Gaullist naval governor had arrested the equally De Gaullist civil governor, had set him aboard a ship by force and sent him to London.

The disastrous impression made by these incidents was not easily erased and the disturbance continued indefinitely on the island— all the more as the De Gaullists tried to create a diversion by opening up a propaganda campaign against the Americans. Relations between the Americans and the French authorities became almost as bad as they were in France between German and French officials, despite the fact that the Japanese were speeding up their preparations to seize New Caledonia.

On December 24, 1943, the New York *Times* published a dispatch from Nouméa which read:

American troops stationed here and their administration were sharply criticized today by Governor Christian Laigret of New Caledonia, French colonial possession in the Pacific.

Governor Laigret issued a prepared statement, and later, in answer to questions, criticized particularly American Negro troops.

Major General Rush Lincoln, commander of the American forces on the island, declined to comment. Officers who have been here since the first American forces arrived in March, 1942, agreed, however, that most of the friction points had been minor and that relations between civilians and American troops had been generally good.

As an example of the good-will of American servicemen towards civilians, it was pointed out today that American troops were staging Christmas parties for orphans, needy children, old folks and even lepers. . . .

M. Laigret, who will leave soon to accept another post with the French Committee of National Liberation in Algiers, said in reply to questions that "one situation that has become quite intolerable is the American colored troops; we have many proofs of lack of discipline among them."

M. Laigret said he had asked that the City of Nouméa be designated as "out of bounds" for Negro soldiers and that they be restricted to camps outside of Nouméa.

"The colored troops are the terror of the white women of New Caledonia," he charged. "They have attacked them even in the company of their husbands and brothers. Our women are afraid to go out of the house after nightfall, though recently General Lincoln took action and the situation is a bit better."

M. Laigret also complained about the establishment of American canteens in Nouméa buildings. . . .

Every Frenchman who has lived in America can testify that while incidents may sometimes occur where American Negro troops are garrisoned, such incidents are quite rare and almost always of slight importance. Besides, it is impossible not to be struck by the resemblance between a propaganda campaign of this type and the propaganda the Germans have always carried on against colored French troops. If there is any difference between the two situations, it lies in the fact that the French colored troops are Africans, recruited sometimes from highly primitive tribes, whereas the American colored troops are United States citizens who were born in

America and have participated in its civilization for generations. But the anti-American propaganda at Nouméa, as well as in the rest of the De Gaullist territories, was ordered by the Cagoulards in London.

From New Caledonia the scandal spread to the island of Tahiti. Since there were no American troops on Tahiti, the De Gaullists there could only fight among themselves.

The De Gaullist *coup d'état* on Tahiti was organized in September, 1940, by Dr. de Curton—who was promptly elected governor—Chief Magistrate Sénac, Dr. Jacques Gilbert, and M. Elie Martin. Shortly thereafter a new governor, M. Jean Brunot, was appointed by London. M. Brunot had scarcely reached the island when violent quarrels broke out, whereupon he arrested M. Sénac and most of the other men responsible for swinging the colony over to De Gaulle. The arrested men sent a note to Admiral d'Argénlieu, High Commissioner for Oceania, in which they said:

> We have been illegally imprisoned, in total violation of the laws of the Republic. No complaint has been filed against us. We are allowed no means of defense. . . . We cannot believe that the admirable proclamations of General de Gaulle are intended to cover up a fascism like that against which we have risen in revolt.

There was no reply. Admiral d'Argenlieu sided with Governor Brunot. Sénac, however, escaped to New Zealand.

The persistent protests of Gilbert finally found an echo in the Oceanic vastness. A serious incident had occurred in Papeete, where anti-British propaganda was raging—a De Gaullist attack on the British consulate. In addition, there were unfortunate rumors regarding "the influence of certain private interests in De Gaullist circles." De Gaulle ordered an investigation and sent out his High Commissioner for War, General Legentilhomme. The new De Gaullist governor, M. Brunot, had just imprisoned the former De Gaullist governor, De Curton.

At that moment, a British official on Tahiti was warning his government that "the De Gaullists have engaged in all sorts of abuses and the situation may take a turn for the worse from one moment to the next, including an outbreak of individual crimes and of riots." In fact, riots had occurred in Nouméa on May 20, and as soon as this was known on Tahiti the general excitement increased.

General de Gaulle therefore hastily approved all the conclusions of the Legentilhomme report on July 17, 1942.

Other scandalous incidents broke out, however, in the two French colonies in America causing not only violent conflicts between French patriots but also an extreme tension between De Gaullists and Americans.

First, the affair at Guiana.

On March 18, 1943, after a popular uprising against Vichy, the mayor of Cayenne cabled his allegiance to General Giraud. The Americans learned of this through General Béthouart on the 19th of March and were very pleased. Giraud, as far as they could see, had no part in the kind of political agitation that followed on the heels of De Gaullism. Besides, American public opinion had been unfavorably impressed by the arrival, in various islands of the West Indies, of a number of escaped convicts from Cayenne who immediately proclaimed vociferously their enthusiastic allegiance to De Gaulle. Be that as it may, De Gaulle promptly protested against the choice made by the American government.

On March 21 the New York *Times* published the following report from its Washington correspondent:

The situation surrounding the French positions in the Western Hemisphere has been thrown into confusion, according to frank admissions here today, by an announcement from London of a sudden turnover of French Guiana to General Charles de Gaulle, head of the Free French.

The Free French statement reporting the adherence of the South American colony to General de Gaulle and the appointment of a De Gaullist Governor, followed an announcement made on Thursday by the French mission here that the colony had declared its allegiance to General Henri Giraud, High Commissioner for French North and West Africa.

General Giraud has designated Colonel Albert Jean Paul Lebel, of his military mission here, to proceed to French Guiana and assume the

Governorship. . . . The State Department has been backing General Giraud and collaborating in the effort to have not only French Guiana but also Martinique align themselves with the United Nations.

General Giraud had actually appointed M. Rapenne, stationed in the Sudan, and Colonel Lebel was to fill in the interim.

Two days later Colonel Lebel flew from Washington to take possession of the post in Guiana in the name of Rapenne. Colonel de Chevigné, De Gaulle's military attaché, immediately followed on an airliner to take over in the name of M. Collat. Under the eyes of the whole world and at an hour when France was writhing in agony, two French colonels were racing from Washington to Cayenne to seize for a faction the capital of a penal colony. At the same time another race began between Rapenne flying from the Sudan and Collat flying from the Cameroon. An official of the State Department said to me in Washington:

We are trying to free France, but the French who set themselves up as the incarnation of French liberation, do nothing but complicate our task. Sometimes they act as if they were really trying to discourage us and to make us relinquish our efforts.

Actually, not one of the colonies passed under De Gaullist control without dramatic incident. The same thing happened in the taking of Saint-Pierre and Miquelon.

These two French islands, only a short distance from Canada and Newfoundland, had remained loyal to Vichy. It is likely that they were being used as a spy center and observation post for German submarines. The English and the Americans were therefore interested in having them in the hands of the Free French. But it was quite evident that the Allies had to control the means of and choose the moment for taking them. Now, De Gaulle, for reasons of personal prestige and to help efface the persistent memory of his deplorable setback at Dakar, decided in July, 1940, to strike the blow as quickly as possible. He ordered Admiral Muselier to go to Canada under a pretext and to take advantage of his stay there to seize the islands.

Accordingly, in November, 1941, Muselier went to Montreal and Ottawa and laid his plan before the Canadian authorities. The latter at once raised the objection that the Washington government was the only one qualified to make any decision regarding a strategic move in American waters. Muselier thereupon called on the American minister in Ottawa, who referred the matter to the State Department.

Now, this took place at the time when President Roosevelt was, quite rightly, clinging to the idea of avoiding a break with the Vichy government in order to retain an observation post in France and a sort of diplomatic *pied à terre* in Europe. The American Intelligence Service in particular was working actively and very effectively. The State Department considered Admiral Muselier's proposal extremely inopportune and turned it down.

The admiral referred the matter to De Gaulle—who promptly entered into an argument with the Americans about it; in addition to everything else, he saw in the situation a good chance to involve Admiral Muselier in a diplomatic *impasse* and thus to get rid of him.

The full details of what happened are not yet known. It is certain that Muselier carried out De Gaulle's order, despite the strict veto by the Americans, after receiving from him the following cable on December 18, 1941:

AS REQUESTED HAVE CONSULTED BRITISH AND AMERICAN GOVERNMENTS STOP WE ARE CONVINCED CANADIANS THEMSELVES INTEND TO DESTROY RADIO STATION ST. PIERRE STOP THEREFORE I ORDER YOU CARRY OUT RALLYING OF MIQUELON ISLANDS WITH MEANS AT YOUR DISPOSAL WITHOUT APPRISING FOREIGNERS STOP I ASSUME COMPLETE RESPONSIBILITY FOR THE OPERATION STOP INDISPENSABLE SAFEGUARD FRENCH POSSESSION STOP

This occupation brought a vehement protest from the State Department. And De Gaulle used that protest as a weapon against the admiral.

Warned by Commandant Morel, his representative in London, of the plot against him, Muselier left Saint-Pierre in haste and returned to the British capital. There he discovered that the leader of the

De Gaullist Cagoulards had bought the cipher of the Navy code, which the admiral had used in his communications with Commandant Morel. Thereafter, at a meeting of the National Committee, disgraceful scenes took place between De Gaulle and the admiral. "You go about things in a detestable way, General," said Muselier. "You use the methods of the Gestapo." According to a witness De Gaulle replied by banging his fist on the table, smashing his chair and all but jumping at the admiral's throat. It is a fact that on leaving that memorable meeting, De Gaulle demoted the admiral—his superior in rank—took away his command and appointed him "Inspector General of the Navy"—just as, later, in breaking General Giraud, he appointed him "Inspector General of the Army." Admiral Muselier refused with dignity as General Giraud did. He went into retirement without pay and without position.

So ended the affair of Saint-Pierre and Miquelon. It had widened the split in the De Gaullist ranks in London, caused most serious difficulties to the Canadian authorities anxious to remain on friendly terms with America, provoked the lively resentment of the State Department—and presented German propaganda, which quickly knew all the facts, with a marvelous theme.

By this time the De Gaullist movement had reached such a state of decay that the British and the Americans were considering means for its eventual replacement.

On May 2, 1942, the New York *Times* had said:

There also have been signs of deterioration within the Free French delegation here [Washington].

But the deplorable incidents in Equatorial Africa, New Caledonia, Tahiti, Saint-Pierre and Miquelon, and Guiana were nothing compared to the infinitely more disastrous events that were to break out in Syria and in North Africa. The North African events are analyzed at length in various chapters of this book. Those that took place in Syria led to revolt, then to a breakup and a dismembering of the French Empire—when Syria and Lebanon, exasperated to the last degree, finally broke all ties with France.

The Syrian drama began in the month of June, 1941, with the British campaign to pluck from Vichy the administration of one of their most important strategic positions in the Mediterranean.

We shall not question here the necessity for English intervention in these territories. If they had not intervened, there is no doubt that the Germans would have attempted to gain a foothold in Beirut and Damascus—they had openly stated such intentions. The day after France fell they had sent their most skillful agents to Syria with orders to act under cover of the Italian Armistice Commission. Their espionage service was headed by a German subject, Roland Eilander, a native of Beirut. In September, 1940, another German, also a native of Beirut, took over as chief of the Gestapo. After November of that year the infiltration of military men under the leadership of a certain Major von Pratt began. Finally, in January, 1941, von Hentig, a noted specialist in Oriental questions, was appointed Minister of the Reich, to Beirut. Von Hentig undertook an extensive agitational campaign among the Arabs with the aim of discrediting the French. He stirred up riots at Homs, Aleppo, and Damascus. In May, 1941, Admiral Darlan gave the Germans permission to use the air bases of Syria, including the great airport of Nerab, near Aleppo. Shortly afterwards, sixty-six pursuit planes and forty transports landed there and hoisted the Swastika. General Dentz, commanding the French forces, had received explicit orders to offer no resistance to German and Italian aircraft, but "to resist by all possible means at any sign of British planes flying over." During the spring of 1941, German infiltration increased. Syria became a regular turntable for the whole German strategy in the Near East. From Beirut and Damascus the Reich backed the rebellion of Iraq, which imperiled Great Britain's oil supply and threatened to spread the flames far along the road to India. From Beirut and from Damascus, Germany encircled Turkey, supplying the terrific pressure von Papen exercised on Ankara. Finally, Beirut and Damascus constituted an immediate and terrible menace to Suez.

The English, then, cannot be blamed for seizing the initiative and attacking Syria and Lebanon in June, 1941. And the little De

Gaullist army should undoubtedly have been held aloof from the military operation for reasons both of French high policy and of local policy. French policy—because the arrival of the De Gaullists in Syria and Lebanon led to an inevitable battle with the regular French forces and created *de facto* a civil war among Frenchmen, which was not absolutely necessary, and which delighted the Germans, who were seeking every opportunity to divide France and to cause irreparable bloodshed between French factions. Local policy —because it was to the interest of Free France not to assume visible responsibility in a war that would inevitably bring to one part of the moral Empire of France, the usual train of suffering, misery, and ruin, and would consequently arouse the resentment of the population against her.

The first clause in the Churchill-De Gaulle agreement of July 1, 1940, specifies that:

General de Gaulle is engaged in raising a French force composed of volunteers. This force, which includes naval, land and air units, and scientific and technical personnel, will be organized and employed against the common enemy. This force will never be required to take up arms against France.

In September, 1940, as De Gaulle withdrew before the guns of the *Richelieu* at Dakar, he declared: "I shall never be responsible for making my soldiers shed French blood. For that matter, the solemn promises I have given and my own treaty with the British forbid me to do so." What made him forget, then, in June, 1941, his words, his writings, his act, the agreements he had made—and caused him "to take up arms against France"?

Obviously, he expected a swift and crushing victory. He anticipated that the French regulars would rally to him enthusiastically and that the population, lured by his promises, would follow suit. These hopes and calculations were tragically frustrated.

On June 1, 1941, he made up his mind to throw the Free French forces against Syria, appointed General Catroux his representative in the Levant, and instructed him to issue a proclamation granting full independence to the peoples of Syria and Lebanon. His proclamation was:

At the moment when the forces of Free France, together with the forces of the British Empire, our ally, are entering your territory, I declare that I assume the powers, responsibilities and duties of France's representative in the Levant. This I do in the name of Free France, which is the true and traditional France, and in the name of her leader General de Gaulle.

In this capacity I have come to put an end to the regime of the mandate and to proclaim you free and independent.

You will henceforth be sovereign and independent peoples, and you may either divide into separate states or unite into one single state. Your sovereign status will be guaranteed by a treaty, in which our mutual relations will be defined.

It is said that as General Catroux was about to sign this historic document, so pregnant with meaning, he came close to refusing. In failing to do so, as in many other instances, he showed a culpable docility.

The independence of Syria and Lebanon has had most resolute partisans and most determined opponents in French political and diplomatic circles. Neither Poincaré, Herriot, Tardieu, nor Blum, the greatest Premiers of the era between the two wars, men of the Right and men of the Left, could bring themselves to grant it, despite the heavy pressure to which they were so often subjected. This comes down to saying that France could never make up her mind to take that step.

How, then, could a brigadier general who had received no political authority from France consider himself qualified to make such a promise without the consent of the French people?

De Gaulle expected his offer of independence to stir up a wave of immeasurable enthusiasm in Syria and Lebanon. Delirious crowds, he imagined, would welcome him as a hero and liberator, shower him with flowers and open wide to him—like triumphal arches—the doors of churches and mosques. The prospect of such glory went to his head; it seemed to him that it would re-echo throughout the world, augmenting his renown, his legend, his prestige. To win

that prestige—obsession and evil genius of all usurpers in history—
he assumed the right to dispose of the French Empire, to scatter
its pieces to the winds. Unfortunately, in so doing he was sowing
the seed of innumerable disorders. An unconsidered gesture set in
motion the gears of political complications which one day would
unsettle France and turn her violently against Great Britain and
America; awaken burning aspirations in the depths of the Arabian
peoples; and in a world already in revolution cause a new earthquake that would be felt from the Atlantic to the Indian Ocean
and would pose difficult problems for the Allies at war with Japan.

Later De Gaulle was to try to clear himself of his irreparable
mistake by accusing the British of having forced him to make his
inflammatory promise to the Lebanese and Syrians. All diplomatic
documents establish, however, that the British refused to grant
De Gaulle political recognition and, in consequence, the right to
represent France and to pledge her future. If, therefore, Britain had
exerted pressure on De Gaulle it would have been in such obvious—
such flagrant contradiction to the attitude of the Foreign Office
that it would have had no force, value, or power. Besides, De Gaulle
was in that phase of his adventure in which he was already violently
opposing Churchill's wishes on every occasion. Not once did the
De Gaullist propaganda, which so often stressed his grievances
against Great Britain, dare to suggest at that time that the offer
to Lebanon and Syria was provoked by British intrigue. They hailed
it as an example of the general political conceptions and revolutionary inspiration of the hero of the liberation.

My distrust and fear on learning in New York of the Catroux
proclamation are expressed in a letter which, as a member of the
Commission on Foreign Affairs, I wrote at once to French Headquarters in London—addressing Admiral Muselier—in the absence
of General de Gaulle, whom I did not know where to reach:

France has no authority to offer or to grant independence to Syria ·
and to Lebanon, whose fate depends on the League of Nations. The
League has given France a mandate which she can accept or refuse, and
nothing more. . . .

If Lebanon does not belong by right to the French Empire, it does belong to its moral Empire for indisputable historical and sentimental reasons. Throughout the ages Lebanon has been the main foundation of the French Empire. I consider it a major political error to provoke this separation. If General de Gaulle grants independence so easily to 800,000 poor Maronite peasants who have never constituted an independent state, how can he refuse it later to millions of Moroccans, Tunisians and Annamites who for centuries maintained free and flourishing kingdoms and empires? I urge you to point out to the general the danger of a concession which amounts to the first dismemberment of our Empire and gives the signal for an even greater dismemberment.

Let me add that I see in the present situation a moral anomaly which may have very serious results. For the Vichy soldiers appear to be fighting to preserve Syria and Lebanon for France, whereas General de Gaulle's soldiers are fighting to separate Syria and Lebanon from France.

And De Gaulle's political maneuver did have the distressing effect of exasperating the French Army of Vichy, who were told: "Defend Syria and Lebanon, which are lost to France if England and the De Gaullists win!" Captive France, dismayed by this fratricidal war, was thrown into new misery. And German propaganda chalked up one of the great psychological triumphs of the war.

Then came the inevitable epilogue of disaster.

De Gaulle suddenly realized the immense mistake he would be making if he carried out the promise he had made to the Syrians and Lebanese. How could he blame Marshal Pétain for having compromised the Empire and having lost Indo-China if he tolerated the separation of Syria and Lebanon? He therefore decided to go back on his word. He appointed a high commissioner—M. Helleu—for Syria and Lebanon, and informed the dejected populace that their fate would not be decided until after the war.

Unfortunately, too, the De Gaullist administration showed itself to the Lebanese and Syrians in the worst possible light. The De Gaullists took over the positions of the Pétainists without bringing the least moral change, the least sense of reconciliation and French unity, the least spirit of heroism. And they did bring fanatacism and corruption. The native populations saw in his partisans merely a new revolutionary faction, in which they sought in vain the features of traditional France, and whose authority and right they questioned. It is a law of history that illegitimate powers are never readily accepted in protectorates or in imperial colonies. The French Revolution of 1789 was responsible for the uprising in Haiti and the loss to France of that pearl of the Antilles, that most beautiful gem in the crown of the Kingdom. Napoleon was obliged to cede Louisiana. If, in the present war, England had lost her old legitimate institutions, Canada, Australia, and the maharajas of India would never have remained within the grip of a brigadier general or a rear admiral risen from chaos to replace the King, and the British Empire would have floundered in the greatest shipwreck in history. To keep Syria and Lebanon, the chief need was for De Gaulle to appear as the continuator, the defender, and the heroic savior of French legality.

The revolt soon spread. It reached Lebanon, whose Christian peoples have never since the Crusades failed to show the deepest friendship for France. The Maronites with their thousand-year-old traditions, who live grouped about their old patriarch in their lofty mountains around the gorges of the Orontes, from the valley of the Anachorites and the historic cedars beneath which Solomon sat—accustomed to defy the infidel Turks and Arabs and to seek French aid against them—these Maronites were reluctant to turn toward the new master sent them by the exile. There were demonstrations in Beirut. Students shouted: "Down with France! Down with De Gaulle!" Their cries re-echoed far beyond the city among the high mountains and in the red desert. Since the collapse of the Frankish kingdom of Jerusalem, never had voices hostile to France reverberated in those spaces. Most Lebanese in Egypt, in America, and throughout the world sided with their brothers.

M. Helleu informed De Gaulle of the gravity of the situation. De Gaulle, who was then in Algiers, fearing the political repercussions of these events among the Arabs of North Africa as well as in French circles in London and Algiers, thought he was in a posi-

tion to use stern measures. He arrested the President of the Lebanese
Republic, Bechara el Khoury, his prime minister, Ruad Solh, and
the leading cabinet ministers and deputies. Helleu objected that this
fantastic decision might have serious consequences. De Gaulle repeated the order and it was carried out.

The British minister in Beirut at that time was General Spears,
the British M. P. who had flown De Gaulle from Bordeaux to
London in June, 1940. Spears warned Churchill that the anger of
the Lebanon and Syrian populations against the French was reach-
ing the boiling point, that it was producing reactions throughout
the Near East and that it was jeopardizing one of the most sensitive
theaters of the war. Churchill asked De Gaulle to release the
Lebanon prisoners immediately and to make every effort to restore
calm.

De Gaulle refused.

Armed revolt broke out at once. Regular Lebanese troops, students, revolutionaries, priests, took to the mountains and guns
went off. Next Syria, inhabited by Mussulmanic peoples much less
devoted to France than the Maronites, rose in rebellion. Finally,
the tumult covered the whole Near East. Then the Prime Minister
of Egypt, Nahas Pasha, sent a letter to De Gaulle advising him
that the Egyptian government could not accept the attitude of the
French in Beirut and that unless matters were improved Egypt
would change her attitude towards France. A few days later the
Prime Minister of Iraq, Nuri es Said, announced the rupture of
diplomatic relations with the French authorities in Lebanon. From
Mecca the King of Saudi Arabia wired Churchill that he would
not tolerate De Gaulle's broken promise to Lebanon. Finally, in
Turkey, sore spot of diplomatic strategy, demonstrators paraded
through the capital shouting: "Down with France! Down with De
Gaulle!"

These developments, naturally, created much uneasiness in Great
Britain and the United States. An official American note went so
far as to say:

The French Committee of Liberation was reminded that the United States would be unable to understand how a nation suffering from oppression on its own home soil could take a step that might infringe on the liberties of another people.

De Gaulle was obliged to yield. On November 22 he ordered the Lebanese prisoners released, and dismissed his representative, M. Helleu.

Questioned by correspondents of large news agencies and American newspapers, Helleu said: "Everything that's happened is very distressing, but I am not responsible for it. I warned General de Gaulle that the arrests would have the gravest consequences. But he refused to listen."

Thus, after causing French blood to flow, after embroiling themselves irreparably with the Syrians and with the Lebanese—friends of France for a thousand years—and then with the authorities of Egypt, Turkey, Iraq, and Arabia—not to mention serious difficulties with Great Britain and America—the De Gaullists were still quarreling among themselves.

One might well reflect, then, on the proud reproaches De Gaulle addressed to Marshal Pétain on February 28, 1941, at the time France lost Indo-China:

The Free French will never recognize any violation of the integrity of the Empire, nor any territorial or political modification of Indo-China or any other colony. . . .

The gory incidents that broke out in 1945 need not be discussed here, for they were but the inevitable result of the facts related above.

6. The Americans in North Africa

France has lost a battle; she has not lost the war.

GENERAL DE GAULLE

Tell the truth, general. France did lose the war but her allies will win it.

ANTOINE DE SAINT-EXUPERY

THROUGHOUT the summer of 1942 the situation of the Allies on all fronts appeared to be, if not desperate, at least tragically critical. One by one they were losing their positions in the Pacific, and Australia was threatened by invasion. In Europe, Russia seemed beaten and the Germans had reached the outposts of the Caucasus and the suburbs of Stalingrad. In Washington the Soviet Ambassador, the eminent Litvinoff, was urging Americans to send aid and especially to open a second front before it was too late. "We are on the verge of collapse," he said. "Our heroic efforts will be wasted if the democracies cannot take a more active part in the war before winter." The British were falling back in Libya, and Egypt, gateway to their African Empire and key to the road to India, seemed at the mercy of Rommel.

What could the Anglo-Americans do? Their armies, in particular the American Army, were not ready. The latter, hastily improvised, had been in existence only one year. Officers and men were totally lacking in experience and confidence. Moreover, submarines were inflicting heavy losses on Allied shipping. It appeared impossible for the Allies to risk a big well-trained army on the European Continent, where the Germans still had large forces of unquestionable strength. To those familiar with the tactical and strategic elements of the situation, any attempt at a landing in France appeared premature and almost certain to result in disaster.

For that reason I did my best to stir up interest in an Allied attack on North Africa. I went to Washington and called on several important men who might be in a position to influence military decisions. In addition, since public opinion is all-powerful here, I tried to win it over. With this in mind I wrote several particularly vigorous articles. On August 15, 1942, *Pour la Victoire* published under the title of "Eurafrica" my first public plea favoring the expedition:

If the Anglo-Americans should succeed in getting a foothold in Algeria and Morocco, they would find in Africa:

(1) Air bases that would give them absolute mastery of the Mediterranean, the life line of Europe; these bases would put all parts of the European Continent within striking distance of their planes.

(2) Naval and military bases useful in launching an expeditionary force toward some point in Europe.

(3) The possibility of knocking out Italy almost at once; of preventing Spanish intervention, which would be Hitler's immediate objective in case Russia is defeated; of bringing Turkey into the Allied fold.

(4) The possibility of getting military aid and supplies to Russia by way of the Black Sea.

(5) The possibility of recruiting between 500,000 and 1,000,000 soldiers among native populations—a fundamental problem, for according to whether that enormous military mass is placed on the Axis side of the scales (should the Germans occupy Africa) or on the Allied side (if the Allies occupy it) the equilibrium of military forces will be decisively affected.

(6) The possibility of transporting American military power to the threshold of Europe, thus furnishing the United States with the battlefield they need in order to put their enormous forces into operation.

On September 5 I published another article; its title speaks for itself: "Victory through Africa."

Let us assume that the British are barricaded in their island and masters of the seas, the Russians are thrown back to the East but holding firm and that the Americans and their allies are in control of North Africa from Casablanca to Cairo and from Casablanca to Dakar. Under this hypothesis, Germany is encircled in Europe, blocked on the North, on the East, and on the South. Surrounded on all sides, cut off .from Asia, Africa and America, with no access to any free waters, she suffocates. Not only that, but she lives under constant threat of aerial bombardment and possible invasions by sea or from the sky. She is turned in upon herself, that is to say upon areas ruined by war, poverty and famine. The peoples she has enslaved rebel, paralyze and sabotage her home front, thus adding to her perils. If she cannot break this encirclement, she must die. . . . The important point, therefore, is to encircle Germany.

Conclusion: there is a good chance that the next phase of the war may be decided in Africa. . . . Nowhere in the world are conditions more unfavorable for the Germans.

Following the accepted journalistic tactic of repeating one's leading ideas like hammer blows, I continued my campaign in the next number of *Pour la Victoire,* under the title "The Problem of Dakar." This time I insisted on the occupation of the great port of West Africa, which was vitally important to security in the Atlantic Ocean and of the countries of Latin America. I was advised, however, not to go on with that subject. I thought I understood the meaning of the suggestion—and I stopped writing along this line.

Two months later, on November 8, 1942, the Anglo-American Army landed in North Africa!

I do not wish to give the impression that my persistent efforts had the slightest influence upon that tremendous event which was "to turn the tide." The opinion of an exiled French deputy could not have weighed very heavily with President Roosevelt and his advisors. But I allow myself to think that it did not discourage them. In any case, of all French exiles, of the entire De Gaullist press and of the press in America, where I was among so many prominent journalists and American military analysts, I was the only one who urged repeatedly and with firm conviction the solution from which victory finally emerged. And from being alone in this, I conclude—as I do from every other incident of my self-imposed mission while in exile—that perhaps one day my fellow countrymen may realize that

I served them to the best of my ability during the days of their captivity and their martyrdom.

Be that as it may, the fact that I had run such a campaign no doubt inspired me to show more enthusiasm than others for the glorious news of November 8, 1942. A drop of personal satisfaction was legitimately mixed with my patriotic joy at seeing "America leap to Africa and seize a foothold on the French portion of the Mediterranean shore." Of course, the entry of the Anglo-Americans into Algiers and Casablanca, the overwhelming news that went with it, the arrival of General Giraud on the battlefield, the victory, the first victory of the war after a long period of defeat, desperation and darkness—all this was an intoxicating and stirring experience to every French patriot.

I read the news in the New York *Times* the morning of November 9. My excitement knew no bounds. Jumping into a taxi I gave the address of the French Delegation at 526 Fifth Avenue (headquarters of the De Gaullists).

The elevator whisked me to the fifth floor. I rushed into the office.

"Where is M. André Philip?" I asked.

(André Philip, the deputy from Lyons, had recently escaped from France, had been appointed Commissioner of the Interior by De Gaulle in London, and was temporarily in America on a special mission.)

"My dear fellow!" I shouted, bursting into his office. "What a great day! . . . Let me embrace you!"

To my utter consternation, Philip stopped me with a gesture. I looked at him. He was gloomy, tense; his eyes did not meet mine and his mouth was drawn in a bitter line.

"But what's the matter?" I cried. "Haven't you heard?"

"Yes . . . yes . . . I know," he answered. "It's all very unfortunate. . . . What are the Americans doing in Africa? . . . And why have they chosen Giraud? . . . Giraud! He is a Fascist! . . . The Americans may have won a military victory, but they have called on the forces of fascism, and they are going to lose the political war. . . ."

"What do you mean, Philip? Giraud is a magnificent French soldier. He is no more a Fascist than you or I. He is no more of a reactionary than Joffre, Foch, Castelnau, Mangin and all the generals who won the last war . . . I have known Giraud since 1915, and I can testify to his hatred for the Germans. . . . In getting his help, the Americans have pulled off a master stroke. . . . As to their victory in Africa, that means actually the beginning of final Victory."

"Don't you see, they failed to call on General de Gaulle?"

"Have a little sense, Philip. Two years ago De Gaulle tried to take Dakar. He failed completely. Moreover, a good section of the French troops stationed in North Africa are regular-army men from Syria who fought the De Gaullist soldiers and hate De Gaulle. From the American point of view, if there was one man it would have been unwise to choose when they were trying to cut down difficulties with the French, that man was De Gaulle."

"I have just been in touch with him in London. He was not even informed. . . ."

"That first unlucky experience at Dakar proved that De Gaulle's crowd was filled with spies. The leakage from De Gaullists tipped off the Germans and the Vichyites about the British preparations, and the expedition failed. Why should the Americans have run the same risk? They were out to succeed. That's all."

For a moment I was silent. Then I went on:

"You are not in the proper frame of mind, my dear Philip. You have no right to show such bitterness and resentment on a day of victory. Frenchmen in France are leaping for joy today at the news. Frenchmen in exile ought to thrill with the same emotion and the same enthusiasm. Take my advice! Pull yourself together. And cable De Gaulle that his sole duty is to rush at once to the side of General Giraud and the Americans, and take part in the battle of Africa which is inevitable now that German airmen have landed in Tunisia."

"Never! De Gaulle shall not go to Africa! De Gaulle shall stay in London. Even if he wanted to go to Africa, we who represent the

Resistance would stop him, because De Gaulle is a political symbol."

"If he is a symbol, he is a symbol of the fight to the finish. And would you have him hold aloof from the battle which will decide the fate of French Africa?"

"De Gaulle is first of all a political figure and he has no business to fight."

"De Gaulle is first of all a soldier and he must fight."

"You are not 'pure,' Kerillis!"

"'Pure'? What do you mean?"

"A pure De Gaullist!"

"I assure you, Philip, you are talking through your hat. I am a Frenchman and I want to see the French stand together to drive the Germans out of France and free my countrymen. That's all I am."

Thereupon I left my former parliamentary colleague. Though disturbed by our conversation I attached little importance to it, for I remembered that André Philip had never had the reputation in Parliament of being very level-headed or having very sound judgment. Quickly regaining my enthusiasm, I sent off two cables, one to De Gaulle, in London, congratulating him on an event which justified his magnificent order of the day of June 18, 1940, the other to Giraud, in Algiers, expressing my compliments, my good wishes, and my gratitude as a Frenchman.

But events of the following days were to be amazingly revealing. For the Philip incident was not an isolated case. The De Gaullists I met and those who wrote to me from the most distant parts of the two Americas, all spoke the same language. A strange psychological phenomenon (which I was to observe later in many situations) gave rise to the same immediate reactions in men who did not know each other and could not even have been influenced by one another. De Gaullism had definitely stirred up an incredible fanaticism, deeply deforming consciences and tragically corrupting minds. Party spirit, with all its dangerous mental quirks, had been formed and developed in exile. A De Gaullist in New York and a De Gaullist in London, Cairo, New Caledonia, or Algiers reacted towards events in exactly the same abnormal way. Not one of them was thinking of France: all were thinking of De Gaulle. The moment the African campaign got going without de Gaulle and threatened to raise another general to fame, De Gaullists could not rejoice in it and even felt a furious resentment.

I know of no more striking example of that state of mind than the one which occurred in New York three days after the landing in Africa, on Armistice Day, November 11. France Forever, the De Gaullist group in New York, had organized a large public meeting which was attended by nearly 3,000 persons. Five speakers—four Frenchmen and one American—addressed the crowd. Not one of the French speakers even so much as referred to the battle of Africa, to General Eisenhower's victory, or to General Giraud. Adrien Tixier, General de Gaulle's representative in Washington, did not attend the ceremony, but asked to have his speech read. That speech contained not one word of gratitude toward General Eisenhower and the Americans, not a fraternal word for Giraud, not a word of hope at the first gleam of victory in the war. The reader may refer to documents published in connection with that rally and to accounts of it which appeared in the New York newspapers on November 12, 1942; they bear witness to this inexplicable silence.

In London, however, the first reactions seem to have been a little better—a little more French. Dispatches from American correspondents noted the satisfaction of the De Gaullist groups. But that satisfaction did not last, and very soon they began to feel "uneasy." That "uneasiness" was the beginning of a ghastly quarrel between generals, of a great moral drama which was to tear asunder Frenchmen in exile and the French Army at war; it was complicated by wide international repercussions, and it shocked the whole world.

For the second time I cabled to General de Gaulle:

URGE YOU NOT ALLOW YOURSELF BE INFLUENCED BY BLIND AND FANATICAL PARTISANS STOP EVENTS IN AFRICA BRILLIANT CONFIRMATION YOUR ATTITUDE AND MAGNIFICENT MORAL VICTORY STOP YOUR PLACE NOW IS ON THE BATTLE-FIELD OF AFRICA ALONGSIDE GENERAL GIRAUD AND FRENCH SOLDIERS WHO WILL DRIVE BACK THE GERMANS STOP IMPLORE YOU GO AS FAST AS POSSIBLE TO FRONT LINE STOP FUTURE OF FRANCE IN BALANCE DOWN THERE STOP

HISTORY WILL JUDGE YOU IN THIS DECISIVE HOUR STOP MORE THAN EVER
REST ASSURED MY ENTHUSIASTIC DEVOTION AND TRUST STOP

HENRI DE KERILLIS

De Gaulle answered this, in a letter dated December 20, 1942, as follows:

I must tell you that I do not wholly share your point of view. What you don't seem to understand is that the whole business was deliberately staged without our knowledge. If, as you suggest, I had wanted to betake myself to Algeria and Tunisia with tanks and guns in order to join in the battle, our Allies themselves would have prevented me by every means at their disposal.

This letter filled me with astonishment. Could De Gaulle be so ill-informed regarding American views? Was he sincere? Could he believe that Eisenhower would stop him if he wanted to fight von Arnim?

I replied at once—January 20, 1943:

An extraordinary and regrettable misunderstanding is arising. I feel it my duty to set things straight and I beg you to take fullest account of my statements and assurances, which represent a totally disinterested point of view.

(1) The Americans organized the North African landing without consulting you because of late you have been playing a political role which could not help them in any way in the African theater—on the contrary. They have no ill feeling towards you. They are convinced that you were not the man to swing General Noguès, Governor Chatel, Admirals Fenard, Estéva, and Governor-General Boysson over to their side. And you know very well that this is true.

(2) If you go to Algiers to fight the Germans, the Americans will not "prevent you by every means" but they will help you "by every means."

Let me tell you in all sincerity that the men about you or your diplomatic representatives who have misinformed you so completely on the question of the American attitude, are traitors to your own cause; for if you allow the battle which will decide the war to be fought without doing your duty as a French general and rushing to arms, you will no longer have the right to stand as the symbol of the fight to the finish.

Let me add that if you really think the Americans are capable of hindering you in the accomplishment of this sacred duty, well then, run the risk and go anyway, and if they refuse you the right to serve as a general, ask permission to serve as a simple soldier.

At the time I still had not the faintest idea that De Gaulle had definitely decided to swap his role of general for that of a politician. I had noticed his absence from the battlefields of Syria and Libya, and had thought it accidental. In any event, I had reached this point in our pathetic correspondence when I received a letter from a lady in De Gaulle's intimate group in London, in which she acknowledged receipt of my book *Français, voici la Vérité* ("Frenchmen, Here Is the Truth"), which I had sent to her. She let slip a casual remark which cast a glaring white light on the drama that was beginning to unfold.

"The question is: Who is to be the liberator?"

To this I replied:

"For me, Madame, the only question is: Will France be liberated? Nothing else interests me."

It was one of the most poignant moments of my exile. My faith in De Gaullism had not yet died, but it was wavering like a flame suddenly flickering in the evil wind of passion and human ambition.

I had in the meantime asked De Gaulle to grant me an interview in London. I wanted to have a thorough and decisive conversation with him on his attitude toward the African events and toward American politics. I was ready to cross the Atlantic immediately.

The reply came quickly through his representative in Washington, Adrien Tixier, who wrote:

General de Gaulle has cabled me in code asking me to give you the following message: "I received your letter of December 2nd. I shall be glad to see you in London. *A bientôt.* Signed: General de Gaulle."

General de Gaulle instructs me to inform you that he wishes to defray the expenses of your trip.

With kindest regards,

Adrien Tixier

Such was the text of the letter typed by the official stenographer. Everybody at the De Gaullist headquarters must have known that the general's invitation had been forwarded to me. But Tixier added a postscript in his own handwriting:

General de Gaulle informs me that he will come to the United States very soon.

It was as plain as day. Officially, Tixier invited me to leave at once for London. But semiofficially, he warned me that if I went, I would not meet the general who was about to come to Washington. Through telephone conversations he kept me dangling for two months in this false belief.*

The general did not arrive until two years later.

Whether Tixier was alarmed at the idea that I might tell De Gaulle the truth, or whether he was carrying out instructions from Cagoulards in London, no less alarmed than he, he managed to prevent me from meeting the general.

By the time I discovered the true situation it was too late. Besides, the winding up of the Darlan affair by assassination had by then changed the African situation and had led me to believe that the difficulties would now be smoothed out.

We must here go into the Darlan affair, because in it the good faith of the Americans was put into question and their intentions and their actions misrepresented by a lying propaganda; and above all because it is one of the most mysterious and staggering incidents of the whole war. The De Gaullists were the first to hurl bitter reproaches at our liberators, when they deserved not only the eternal gratitude of Frenchmen but sincere admiration for their skill in improvisation, their political ingenuity, the decisiveness and boldness which they showed at the moment when the vacillating gods were changing sides.

First of all, had they or had they not already made a deal with Admiral Darlan when they landed in North Africa, on November 8, 1942?

* It is true that for three or four days in December, 1942, there was some talk of De Gaulle making a trip to America. But that same talk had kept bobbing up every month since November, 1940, and De Gaulle had firmly made up his mind not to come.

Having had the opportunity to consult the best sources, and having had access to certain documents still unknown to the general public, I can answer positively: "No; when the Americans arrived in North Africa they did not even know whether they could lay hands on the admiral and of course, therefore, could not have anticipated that they would be able to conclude with him the famous transaction that delivered North Africa into their hands."

There is some thought that the American minister, Robert Murphy, who played such a decisive role in the diplomatic-military events that marked the invasion, "knew that the admiral knew" that the landing was imminent, and that he also knew that the admiral had hastened to Africa in the hope of taking a big part in a great adventure and was ready to negotiate with him.

This hypothesis has no merit.

The simplest and most likely explanation is the true one. Having failed in their negotiations with Weygand, the Americans prepared their attack in North Africa in co-operation with Giraud and Lemaigre-Dubreuil. They encountered three surprise elements: on the one hand, the hostile attitude of the Navy, the Army and the French population; on the other, the inability of Giraud, who had turned against Pétain and had been condemned by him, to make the Pétainist armed forces obey him; and finally, the unexpected arrival of Darlan in Algiers, either to visit his son who was sick, or summoned there by Admiral Fenard, Secretary-General of Algeria. Hence Mr. Murphy, knowing the difficulties and hazards of the military operation and alarmed at the weakness of the forces carrying it out, seized the opportunity offered by Darlan's presence, and, on his own initiative, without General Eisenhower's knowledge, started the machinery which led to negotiations with the admiral.

With this point settled, it will be easier to understand the development of events.

When the Americans made contact with the French Army in Africa on November 8, 1942, a large part of that army was loyal to Marshal Pétain. And when the Marshal passed sentence on Giraud and issued orders to the officers to resist the Americans, there was a noticeable wavering in their ranks as well as among the naval personnel stationed in Tunisia, in Algeria, and in Morocco. Certain elements did not hesitate to fire on the American troops. Others uneasily held back. Very few went over to them at once. History will place the responsibility where it belongs. Its judgment will no doubt be harsh but it will perhaps allow for extenuating circumstances in judging the mental victims of such a muddled revolutionary age.

At that moment Pétain's prestige was still practically unimpaired. The Army saw in him the hero of Verdun sacrificing himself to spare his country worse sufferings. They felt that the only duty that stood out clearly in the abyss of disaster in which France was wallowing was that of obeying blind discipline. Moreover, German-inspired propaganda had undermined the officers' old confidence in Anglo-Saxon strength. They considered the British and the Americans equally incapable of making a landing in force in North Africa. These doubts felt by the Army were fairly well expressed in a remark attributed to General Weygand.

"Can we count on you, General?" an American diplomat had asked a few days before the occupation.

"If you come with ten battalions—no. If you come with ten divisions—yes," Weygand replied.

As a matter of fact, the Vichy radio and the German radio tried to reduce the importance of the American invasion by minimizing the number of effectives involved. The most widely publicized theory was that Eisenhower would conduct a few spectacular commando raids and would then retire from North Africa—whereupon the Germans would rush in and carry out terrible reprisals. The rich Algerian colonists, among whom Nazi influences were strong, were openly hostile, since many of them were enjoying financial prosperity through obtaining high prices from Germany for their wine and wheat.

In any event, since General Giraud was not having much success in swinging over the French Army, the situation of the Americans was rapidly becoming critical. The Germans were coming by air from Sicily to Tunisia. Their agents in Spain and Spanish Morocco were stirring up the Riffs—mercenaries and good fighters. The native populations of South Morocco and the high Algerian plateaus were becoming increasingly nervous; and a general uprising of Arabs, aided or merely tolerated by the French Army and backed by the intervention of both the Germans and the Spaniards, might mean catastrophe. . . . It was then that Mr. Murphy got in touch with Darlan, who had been caught in the invasion at his son's bedside in a hospital in Algiers and taken prisoner. It was only when the Americans realized that French soldiers and sailors were welcoming them to African soil with gunfire, when they had reason to fear that the French fleet might rally the Italian fleet to stab their landing in the back, when, in short, they were faced with the danger of a tragic defeat—only then did the Americans venture to negotiate with Darlan.

That landing in Africa was the Americans' first major operation of the war. And one may well imagine that their commanders felt a justifiable anxiety. Their expeditionary force in Africa, consisting of only 50,000 men (against 100,000 Frenchmen and the 300,000 natives who could be mobilized), had been organized, trained, and shipped within a few months. This army could not yet have developed the superb confidence and magnificent courage it was to show later. Everyone knows that the first clash between the Germans and Americans on Tunisian soil highlighted the enormous superiority of Hitler's troops. Representatives of a century-old military tradition, having won their stripes on all the battlefields of Europe, they were, moreover, fanatics of a revolutionary ideology of incredible violence. The American military miracle, therefore, was all the greater and the more disconcerting to the enemy. For in a few months, the American Army proved to be a powerful and formidable force able to meet on equal terms an enemy that had the reputation of being invincible. What the Americans could do in their factories and their laboratories—the wonders of their gigantic production—was well known. But no one suspected that they could, overnight, from the humblest GI to top-ranking generals, reach such a high level of military skill. What the world failed to realize, they themselves were not aware of as they approached the shores of Morocco and Algeria and were, undoubtedly, inclined to avoid unnecessary risks by calling their diplomacy to the aid of their guns in that first hazardous undertaking.

Admiral Darlan happened to be in their path. There has been much discussion about Darlan's personality, his attitudes, his opinions. At the time of the armistice, he had accepted the "neutralization" of the Navy of which he was commander in chief, although he had sworn to "fight side by side with England to the last ship." Later he became servile to Marshal Pétain. He suddenly turned furiously anti-British and "collaborationist." He helped stimulate in the French Navy that spirit of doubt, uncertainty, neurasthenia, and helplessness which was to end in the dramatic suicide of the fleet, an event without precedent in history. Yet the fact remains that he played a singularly useful and decisive role at the most critical moment in the battle of Africa. Assuming his title of representative of Marshal Pétain—a Pétain "virtually a prisoner and unable to express his wishes"—Darlan got the backing of the Army and brought it over to the American side. At his command, French guns turned on the American fleet were silenced. The blood of those who were saving the world ceased to flow. Eisenhower could enter Algeria and Morocco in force. The battle of North Africa, which had been hanging fire for eight days, was won. The effect of that first victory soon spread. Darlan persuaded Governor Boysson, in command at Dakar, to follow the example of North Africa. And while his pleas and his orders failed to move Admiral Laborde, in command of the great fleet of the Mediterranean, Admiral Godefroy, commanding the fleet at Alexandria, and Admiral Robert at Martinique, at least they had the effect of immobilizing them. And he was obeyed by the commanders of the magnificent battleship *Richelieu,* stationed at Dakar, the cruiser *Montcalm* and several destroyers and submarines which joined in the fight.

It must be admitted, however, that events in Africa were disturbing to world public opinion. The understanding that had

suddenly sprung up between General Eisenhower, commander of
the armies of democracy, and Admiral Darlan, a figure thoroughly
symbolic of "collaboration" with the Nazis, stirred deep emotions.
The purists—the partisans of "principles above all else"—complained
that the situation was a scandal. Many had the excuse of being
unaware of the dangers which the American Army had faced. Hence
the flood of criticism, sarcasm, and bitter reproaches poured out
upon Eisenhower, Murphy, the American government, and, especially, Roosevelt.

French patriots should have been the first to appreciate the
wisdom of the American decision. Our liberators had committed
themselves to battle in Africa—they had to win that battle. Had
they been thrown back into the sea—to which they came close—the
war would have lasted two years longer. In negotiating with Darlan,
they had by a subtle and clever political move compensated for the
weakness of their military machine. They had put into practice,
on the soil of Africa, a doctrine that was essentially French—the
doctrine of the illustrious Lyautey, who extolled diplomacy as "the
first weapon of war," and still more that of Napoleon in his dealings with the German principalities from 1802 to 1813. The Americans here set the precedent that was to serve them in their Italian
campaign, when, still militarily weak, they made a deal with Marshal
Badoglio and with one clean sweep won the southern end of the
Peninsula, Naples, Sardinia, Corsica, and the whole Italian fleet.
They did just what the Russians * were to do later in Rumania, in
Bulgaria, and in Finland, when, in a masterly manner, they turned
against the German armies and politicians who had been fighting
for four years by their side. They had used the classic and traditional
method of war-revolutions. . . . Why should the exiles, representing at that time a France that was regaining in this sensational success the three departments of Algeria, as well as Tunisia and
Morocco, plus the department of Corsica, plus an enormous piece
of her North African empire—why should the De Gaullists have

* The Russians approved of the Darlan accord and the Badoglio accord.

suddenly placed themselves at the head of the anti-American campaign?

The New York *Times* of November 17, 1942, wrote gloomily: "Darlan's Role Irks De Gaullists Here." Would the De Gaullists have preferred Admiral Darlan to mobilize the fleet and the French Army against the Americans? *La Marseillaise* took a very bitter tone. Published in the British capital, it had to keep within certain limits, at least until it overstepped them and was banned. But Radio Brazzaville was not inhibited by such petty cares, and its commentators were just as violent against Admiral Darlan and General Eisenhower as those of Radio Vichy. One of them protested: "The occupation of North Africa by the Americans is as much of an insult to France as the occupation of France by the Germans."

The newspapers of Brazzaville, Nouméa, and other places let themselves go completely, in particular *France Nouvelle,* which appeared in Buenos Aires. The basic themes of the De Gaullists were: "President Roosevelt and the State Department are in the hands of Fascists"; "American capitalists and Wall Street insist that European fascism be used to bar the way to communism"; "The American Army and its generals are 'Darlanists' and Hitlerites"; "America came to North Africa as a conqueror, to seize bases, and she will keep them."

In New York and Washington, De Gaullist agents made contact with the American press to supply it with copy in support of attacks against President Roosevelt.

Did that De Gaullist outburst at least have the excuse of sincere fanaticism?

Not even that.

Though De Gaulle bitterly criticized the Americans for negotiating with Darlan in order to win a battle on which the fate of the war depended, he himself thought nothing of coming to terms with the most passionate Darlanist in order to derive a political profit and to climb another rung toward the conquest of power. The story of De Gaulle's relations with Admiral Fenard, former head of Darlan's staff, is most striking in this respect.

Fenard came to America, at the same time as General Béthouard, as the head of Giraud's naval mission.

From London one of the top members of De Gaulle's staff promptly wrote me:

You know that General Giraud has just sent two military men to Washington: General Béthouard and Admiral Fenard.

General Béthouard is a big ·. . . (here followed a series of insulting epithets). As for Admiral Fenard, he is a dangerous figure. He belongs to what was called in Vichy and Algiers the A.D.D., *"amis de Darlan"* [friends of Darlan] or, if yóu wish, "ames damnées de Darlan." . . . He sent a telegram to Darlan on November 3rd, five days before the invasion, which showed the amazing influence he wielded over his former captain of the *Edgar Quinet*. In Algiers, Darlan hid in the Villa Arthur at Guyotville where Fenard was living. Fenard and two other A.D.D.'s, Admirals Battet and Leclerc, were arrested by the patriots. De Gaulle has only one regret—that someone did not put a few bullets through his skin while they were killing his boss. In any case, he will not lose anything by waiting. . . .

You will no doubt run into him; let me know your reaction.

I replied that I had, as a matter of fact, met General Béthouard and Admiral Fenard, that they had both struck me as being very sincere in their support of the war, and that that was all I cared about.

Great was my surprise, a few weeks later, to learn that the Darlanist admiral, the leader of the A.D.D., "for whom General de Gaulle was reserving a firing squad," had become De Gaulle's chief confidential agent in Washington.

He arranged De Gaulle's visit to the American capital in July, 1944, after which he was the *de facto* ambassador of France until he tried to have himself appointed official ambassador in November, 1944.

In the light of the Fenard story, I had to recognize that while De Gaulle had proclaimed to the world that it was a crime for President Roosevelt to make use of Darlan to spare the blood of American soldiers, he thought it perfectly natural to utilize Darlan's man to further his own personal career.

But to return to Admiral Darlan. On December 24, 1942, he was assassinated by one Bonnier de la Chapelle.

There are, to be sure, circumstances in which assassination is a legitimate act of war. Darlan could undoubtedly have been justifiably slain while he was helping to bring about the armistice in 1940, when he was collaborating with Pétain at Vichy, or when he visited Hitler at Berchtesgaden. But he was killed at the very moment when, having ceased to collaborate with the Germans, he was helping the Americans out of a most dangerous situation; when he was handing over to them Algiers, Oran, Casablanca; when he was negotiating for the port of Dakar to open its doors to them and for the battleship *Richelieu* to join their fleet; when he was urging the French Navy—the great squadrons at Martinique, Alexandria, and Toulon—to go over to the Allies; and was appealing to the French of North Africa for united support of their American liberators.

"We have one task before us," he declared on the eve of his death, "which is more important than anything else—to win the war. There are still certain difficulties, a certain opposition. . . . Anyone trying to hinder the war effort will be mercilessly eliminated. All other considerations are of no importance. The effects of the past have begun to disappear. The main thing is that we must again fight the common enemy. I desire all Frenchmen to unite. . . . No man who fights against Germany can be our enemy. . . . I am acting in the capacity of guardian of legal authority, as custodian of the national treasure. The moment France is again free and mistress of her own fate, she alone shall choose her political government and her leaders. When that day comes, I shall have done my duty and I shall consider my role at an end."

Was he or was he not sincere? Can his past mistakes or crimes be forgiven? That was not the question on December 24, 1942. After the war a court would doubtless have tried his case and weighed the extenuating or incriminating circumstances. But at the moment he was struck down the only important fact was that, repentant or not, free or under constraint, he was making an immeasurable contribution to the cause of liberation and to the Americans.

This fact was so generally recognized that the first unanimous reaction throughout the world was that the Germans were certainly behind the crime. Who else had a motive for retaliating against the admiral and terrorizing the military and political elements of Vichy that might be turning towards the Allies? Who else had an interest in breaking up the massive reassembling of the French Army, on which the admiral was working? Who else had anything to gain by poisoning and polluting the political atmosphere in North Africa, and intimidating all the Quislings in Europe by an example of vengeance? Radio Berlin and radio Vichy and the press of Berlin and Vichy were, moreover, acclaiming the murder with vociferous delight: "The traitor has paid. He did not get away with it. . . . The Americans are the real victims of the assassin! . . . Consternation reigns in Washington. . . . North Africa is in revolt against the renegades who have rallied to the Anglo-Saxons!" Such was the language of the commentators and the headlines of the articles inspired by Goebbels.

Now, the world soon learned with amazement that the Germans had nothing to do with the assassination. The assassin, Bonnier de la Chapelle, was, on the contrary, a well-known anti-German, a real patriot, a De Gaullist. He belonged to a "Youth Group" organized by M. Henri d'Astier de la Vigerie. He was chosen by lot (under conditions that are still not quite clear), and after two comrades, chosen before him, had recoiled in fear from the mission assigned to them.

As for d'Astier de la Vigerie, he was also a De Gaullist, a member of the Cagoulards, and, according to several witnesses—including a work of De Gaullist propaganda written by Renée Gosset— *Le Coup d'Alger* * (p. 61)—he had boasted openly of his Cagoulard background. My information about D'Astier de la Vigerie is not sufficiently definite to clarify the mystery of his personality. Lacking

* The English translation: *Conspiracy in Algiers.*

proof to the contrary, I prefer to think of him as an enthusiast, a fanatic, a sincere man, and a patriot. He was undoubtedly anti-German—as were certain other Cagoulards who became anti-German in 1940 not knowing—and perhaps still unwilling to admit even now—that they had naïvely strayed into a German organization. But anti-German as he was, he bore the indelible mark which the Nazi influence had stamped on Cagoulard minds: a taste for police methods, a frenzy for risky adventures, an attraction towards terrorism. He had helped the Allies in their preparations for the invasion of North Africa. But scarcely had the invasion been accomplished when he entered the anti-Allied opposition into which De Gaullism as a whole had been drawn. He was taken in by that beastly propaganda which represented President Roosevelt, the State Department, and Mr. Murphy as favorably inclined toward Marshal Pétain and Vichy. Sincerely, honestly, one may say, he steeped himself in hatred of the Americans. His post at police headquarters in Algiers gave him an excellent position to translate that hatred into effective action.

Certain persons who have inside information on the assassination, and secret Allied reports, openly accuse D'Astier de la Vigerie of having conceived and instigated the crime. I absolutely refuse to associate myself with that accusation. But it is my duty, in a book devoted to unveiling the truth, to report facts that are public property and which support the charges against him.

Below is an extract from a document—whose origin I am not permitted at this time to reveal—which specifically refers to the outside influences behind the assassin, Bonnier de la Chapelle, and which shows him to be the blind tool of a carefully laid plot aimed not only at Admiral Darlan but also—after him—at the American leaders.

Immediately after the assassination (December 24), the assassin was questioned by Commissioner Garinaci. It seems certain that he made a full confession involving several persons and that he mentioned the names of several important Algerian officials. According to the official version, Commissioner Garinaci was so upset by what he heard that the same evening he burnt the documents written and signed by Bonnier de la Chapelle—in the opinion of several neutral investigators, however, he burnt it in obedience to an order.

On the day of the 25th, the assassin received a visit from his lawyer, M. Sausonnetti, one of the few frankly De Gaullist members of the Algerian bar. He was then questioned by Divisional Commissioner Esqueyré, also a De Gaullist and confidential advisor of M. Henri d'Astier de la Vigerie, head of the Police Department. But whereas Commissioner Garinaci had obtained a full confession, Divisional Commissioner Esqueyré was unable, or says that he was unable, to extract anything from the murderer as to his accomplices.

Bonnier de la Chapelle is said to have declared before the court martial that the revolver he used belonged to one of his "Free Corps" comrades, named Sabatier, for whom he was substituting; and that the black Peugeot automobile which drove him to the scene of the crime belonged to M. d'Astier de la Vigerie. But he refused to say any more. He told his guards on several occasions that he had "protectors" and that he "would not be executed because he had killed a traitor." He admitted that he might have to go through with a "faked execution."

At the last moment on December 26th, as they were about to lead him before the firing squad, Bonnier de la Chapelle suddenly became terror-stricken, as if he then realized that his mysterious "protectors" had put one over on him. He asked for a sheet of paper, but as none was available, he dashed off a few words on a visiting card on which he had written the name of Henri d'Astier de la Vigerie.

There is proof, on the other hand, that on the day of the murder a certain Abbé Cordier confessed Bonnier de la Chapelle and provided him with a false identification card in the name of Morand, which Bonnier de la Chapelle used to gain admission to the High Commissioner. Abbé Cordier, a fanatical De Gaullist priest, was a close friend of M. Henri d'Astier de la Vigerie.

The evidence seemed so serious that, with General Giraud's authorization, the arrest of M. Henri d'Astier de la Vigerie, Abbé Cordier, Commissioner Garinaci and several other officials was ordered.

In the opinion of French and American official circles the crime is part of a vast plot hatched by a secret society of De Gaullists. The French authorities are convinced that Mr. Murphy, the American representative in Algiers, is in grave danger.

Having read this report, I naturally tried to verify it. I have never been able to find proof that Bonnier de la Chapelle had pointed to

M. Henri d'Astier de la Vigerie as the chief instigator of the crime by writing his name on a calling card. But aside from that important point, all other facts given are now beyond dispute.

Commissioner Garinaci definitely burnt the assassin's confession—an extraordinary act, without precedent in the annals of the law! It strengthens the assumption that the assassin had mentioned the names of prominent figures.

It is a fact that Commissioner Garinaci was dismissed after attempting to justify his conduct. Also, that Divisional Commissioner Esqueyré, D'Astier de la Vigerie's right-hand man, questioned the criminal a second time and declared that he had not been able to get a word out of him. How can one believe that Bonnier de la Chapelle refused to repeat under oath to one policeman what he had put in writing for another? It would seem that Commissioner Esqueyré was given orders to question the assassin in such a way as to avoid extracting any revelations. Esqueyré, too, was arrested and imprisoned.

It is also a fact that the day of or the evening before the murder, Abbé Cordier, a political associate of D'Astier de la Vigerie confessed Bonnier de la Chapelle and furnished him with a false identification card.

And it is a fact, too, that the French authorities in Algiers were convinced that the assassination of Admiral Darlan was part of a vast plot aimed at the American authorities—first at Mr. Murphy, Roosevelt's representative, then perhaps at General Eisenhower himself. Six days after the crime, General Giraud gave the following interview to the New York *Times:*

"Why have you arrested friends who helped the American invasion?" asked one correspondent.

"I ordered the arrest of those who were plotting," he (Giraud) answered. "I am not looking at the political angle."

"Do you really think there would be other attempted assassinations?" was the next question.

"I am quite certain of it," was his unequivocal reply. "I do not fear for myself, but it affected others, including Mr. Murphy, President Roosevelt's representative in North Africa."

Though it is not mentioned in the report, people mysteriously intervened in the case under various pretexts and took advantage of the political vacuum resulting from Admiral Darlan's death and the complete inexperience of General Giraud, who replaced him, to quash the investigation and railroad the trial through the courts. The murderer was convicted and executed less than forty-eight hours after the crime. Is it customary to act in such haste in dealing with a political crime of such magnitude and, from the evidence, with so many secret ramifications? A determined will to sabotage and suppress the investigation seems definitely present.

Now, the Americans were very much in favor of a full investigation. On being informed of the crime, President Roosevelt made the following statement: "The cowardly assassination of Admiral Darlan is murder in the first degree. All leaders of all United Nations will agree with this statement. Nazism and fascism and military despotism hold otherwise. I hope that speedy justice will overtake the murderer or murderers of Admiral Darlan."

Significant words! On the strength of the first information received, did President Roosevelt refuse to believe that this was the crime of a single individual, or of a madman? Whom did he suspect? The Germans? Perhaps. But did he have other possibilities in mind? What was he hinting at when he spoke of "military despotism"? And was he not suggesting the hypothesis of a widespread plot when he used the words "the murderer or murderers"?

Secretary of State Cordell Hull underscored the President's words:

"Of Admiral Darlan it may be repeated that the part he played in North Africa related primarily to the military situation and was of incalculable aid to the Allied armies in the battle which is still raging. His assassination was an odious and cowardly act."

Now let us look at De Gaulle's reaction.

He did not condemn "the unpardonable crime." He had nothing to say when a man whose action was "of incalculable aid" to the Allies in a "battle still raging" was eliminated. It did not occur to him to accuse the Germans, the collaborationists, or the agents of Vichy, overrunning Algiers, of the slightest responsibility for a crime that upset the plans of the Allied Command. The first issue of *La Marseillaise* to appear in London after the event (December 27) neither attacks nor supports the assassination. British and American newspapermen had crowded into De Gaulle's headquarters in London on hearing the news. Headquarters went no further than to express disapproval of what had happened in Algiers.

On December 26 Raymond Daniell wired from London to the New York *Times:*

The Fighting French officials consider that punishment of men who have taken a leading part in the policy of capitulation and collaboration with the enemy is a question that should be settled properly by the justice of the nation and that this punishment should not be left to individual initiative.

Mallory Brown, correspondent of the *Christian Science Monitor,* also wrote from London:

Should the assassin prove to be a real French patriot, for instance, this, it is pointed out here (in French and Allied circles), would raise the problem of whether those who, in the future rid their country and their cause of quislings, would be court-martialed and sentenced to death in a similar manner. . . .

Fighting French officials here were shocked by the news of Admiral Darlan's assassination, but hesitated, pending receipt of fuller information from Algiers, to suggest any explanation or to attempt any evaluation of its possible consequences.

Suddenly, however, the De Gaullist attitude changed. On January 24 *La Marseillaise* published a report from Algiers protesting against measures taken there to discover those really responsible for the assassination.

On December 29 . . . with Mr. Murphy's permission, the *Garde Mobile* began a wide police investigation, the one the London radio has reported erroneously. The official communiqué states that people have been arrested on three charges:

(1) Being implicated in the assassination of Admiral Darlan.

(2) Organizing an attempt against the life of General Giraud.

(3) Organizing an attempt against the life of Mr. Murphy.

We have a sense of being disarmed, shackled and deserted by our own friends, the Allies. . . .

What have we come to after two months of contact with our British and American friends? We are greatly disillusioned.

How could *La Marseillaise* blame Mr. Murphy and the Americans for trying to get to the bottom of the plot that led to the assassination of Darlan and might tomorrow lead to others, including—to judge by many signs—the assassination of Mr. Murphy himself?

For that matter, De Gaulle went even further. Learning that Henri d'Astier de la Vigerie had been arrested for complicity in the assassination, he sent the latter's brother General d'Astier de la Vigerie from London to Algiers on an official mission. The general, though a brilliant officer, was scarcely fitted, it must be granted, to judge the situation impartially. General d'Astier de la Vigerie visited his brother Henri in the Algiers prison and did all he could to obtain his release. He failed. It was not until several months later, when De Gaulle himself took power, that the prison doors opened miraculously and all those accused of "complicity in the Darlan assassination" were released "for lack of evidence" and the investigation definitely quashed.

That was, of course, to be expected. De Gaulle had appointed another brother of M. Henri d'Astier de la Vigerie, M. Emmanuel d'Astier de la Vigerie, Minister of the Interior!

And soon it became impossible to hide the fact that De Gaullism was actually claiming the credit for Darlan's assassination. In December, 1942, on the anniversary of the execution of Bonnier de la Chapelle, the Algiers newspapers hailed him as "a martyr to the De Gaullist cause." And on December 26 the Associated Press sent the following dispatch:

Many high officials of the French Committee of National Liberation and De Gaullists paid silent tribute today at the tomb of the young university student who assassinated Admiral François Darlan on December 24, 1942.

A group of about fifty persons, almost all of whom held Government offices of one type or another under General Charles de Gaulle, marked the anniversary of the execution of Fernand Eugène Bonnier de la Chapelle, who shot Admiral Darlan, by placing a wreath on his tomb and observing a minute's silence.

There were many prominent persons at the ceremony. Among them was Emmanuel d'Astier de la Vigerie, Interior Commissioner of the French Committee of National Liberation. . . .

In sum, Henri d'Astier de la Vigerie had been imprisoned in Algiers for complicity in the assassination of Darlan. His brother the general had been sent from London to try and obtain his release. His brother Emmanuel, a member of the Committee of National Liberation, was sent by De Gaulle to place flowers on the assassin's grave.

We now have a general outline of what actually took place:

(1) Darlan's assassination was carried out by De Gaullists. At first in order to divert public attention, the De Gaullists disapproved of the act, then openly commended it, and finally paid homage to it.

(2) There seems no question but that the Cagoulards had a hand in the murder, though this point is not yet completely clarified.

(3) The investigation to discover responsibility for the crime was systematically suppressed.

(4) The American government and its High Command considered the assassination a blow of "incalculable" effect, directed against the North African invasion at the very moment when the expedition was encountering critical difficulties.

(5) According to all the evidence, Darlan was struck down without regard to his service to the Allied cause in the North African invasion, and solely because he was an obstacle to De Gaulle's climb toward the New Power.

7. Before Casablanca

Periods of war are not periods of law.

JULIUS CAESAR

THE De Gaulle-Darlan drama seems almost an operetta compared to the De Gaulle-Giraud drama.

We have seen that on November 9, 1942, a representative of De Gaulle, André Philip, burst out in denunciation of the famous French general who had escaped from a German prison and later landed in North Africa. But what exactly did De Gaulle himself think of Giraud's escape? What was his first reaction? What passed through the mind of an officer whom even a political adventure could not have completely estranged from the great traditions that ennoble the Army?

Let us refer to the dispatches of foreign correspondents.

On November 8 James MacDonald cabled the New York *Times* from London:

General Charles de Gaulle, leader of the Fighting French forces, acclaimed General Giraud's action in a broadcast tonight. It was recalled that when General de Gaulle learned about General Giraud's escape from the fortress of Koenigstein last April, when he was making his way under an assumed name through Switzerland to France, the Fighting French leader unhesitatingly expressed his willingness to serve under the man who commanded the Seventh French Army in 1940. . . .

A very fine beginning!

But by the next day, November 9, certain ideas had already begun

105

to make headway. An Associated Press dispatch from London considerably amended the sense of MacDonald's story. It was no longer a matter of Brigadier General Charles de Gaulle going to Algiers and placing himself under the orders of General of the Army Henri Honoré Giraud, as required, after all, by army discipline, but of General Giraud joining the ranks of the Fighting French. Then an arrangement could be made between the generals by which the delicate question of superiority of rank would be readily settled.

The Associated Press story said:

Fighting French sources here indicated today that General Giraud would be welcomed in Fighting French ranks.

Responsible French quarters said they did not know whether Fighting French leaders had been approached in connection with the appointment, but said General Giraud was recognized as a Fighting French, and it also was well known that he had great influence in North Africa.

"There has been no direct contact between General de Gaulle and General Giraud as yet," one source said, "but as soon as they do get together the question of how Giraud can best serve with De Gaulle will be settled rapidly. You can be sure no superiority of rank will play a role between two such men in the present cause."

This source added that General de Gaulle's broadcast yesterday appealing to North Africa fighting men to join the Allied forces, "doubtlessly replies to any question about the attitude of the Fighting French towards General Giraud. . . ."

But in a time of revolution, emotions succeed one another with the speed of a tornado. One day more and the Fighting French all over the world will have received the sign from London to start their campaign against Giraud. On November 11, 1942, a Fighting French journalist wrote for the New York *Times*:

All Frenchmen opposed to Germany who at the same time want to save the Vichy regime and prevent the restoration of the Republic will flock to General Giraud, while former republicans take their stand by General de Gaulle. As a whole, General de Gaulle, because of his antagonism to the High Command in pre-war days, was prone to associate with the Left. On the contrary, General Giraud belonged to the extreme Right. On his staff of the Seventh Army was Guy de Wendel, who was wont to exclaim: "Between Hitler and Stalin I don't hesitate. I am for Hitler."

Within the ranks of French patriots, seeds of dangerous division could easily develop. Will General Giraud agree to perform his task, which is likely to grow in proportion to American control over North Africa, within the frame-work of the National Committee in London? Already that question has become a live one.

· Right here were distilled the first drops of the deadly poison that was to destroy reconciliation, fraternity, military unity, and the solidarity of the French against the Germans. General of the Army Giraud and Brigadier General de Gaulle were to be judged by public opinion according to their views, or rather their so-called political leanings. The De Gaulle who was a former follower of the *Action Française* and frequenter of the offices of the *Echo de Paris,* and a former friend of Paul Reynaud, was now classed as a Leftist, while Giraud was labeled as a Rightist—and considered even more than a Rightist—for he was represented as being surrounded by Nazi influences on account of a subaltern reserve officer (De Wendel) in his army, whom he himself had not chosen. The heroic general who, after escaping from Germany, defied the threats of Abetz and Laval at Vichy and who threw himself boldly into the African war was greeted by the De Gaullists with scowls and made the object of the odious suspicion that he might well be in agreement with those who said: "Hitler is better than Stalin." The article in the New York *Times* unleashed a storm of hatred against him.

But the situation in Algiers took an unexpected turn. Giraud had been unable to get control of the French Army and the Americans had therefore dealt with Darlan. Immediately, the Fighting French changed their tune and turned on the latter. And simultaneously Giraud was once again a "good Frenchman," qualified to unite the French "locally." The London correspondent of the New York *Times* cabled his paper on November 13:

Fighting French spokesmen said they were shocked by the announcement by Admiral Darlan that he had assumed command in French Africa and pointed out that the report made no mention of General

Henri Giraud, who Lieut. Gen. Dwight D. Eisenhower said on Tuesday would organize the French colonial army to fight against the Axis.

The Fighting French feel that General Giraud was the most logical figure to unite French resistance in Africa rather than Admiral Darlan whom they described as "not symbolic of the spirit of resistance," and whose leadership of a North African government "will not be acceptable to the mass of French people who are loyal to the Allies."

Was that the end of it? Was that De Gaulle's final attitude toward Giraud? Did he now accept the need for unity against the Germans invading Tunisia and making ready to strike at the heart of the American expedition by marching on Algiers? Not at all.

On December 24 Darlan was assassinated in Algiers. The De Gaullists once more found themselves confronted by Giraud alone. They hesitated about the next step. On December 29 De Gaulle declared, on the radio, from London, that, as a member of the Reynaud government, he had been a witness to the esteem in which Giraud was held. "Had he not been taken prisoner," De Gaulle observed, "the Minister of War would have made him Commander in Chief of the French Army." But on December 30 the wind veered again, this time permanently. The New York *Times* learned in London that De Gaulle's spokesmen did not believe an accord between the two generals was possible. And now the struggle began in earnest—that implacable struggle that was not to end until Giraud, stripped of all authority and of his command, wounded by an assassin's bullet, lay in agony in Algiers at the moment when De Gaulle was marching into Paris under the Arc de Triomphe.

The first phase of the De Gaulle-Giraud struggle was to last from December 30, 1942, till January 24, 1943, the day of the Casablanca Conference.

To grasp their personalities we must place the two men in their respective settings.

The day after Darlan's death, Giraud found himself in a difficult position in Algiers. Marshal Pétain had condemned him in the following terms:

"General Giraud, who has betrayed his officer's oath and who is dishonored, now claims to have been installed in command of the army in Africa. The title he has assumed comes to him from a foreign power. I forbid General Giraud to act in my name and to invoke my authority. Officers, noncommissioned officers and soldiers, do not become accomplices of his treason. Refuse to obey him. I am, and I remain, your leader."

This denunciation troubled many officers of the Army, Navy, and Air Force; and it was some time before they could shake off the spell of the Pétain legend and the effects of Vichy propaganda. It worried Giraud—himself a soldier trained in the traditional school —who, while he certainly had no affection for the old Marshal and had been deeply outraged by him at their meetings in Vichy, yet recognized him as his superior in rank and as head of France's legal government.

After Darlan's death, the Council of the Empire, comprising the governors of the colonies, had chosen General Giraud to be civil and military chief in Algiers. These men, however, were jealous of Giraud and hated him. All North Africa was a hotbed of monstrous intrigue—everybody plotting, suspecting everybody else, denouncing and betraying. The Vichyites, the P.P.F.,* the Legion, the Cagoulards, the Royalists, the De Gaullists, and the Communists carried on savage wars, faction against faction. The city walls were covered with scrawls: "Long live De Gaulle!" "Long live Pétain!" "Long live the King!" "Long live the Americans!" "Down with the British!" "Down with the Americans!" "Long live the British!" "Long live the Legion!" "Long live the New Order!" "Long live Doriot!" The colonists resented getting back into the war, which ruined business. Officials kept trying to find out which way the wind was blowing, which direction was best for their careers. Housewives were being driven mad by the rising prices of the Black Market and the competition of the American dollar.

In the middle of all that, the honest General Giraud was practically helpless. He had only one motive—hatred of the Germans.

* *Parti Populaire Français*, a French Fascist party led by Doriot.

And at every step he found himself floundering in the putrid sea of French animosities. A magnificent soldier, he would have liked to lead the life of the army camp, to spend day and night with his troops—those troops without guns, without tanks, without ammunition, that he, a marvelous inspirer of men, had called forth from their barracks, from their moral bewilderment, their defeatist mentality, their myth of Pétain, and had hurled into a bloody war. But politics, which pursued him and never allowed him to escape, had snatched him from the battlefield and brought him back to Algiers. He had been in every sense tossed and buffeted about by events. At Gibraltar he had run up against his first misunderstanding: he was not Commander in Chief of the Inter-Allied Expedition, as he had understood from his negotiations with the Americans, but just plain Commander of the French troops—who at first refused to obey him. Darlan turned him out and took his place. Then Darlan fell and Giraud was given his command. But the Vichyites, the Darlanists, the collaborationists, fought him relentlessly; and he turned to De Gaulle—in vain. He thought that if De Gaulle came to Algiers to help him and march to battle with him, the moral atmosphere would improve at once. But De Gaulle joined with the Vichyites, the Darlanists, and the collaborationists, in attacking him; refused to fight, and, more than anyone else, stabbed him in the back.

Giraud was also disappointed in the Americans, without realizing that he in turn had disappointed his protectors. Actually, the Americans backed Giraud—in preference to De Gaulle, whom they did not hold in high regard—because they knew him to be honest, courageous, completely selfless, and interested only in getting into the fight. In Giraud they recognized an out-and-out soldier, a successor of Joffre, of Rochambeau—and they liked him. But to hold his own against De Gaulle, who had nothing of the soldier in him, nothing of the *condottiere,* but whose temperament is that of a great agitator, Giraud would have needed precisely a little political acumen, a bit of ambition and a pinch of Machiavellism. At every step, however, Giraud repeated: "Politics is not my affair. I want nothing to do with it. What I want is to march into Metz at the head of my troops. After that I shall retire."

Met with such an attitude, it was not surprising that the upstarts, the ambitious, turned to De Gaulle, who virtually assured them that as far as he was concerned this war was a means to his becoming President of the Fourth Republic. "Those who have stood by me will get the positions, the honors, the service stripes. . . ." Yes, there is no doubt that the struggle between the two men was decidedly unequal.

If only sentimental considerations had counted! Giraud is first and foremost a fighting general. Giraud has known the torture of German prisons—that grand old man of sixty-three escaped by sliding down at night from the top of a fortress one hundred and twenty feet high, with German sentries around him. He possesses as much moral as physical strength, for he stood his ground at Vichy against the threats of Laval and Abetz. "If you want me to go back to prison," he said contemptuously to the latter, "free 100,000 French prisoners, and free them first, because I do not trust your word." He infuriated the Vichy police and the Gestapo as he had his Prussian galley sergeants. The Germans took ferocious revenge upon him. They confined his wife, his children, and his grandchildren in concentration camps; they caused his daughter to die there. Yes, Giraud has suffered all the horrors of the war. He is the true symbol of the martyrdom of France. He is the greatest of the "resisting" generals. In the return to balance that has taken place in the depths of French consciousness, in the mounting revolt that has swept out the invader, Giraud represents the great French Army, whose chivalrous, heroic, and indomitable spirit he revived even before it was restored physically.

But De Gaulle who deserted the battlefield to which he had summoned the finest flower of France, who made a "daring" but safe escape from Bordeaux in General Spears' plane, who for two years of the war stayed in London, surrounded by his family, while he took advantage of circumstances to carve out for himself a sham glory and a political fortune—this general, subordinate in rank to

General Giraud, was to attack the latter treacherously, overwhelm him with new torments, crush him and drive him out of the Army. The hero of an order of the day issued without a battle was to beat down the hero of nameless battles waged without pomp or glory in German prisons. A false symbol was to triumph over a true symbol. . . . We live in an age when uprooted men, distraught and maddened by misfortune, have lost their sense of fair play and their love of the beautiful, for very few were shocked or disturbed; and the stupid, fanatical crowd of exiles took sides against Giraud.

The scales were tipped even farther in De Gaulle's favor because of the fact that during his two years in London he had had plenty of time to master the profession of political adventurer, whereas Giraud, in his German prison cell, had learned absolutely nothing about this profession which, moreover, attracted him not at all. He was to make mistakes which may be forgiven him, for he was always their principal victim. He knew how to fight the Germans, but he did not know how to fight the French. He was tricked by his advisors. He chose his associates maladroitly, as, for example, the banker Monnet who went from Washington to Algiers ostensibly to support him, or Peyrouton, in whom he naïvely saw "the man who tried to lock up Laval." He did not know how to discard the whole mass of monstrous laws passed by Vichy. He was too slow in dealing with the Jewish problem. He was too honest, too good, too candid, too soft—this man of steel—for this age of trouble, storm, disorder, gangsterism, and terrorism.

By January, 1943, the battle had been raging in Tunisia for seven weeks. Giraud was in command of the small French Army which, at frightful cost, was holding Von Arnim. De Gaulle, who had under his command about 15,000 admirably equipped men—not 100,000 as his propaganda had previously given out—refused to help the French and Allied soldiers who were waging a bitter battle on the soil of the Empire. He demanded political concessions in return for coming to the aid of his superior in rank.

During that first, brief period of the struggle that was to end in the complete break between the two generals at Casablanca on

January 25, the points of disagreement were many and varied. De Gaulle demanded the dissolution of the Superior Council of the Empire, made up of the governors of Algeria and West Africa, the High Commissioner of Morocco, and the Resident General of Tunisia. He also demanded the dismissal of General Juin ("General June, '40" as he called him), whom he accused of "Vichyism" and pro-Germanism though he was serving gloriously in Tunisia.

The problem of political prisoners also arose. De Gaulle accused Giraud of being slow to open the concentration camps established by Vichy, and even of imprisoning De Gaullists. Giraud replied that the political prisoners had been mixed with common criminals and that, in such a disordered situation, he was obliged to use caution in releasing prisoners behind the backs of soldiers facing the Germans.

Ought not the two French generals have met, talked things over and quietly adjusted their differences, which were becoming a scandal in the world press and lowering war morale? That proved to be impossible.

One issue stood out. Giraud intended to maintain a provisional military administration in Algiers and not a government; whereas De Gaulle, who declared himself "civil authority" and the New Power, wanted to build up a more or less governmental structure with himself as the head. De Gaulle's claims were frequently just and legitimate—except, obviously, those that had to do with his pretensions to political power. The fault lay in posing them in the form he did; in airing the quarrel in public; making it a focus of international disturbance, which annoyed and exasperated the British and Americans; and particularly in refusing to wait until the battle of Africa had been won.

The New York *Times* said in its issue of January 3:

It is therefore believed by some officials here that the United States and Great Britain may be obliged to warn the anti-Axis French leaders that . . . it may become necessary for the United Nations to break the chain of French sovereignty with a formal military occupation of North Africa and West Africa.

On January 5 the New York *Times* noted:

> General de Gaulle's proposal for a "temporary and enlarged central
> power" in North Africa . . . was interpreted in some informed quarters
> here as a demand for a political upheaval that might hamper military
> operations.

On January 6, in the same paper, Anne O'Hare McCormick
wrote: ". . . we, too, are divided by the French division. . . ."

On January 14 the New York *Times* declared that the De Gaulle-
Giraud quarrel was hindering the rearmament of the French Army.
And on the same day Raymond Daniell cabled the *Times* from
London:

> Reports of an imminent quarrel between Downing Street and the
> White House over American policy in Algeria and Morocco are causing
> so much concern here that Brendan Bracken, Minister of Information,
> went so far today as to allow himself to be quoted, thus departing from
> the general practice of talking off the record. The British government
> has given General Eisenhower the power of attorney and will support
> him unquestioningly, whatever he does.

On January 22 Harold Callender reported that General Eisenhower
approved of General Giraud's attitude, since all political questions
had to be held in abeyance until the final liberation of Africa.

On January 23 Drew Middleton sent these words, so eloquent
in their simplicity:

> The drama played here during the last two months would be rela-
> tively unimportant were it not for the fact that 40,000,000 French are
> inextricably connected with it.

These comments from American newspapermen indicate the surprise, uneasiness, and annoyance caused by the French dispute, the
motives for which seemed obscure and petty. France, just coming
back to life, was already surrounded with an atmosphere of scandal.
Relations between the French and the Allies had worsened. Problems involving the Army—its provisioning, the general mobilization
—were affected by it. Meanwhile, the war with the Germans was
at its height and De Gaulle, stubbornly pursuing his political objec-

tive, was apparently not even interested. During that lengthy period, not a single London dispatch concerning De Gaulle mentioned the subject that was keeping the rest of the world on edge: when and how would von Arnim be driven out of Tunisia? Could he be thrown into the sea before the Italians in Tripoli and, particularly, Rommel were able to join forces with him?

Churchill and Roosevelt made no effort to hide their extreme dissatisfaction. And, unexpectedly, they made a great decision: to go personally to Casablanca to confer on French affairs and oblige the two generals to join in the discussions. Giraud welcomed the proposed meeting with keen satisfaction. De Gaulle began by protesting. Churchill insisted. De Gaulle would not give in. Finally Churchill informed him that he had had enough: if things continued in this manner he would ask the Fighting French to leave London and take their quarrels to the French colonies. General de Gaulle replied that he was ready to go to Brazzaville. However, he yielded and left for Casablanca.

There he told Giraud: "The situation is quite clear. I am Clémenceau; you are Foch."

Dumbfounded, Giraud replied:

"Considering the immense disasters that have overtaken France, we are not the great men you think we are. Believe me, we are neither Clémenceau nor Foch; we are just two ordinary French generals whose sole duty is to fight for our country."

Beginning on this note, the meeting ended in bitter words. Roosevelt and Churchill made no secret of their disappointment. As for the results achieved by the conference, here is what the newspapers had to say:

On January 27, the New York *Times* reported that De Gaulle had returned to London with "just about as much brimstone snorting from his nose and sparks flying from his heels as when he departed." He had demanded that Giraud disband his political followers in North Africa and "show his respects to the Third Republic." The same day Robert Post cabled the *Times* from London:

Only in so far as the question of France is concerned does the conference appear to have been a failure. It should at least be recorded that the atmosphere at Fighting French Headquarters was most gloomy today. General Charles de Gaulle and General Henri Honoré Giraud met and talked out the whole question but, for the moment at least, it can be said that there are no signs that they found any common ground. Of course, some agreement may be worked out, and that is hoped here. It is hoped, too, that perhaps the exchange of military and economic missions may lead to some real unity. The Fighting French are going to send their best men on the mission. North Africa, of course, is a small part of the French world, and it may be that inside France something may happen; some man may arise who will clear up the whole tangle.

On January 30 Drew Middleton, in London, wrote to the New York *Times:*

Both generals are exceedingly stiff-necked, but even those who have hitherto been admirers of General de Gaulle are inclined to believe that the dashing of Allied hopes of French unity after the splendid beginning at the Casablanca conference is more the work of General de Gaulle than of General Giraud.

On January 29 General Giraud, who had returned to Algiers, sadly told American newspapermen that he was ready at any time to reach an understanding with De Gaulle provided the latter refrained from raising political problems that had nothing to do with the fighting going on in Africa. And he summed up by saying: "This is not the time for political agitation but for patriotic discipline. There is only one policy for France: to fight and win the war."

This expressed the view of all parties, including the Communists. It was the policy of all the French in exile who had avoided the madness of De Gaullism. Above all it was what the 40,000,000 French prisoners must have been thinking when they heard the jeers of German commentators on the radio—and who must have wept to know that, at the gates of their prison, their brothers were abusing one another and forgetting them—to the disgust of the whole free world.

8. The *Richelieu*

IT was indeed a thrilling day for the exiled French patriots in New York when the *Richelieu*, sailing under General Giraud's orders, arrived from Dakar for repair of the damage inflicted by the British in June, 1940. Saluted by guns of shore batteries and ships, the handsome battleship swung majestically into the Hudson River. The American press welcomed her with the same consideration it has never failed to show France at every stage of her misfortune and her recovery. The arrival of the *Richelieu* in New York waters was hailed as the "symbol of France's return to American friendship," as the "living proof that French maritime power would rise again," as "a triumph for France." The New York *Times,* the *Herald Tribune,* and the *Sun* outdid one another in those phrases so pleasing to French ears. The Secretary of the Navy, the mayor of New York, high military and naval authorities, went aboard the *Richelieu,* and added their friendly greetings.

From the moment they landed in New York, French sailors were tremendously popular. The prettiest girls went to theaters and dances with them. Americans on every social level polished up the few words of French they had learned in high school or had brought back from their visits to France and offered to act as interpreters or invited the sailors to their homes. Candy shops on Fifth Avenue brought out de luxe boxes, round and blue and topped with a red pompon. The red pompon also appeared on the hats of smartly dressed women. The American welcome had a sweetness, imagination, and charm that stirred French hearts deeply.

Then De Gaullist officials in New York, alerted by instructions from London, began to call on the editorial rooms of American newspapers to point out that the officers of the *Richelieu* had alarming intentions, that they "preferred the Germans to the Americans," that they "were plotting" and "were getting ready to go over to Hitler the moment the ship was repaired."

Following these rumors, strange things began to happen. The attitude of the sailors, their behavior on the streets, changed. Many removed their ship's ribbon from their berets. Others sported a new ribbon bearing the initials of the *Forces Navales de la France Combattante* (Naval Forces of Fighting France). Some collected on street corners, attracted a crowd, and delivered speeches against their officers or shouted praise for De Gaulle. Soon it was no longer possible to conceal the fact that numerous desertions had taken place. The De Gaullists passed out money in bars frequented by the sailors, got them to drop in at their delegation's headquarters on Fifth Avenue, had them sign an "oath of allegiance to the general" and steered them towards London by way of Halifax.

For four months these painful incidents multiplied, to the embarrassment and genuine distress of the Americans, accustomed to the discipline of their own sailors and to a quite different conception of France. The Algiers authorities had sent to Washington as naval attaché Admiral Fenard, the former close associate of Darlan, whom we have spoken of above. Later he was to become the most fanatical De Gaullist in America.

"The De Gaullists have induced 120 of my men to desert," he told me. "If they succeed in taking off a hundred more, the *Richelieu* will be tied up here for months and will be unable to take part in the Battle of the Atlantic."

One day I received a visit from a delegation of five sailors from the *Richelieu.*

"*M. le Député,* is it true that you, too, advise us to go and join De Gaulle?"

"Who told you that?"

"Some ladies who came to the canteen yesterday."

"My friends, that is a lie. Sailors must never desert their ship.

Don't expect me, the son of an admiral, to encourage your wretched demonstrations against discipline—especially here, under the eyes of our Allies."

"But our officers are anti-British and anti-American."

"In the first place, you probably know nothing about that. And besides, if your officers have been influenced by Vichy propaganda, they cannot be cured at one stroke, and it's all the more to their credit that they have come back into the war."

"General de Gaulle wants us to come to London. He has promised us good pay. If a man like General de Gaulle gives us an order like that, he must have his reasons."

"I'd rather not think that a French general would order you to quit your ship at a time like this. I am a De Gaullist, but to me De Gaullism means the restoration of discipline, French unity, and a fight to the finish against the Germans. If you desert, if you succeed in tying up your ship, the Germans will be the gainers. Don't ask me to give you the advice of an agent of Hitler in New York."

The sailors went away, but I learned that they remained at their stations and I was very happy about it.

Following this incident, however, I telephoned the De Gaullist delegation in Washington and urged them to call on the general to put a stop to the desertions.

"Impossible," was the reply. "Those are the orders from Admiral Auboyneau [the De Gaullist Naval Commissioner in London] to Captain Gayrald [the De Gaullist naval attaché in Washington]. Besides, General de Gaulle himself has been consulted about this three times and we can't bother him with this business any more."

What was De Gaulle's real motive in giving the order to provoke those shameful incidents and the desertions from the *Richelieu?* To answer this question we must go back to similar incidents and desertions which he instigated in the army in Africa while that army was fighting the Germans—these are described in an official military report which we shall consider in another chapter. In the crushing indictment which history will undoubtedly draw up against De Gaulle, these facts will constitute the most serious and most tragic charge. They cannot be explained if we retain the illusion that De Gaulle was the prime mover in a fight to the finish against the Germans and that he pursued only the noble aim of liberating France. They become, on the contrary, clear and logical if we recognize that De Gaulle thought primarily (and no doubt exclusively) of building up his political fortune.

We have seen that at the start of his activities in London, De Gaulle took an immediate dislike to Admiral Muselier, then broke him, for the double reason that the admiral, being of higher rank than De Gaulle and in control of a naval force far superior in size to his force, was becoming a dangerous competitor. The appearance on the scene of the French Navy with three or four admirals—one or two of whom were also his superiors in rank—commanding powerful units revived the danger. An official British report notes an extremely significant conversation which one of the officers of Admiral Auboyneau's staff had on this subject with a British admiral when they met at Plymouth.

"We are afraid of the *Richelieu* because she is not De Gaullist," the officer said.

"What difference can that make if she is anti-German and if she is fighting for France?" replied the admiral.

De Gaulle was perfectly aware that the officers of the *Richelieu* had loyally come into the war on the side of the Allies and that they were courageously doing their duty according to the great tradition of the French Navy—as had the sailors of the *Surcouf* who went over to the De Gaullist cause and won glory in the Battle of the Atlantic. He was not in the least disturbed by the anti-British and anti-American remarks which, it is said, sometimes cropped up in the officers' wardroom on board the *Richelieu*—the result of habits acquired at Dakar after the British torpedoed them in June, 1940, and of the propaganda to which the Navy had so long been subjected under orders from Darlan and the Germans. He was the less concerned as he himself was stirring up inside the De Gaullist movement similar propaganda campaigns against the British and particularly against the Americans. At the very moment he gave the order to induce the sailors of the *Richelieu* to desert on account of their officers' anti-British and anti-American sentiments, his newspapers in Buenos Aires, Brazzaville, and Nouméa were insulting America and Great Britain; and his official newspaper in London, *La Marseillaise,* was being banned by Churchill for its anti-American attacks. Actually, De Gaulle, having proclaimed himself the incarnation of "civil authority," saw in "military authority" and in "naval authority" the only serious obstacles in the path of his conquest of the New Power. Logically, he had, therefore, no choice but to fight them and to destroy them. His ruthless war on Muselier, on the officers of the *Richelieu,* on Giraud, and on the officers in the army in Africa are all part of the same struggle for the success of a great personal adventure, the consummation of a *coup d'état.*

However that may be, as the result of those orders, desertions spread to the cruiser *Montcalm,* which had arrived in port at the same time as the *Richelieu,* then to the French merchant marine— and since the Battle of the Atlantic was then at its height, the desertions endangered the shipment of supplies to England, Russia, and North Africa, and proved very costly to the Allies in material and in human lives.

At that time there were in New York several thousand French exiles—people of all kinds. Among them were distinguished intellectuals, like the members of the *Ecole Libre des Hautes Etudes* (the French section of The New School for Social Research in New York), most of whom were ex-professors of the Sorbonne and of the leading French universities. There were also a few clericals and a large number of wealthy Jewish bankers and merchants. All were aware of the *Richelieu* incidents. It is probable—nay, even certain— that in normal times these respectable individuals, most of them conservative in temperament and highly patriotic, would have been outraged. The great majority, however, were De Gaullists; and they were not even surprised—quite the contrary—at this distressing and discouraging spectacle presented in a strange land by a movement which was in their eyes the guardian of the traditions of honor and discipline of the French Army and Navy. It was disconcerting

enough that they had so easily accepted De Gaulle's failure to appear on the battlefields of Syria and Libya where died the men
whom he had called together from the ends of the earth, promising
to lead them. From that, they swiftly reached the point of approving
his decisions not to take the small well-equipped army he had
organized in London to Algeria to fight on French soil where German tanks were on the move and where a much less well-supplied
French Army was battling desperately. Sliding even farther down
the same slippery psychological slope, they now applauded the effort
to disarm French warships that were making ready to enter the
Battle of the Atlantic against the Germans.

They did not realize the extraordinary dilemma in which the
officers and crews of the *Richelieu* and the *Montcalm* had been
placed. For two years De Gaulle had been calling on the officers
of the Army and Navy to abandon·Pétain and enter the war on
the side of the Allies. The majority had refused to listen. The great
French fleet had even been scuttled at the monstrous order of leaders
unable to find the path of duty in the midst of the tragic moral
anguish of the revolution. And now that two fine ships had come
in, the only two ships of the grand fleet that had managed to shake
off the fatal inclination towards cowardice and treason, they were
welcomed with insults and treated as enemies. Unfortunately, the
French Admiral Robert was then in Martinique with two warships
that had been immobilized since June, 1940. On November 9, 1942,
they were on the point of steaming into American ports. Hearing
about the shocking events that were taking place in New York, the
admiral used them as a pretext to hold back his officers and crews.
The same thing happened in Alexandria, where Admiral Godefroy's
squadron, which was out of commission, learned of the incidents in
New York from Robert's reports. At the same time, however, that
De Gaullist propaganda was insulting the sailors of the *Richelieu*
who were bravely entering the war again, it was also insulting those
who refused to go in and was clamoring for "Robert's and Godefroy's
hides." This De Gaullist propaganda was conducted in New York

by a corps of agents who proclaimed that in De Gaullism "politics comes before the Army."

From the officers of the *Richelieu,* labeled as "Vichyites and traitors," the attacks were now aimed higher up, against their leader, General Giraud—he was called a "coward," an "escape artist," an "agent sent out by Pétain to divide the French," a "Nazi," an "assassin." At that time a leading New York evening newspaper printed an article, inspired by the De Gaullist propaganda service, according to which Hitler had sent General Giraud * to North Africa in June, 1940, to persuade General Noguès that Morocco should resist being split by the De Gaullists—which led the reader to conclude that General Giraud returned to North Africa in 1942 on behalf of Hitler.

From the Giraud level, the propaganda then rose to the top—to Roosevelt; for if Giraud was the "boss" of the *"Richelieu* traitors," Roosevelt was the "boss" of the "traitor" Giraud. And President Roosevelt was a "Fascist," an "agent of the Wall Street Bankers," who was trying "to use Hitler and the French Nazis to ward off the Communist danger in Europe." Thus an unbelievable state of mental excitement was produced, spread from one mind to the next, and turned into a mass phenomenon that clouded the intellect and left no room for free judgment. Day after day I received at *Pour la Victoire* a flood of furious and impassioned letters. I have preserved them all. They will be valuable material for psychiatrists and historians who may some day seek to analyze that strange pathological paroxysm characteristic of revolutionary madness.

Meanwhile, on board the *Richelieu* and the *Montcalm,* the situation was growing worse. Sailors were continuing to jump ship. And the mass desertions produced unimaginable chaos among the crews. Brawls broke out. The ships' officers were abused. An officer of the De Gaullist delegation, named Brunswick, a good fellow for that matter, who had gone to London a captain and returned a swivel-chair lieutenant colonel, was put in special charge of receiv-

---

* Intentionally or not, the reporter was led to confuse General Henri Giraud with General Henri Joseph Eugène Gouraud.

ing deserters and sending them on to England. In England there
was no French battleship for these sailors to serve on, and they were
lodged in barracks. Some of them regretted their decisions, and
having deserted the "Giraud Navy," they now deserted the "De
Gaullist Navy." Several tried to volunteer for the British Navy.

The American police kept a close watch on the situation. They
mingled with the workers repairing the ship. They infiltrated among
the crew. They watched bars and canteens where the corruption
was at work. It was not long before they were sending in alarming
reports. They feared that the desertions would increase so rapidly
that the *Richelieu* would be completely immobilized. Englishmen
in America also followed those events with growing apprehension.
A top-ranking officer of the Royal Navy, temporarily in New York,
wrote to an admiralty official in London:

> At a time when Allied naval forces, and the British Navy in par-
> ticular, are suffering considerable losses and when an ever greater effort
> is required of the crews, it is impossible to be indifferent to the crisis
> which is developing in the French Navy. In New York, Halifax and
> London, those rebel sailors are fraternizing with American, Canadian
> and British sailors and are setting them the worst example. I myself
> have seen French deserters walking on the streets arm in arm with
> British sailors. . . . If rigorous measures are not taken at once, we can
> expect the most regrettable incidents and very serious developments. . . .

The British Admiralty had already been warned and was worried
about the desertions that were also taking place in British ports
on the arrival of French merchantmen from Algeria.

It was shortly after this that American authorities, having patiently
made every effort at friendly persuasion, came to the conclusion
that the situation was serious enough to endanger success in the
Battle of the Atlantic, and decided to intervene. It was announced
officially that desertions from French ships would no longer be
tolerated. Then, as the desertions continued, the New York police
arrested twelve sailors from the *Richelieu* just as De Gaullist officials
were about to send them off to England (February 22, 1943). De
Gaulle's representative promptly protested. But on March 3 the

United Press published a story reflecting the official position of the United States:

> This government takes the view that friction between various French factions in this country is impairing the war effort and will move to suppress it.
>
> The UP informant said emphasis ought to be put on the fact that the United States is helping to rehabilitate the French ships which are expected to be of great use in the common war program and that they are decreasing the efficiency of those ships.
>
> The quarreling between French elements is doing nothing except impair the general war plans, and this government wishes to have it ended, the informant said.
>
> The arrests of deserting sailors are being handled by the Justice and Navy departments, and today twelve Frenchmen from the ships were being held at Ellis Island, it was said. Deserting sailors will be classified as undesirable aliens illegally in this country and subject to action by the immigration authorities, according to the official view.

Far from coming to an end, the agitation redoubled. De Gaulle's representatives defied the American authorities, speeded up the desertions, took the sailors to newspaper offices and had them give interviews in the course of which they insulted their officers and General Giraud.

On March 13 Secretary of the Navy Frank Knox felt it necessary to make the following statement at his press conference:

> The French naval vessels now being repaired in American naval shipyards were brought to this country under an agreement that they would form a part of the naval forces of the United Nations fighting the Axis powers.
>
> The American Government, through the Navy Department, is undertaking the repair and reconditioning of these ships. It is doing so for the express purpose of making them serviceable against our Axis enemies.
>
> These vessels cannot be put back into service without a full complement of trained crews. As a result of various circumstances there have been numerous desertions.
>
> If the desertions continue the vessels will be so understaffed that they will be virtually immobilized, inasmuch as there is not a reservoir of French naval personnel readily available to replace those who have jumped ship.

The enemy would profit directly from the immobilization of these vessels regardless of the cause. It follows therefore that the greatest service which their crews can render to France and to the United Nations is to stay with their ships. These vessels are pledged to fight on our side against the common enemy.

This public warning to the De Gaullists was a solemn and impressive one. In it the American government was accusing them of responsibility for an action directly benefiting the enemy. The official warning was accompanied by a most urgent protest to Tixier, De Gaulle's representative in Washington, demanding that he not only put a final stop to the encouragement of deserters by giving them passage to Great Britain, but that he publish an official declaration formally reprimanding the guilty sailors.

Tixier pretended to be helpless, and the desertions went on.

On March 20, 1943, Mr. Knox made another statement at his press conference. He emphasized the fact that the ships were being repaired with "good American money." This time he told the public a few tragic facts: One ship, he said, had recently sailed short of 40 per cent of her crew, which "added to the perils of her voyage." Another merchant ship lost eight out of ten of her gun crew and later was sunk, with her American cargo (the New York *Times,* March 20, 1943).

That day I wrote in my notebook:

"The American government, through its Secretary of the Navy, openly accuses the De Gaullists of playing the game of the Germans by turning sailors from their duty and disarming French ships in the midst of war. Mr. Knox disclosed that a ship has been sunk because her gun crew had been induced to desert. . . . In June, 1940, I enthusiastically joined a De Gaullism that summoned all Frenchmen in France and throughout the world to lay aside politics and, in a spirit of abnegation, self-sacrifice, and honor, to enter the supreme struggle on the side of the Allies. Today I am through forever with a De Gaullism that sets Frenchman against Frenchman, arouses the indignation of our allies, and is responsible for a German victory over a French ship. *Adieu,* De Gaulle! . . ."

9. The Downfall of Giraud

As long as he still breathes, I am only half alive.

RACINE

W E left De Gaulle at the end of January, 1943, returning from Casablanca to London more than ever at odds with Giraud and, consequently, more estranged than ever from the Americans.

The war in North Africa had been raging for three months. Von Arnim was making the desperate stand before Tunis and along the North-South corridor towards Tripolitania which was to keep the way open for Rommel in his retreat from Egypt.

The two French generals should have joined forces in that battle. Granted that they could not get together on political problems, they could at least have fought side by side as good soldiers. Had they done so, they would have formed habits of working together which would have served as a prelude to future conversations once the Germans were driven from Africa. But De Gaulle remained in London and from there continued his dramatic duel with Giraud.

And so, month after month went by and the situation showed no signs of improving. English and American correspondents sent their papers long dispatches every day, reporting the ups and downs of that painful quarrel, and these were featured under large headlines. Radio commentators took up the subject and discussed it daily. Thus the free portion of the world became an interested witness of the struggle. And in fact the security of the Anglo-American armies in Africa was involved in it; for to fight on a terrain where the

127

political atmosphere is sultry and unsettled adds to the difficulties of both officers and men. The affection many Englishmen and Americans felt for France led them to take a deep interest in a dispute so laden with meaning. Finally, scandalmongers, spurred on by underground Nazi propaganda, took an unhealthy pleasure in it.

To gain a correct impression of the events that marked that period, we might best refer to newspaper articles and, as before, particularly to those appearing in the New York *Times*. The editorial policy of this ardently pro-French newspaper has always been De Gaullist, but in the broadest sense of the term. Its correspondents have known this and have taken it into account. Besides, the greater part of their information in London and in Algiers has come from De Gaullist sources. Their reporting, their comments, and their analyses have thus showed a bias in favor of De Gaulle, though so highly moderate as to win the confidence of men of good will. Moreover, the *Times* is one of the leading newspapers of America and of the world and is renowned for its professional probity as well as the exceptional ability of its correspondents.

General de Gaulle, then, returned to London from Casablanca on January 31, 1943, three months after the American landing in Algiers, without having reached an understanding with General Giraud. Around him a good deal of criticism broke loose. On February 1 his Minister for Foreign Affairs, M. Massigli, gave several statements to the American press which were considered in Anglo-Saxon circles as a direct reproach to his chief. On his return from Casablanca, M. Massigli said in effect to Milton Bracker:

Frenchmen say "Vive De Gaulle et Giraud" and cannot see any difference. It is Vichy that tries to create that difference, in line with the German aim to keep the French people divided.

At his press conference on February 2 President Roosevelt repeated Massigli's statement, but more pointedly, and added that the dispute between De Gaulle and Giraud was a positive help to the enemy.

On February 3 Eden was called upon in Commons to answer

questions of the opposition, which had been influenced by the violent attacks of the London De Gaullists on Giraud. He made the following statement:

I think General Giraud is an extremely gallant soldier. I should feel very proud if I had his record in fighting Germany. . . . We are doing our best to bring about unity of Frenchmen who want to fight Germany.

Thereupon, from London,.De Gaulle appointed an "ambassador," General Catroux, to treat with Giraud; for obviously an intermediary was needed between these two French generals who could not come to terms in their private meeting and were conducting themselves like two hostile powers.

On February 10 Raymond Daniell wired from London to the New York *Times* that De Gaulle had just held an important press conference, the first in many months. The general had declared that when freedom of the press and the right of assembly were restored in Algiers, he would be able to come to an agreement with Giraud. He had also laid particular stress on a complete restoration of the laws of the Third Republic.

These explicit statements of De Gaulle, repeated a score of times and thoroughly reconsidered, should be underscored; for no sooner did he become ruler of Algiers than he completely suppressed freedom of the press and abolished the laws of the Third Republic, replacing them with amazing legislation of his own invention as to the press, public liberties, votes for women, electoral methods, and so on—which legislation had nothing whatever to do with the laws of the Third Republic.

The month of February passed in bitter polemics between London and Algiers. On February 25, however, De Gaulle declared that unity was necessary, if for no other reason, he said, than because the London and Algiers radios were giving France, and particularly the Resistance movement, contradictory instructions.

But days passed without bringing the slightest improvement.

On March 14 Giraud delivered an important speech in Algiers, in which he solemnly promised the French people to retire from public life the moment France was liberated. Perhaps he hoped to draw a similar promise from De Gaulle; had that promise been given, the dissension between the two generals would have ended instantly. For their quarrel was caused solely by De Gaulle's political uneasiness as he foresaw in the postwar picture the moral and political rivalry of another "liberating general," and by his jealousy of the high regard in which Giraud was held by the Americans.

On March 14, 1943, De Gaulle ordered a "note" handed to Giraud. In it he renewed the demands mentioned by Daniell. Republican legality, he said, must be re-established. Local republican institutions must be restored. Changes would certainly be made in French political institutions, but these changes could only be brought about by the French people after it had regained the full exercise of its sovereign rights. He suggested as an eventuality, as a profitable solution, the formation of an Advisory Assembly in which those members of Parliament who did not stand for capitulation and collaboration might be consulted.

Now the two French generals, having exchanged ambassadors, were going to exchange "notes," which, naturally, would promptly become public property.

Meanwhile, the De Gaullist press blamed Giraud for not immediately restoring in Algeria the Crémieux law which Pétain had abolished, the law granting French citizenship to all the Jews in Algeria.

The subject aroused deep interest in America, where the Jews are numerous and influential. Certain sections of the Jewish press, the Jewish radio, the large Jewish organizations, egged on by French De Gaullist exiles—several of Jewish origin were particularly militant—turned not only on Giraud but even on Secretary of State Hull and Under Secretary Sumner Welles, whom they accused of failing to support the Jewish cause in Algeria and of leaving Vichy laws intact under the American occupation.

In this situation, as in many others, Giraud was influenced by military considerations. He was afraid of political questions that might stir up Algerian opinion. The Jewish problem seemed to him all the more alarming because the violently anti-Jewish Arab population was against the restoration of the Crémieux law. Could he run the risk of irritating the Arabs at a time when the war was being fought in their land, when their villages and their minarets were being destroyed, their wives and their children being killed by bombs?

Giraud thought it best to resort to a temporary expedient and decreed that Jews desiring to resume their French nationality might apply individually. He let it be known, moreover, that these petitions would in every case be granted. In this way he re-established the Crémieux law by roundabout means and put the Jews on the same footing as the Arabs—which, fundamentally, is sound and reasonable.

The De Gaullists, however, protested in the name of what they called "high principles." It was necessary, they declared, to break with Vichy laws without circumlocutions. More Jewish demonstrations took place in New York. Baron Edouard de Rothschild, a loyal Frenchman who usually knows better, sent a letter of protest to the State Department. Under Secretary Welles replied that General Giraud was right. Excitement ran high. And meanwhile battles were raging in Tunisia.

, Three months later De Gaulle was to take power in Algeria; but though the fighting was then over and the Germans driven from Africa, De Gaulle did not yet dare to arouse the ire of the Arabs. He was to let two months go by before restoring the Crémieux law. Apparently, Giraud had acted wisely.

To express this opinion does not mean that we approve everything Giraud did. The general often showed a lack of flexibility, decision, and even foresight during that period, particularly when it came to eliminating certain Vichyite and collaborationist officials. His lack of political acumen is obvious. But what right has one to reproach a general of the Republic for this deficiency, when his republican tradition itself requires him to suppress such political talents as he may have?

On March 17 De Gaulle accepted Giraud's invitation to meet him in Algiers. Churchill promptly made a speech in the House of Commons expressing his satisfaction.

> Frenchmen everywhere [he said] must be united, and . . . act loyally against the common enemy without one day's needless delay. . . . It now appears that no question of principle divides these two bodies of Frenchmen.

But the beginning of a new incident, on March 20, was to put De Gaulle's journey off indefinitely. That was the revolt of Guiana against the Vichy government and the battle of the governors which we have already discussed in detail.

The African situation became so acute that, according to a United Press dispatch from Algiers on March 29, people there foresaw some new and most remarkable solutions: either a "regency" with a Giraud-De Gaulle-Catroux triumvirate; or a two-headed government with De Gaulle and Giraud; or two separate governments, one military, the other civil. There was even another possibility: to settle the quarrel by appointing General Catroux head of the African administration.

For all that, a certain calm seemed to prevail. On March 31 it was rumored in London that De Gaulle had decided to go to Algiers.

But on April 6 events took a dramatic turn. De Gaulle's luggage was packed and his plane waiting at the London airport when word came from General Eisenhower advising him to postpone his trip for several days. It was in fact the crucial moment in the African war. The two German generals, Rommel and von Arnim, working perfectly together, had just joined forces. Eisenhower had been informed by reports from London of De Gaulle's attitude and he did not want any quarrels between Frenchmen at such a moment.

The incident made a tremendous stir in De Gaullist ranks. On April 5, at his press conference, Secretary Hull explained:

> We knew that we would get into a hopeless tangle if we stopped fighting to take up politics. . . . If the Frenchmen there were fighting or opposing the Axis powers we would work with them and help them militarily as we did with the De Gaulle group when we gave them lend-lease recognition.

A few days later, on April 7, the Washington correspondent of the New York *Times* wrote:

According to what is being said here among informed circles, General de Gaulle has come to be regarded as a disturbing factor, one whose presence in North Africa at this juncture might create more embarrassments than the problems he might help to solve through conversations with General Giraud.

On April 11 the papers announced that Catroux had returned to London greatly discouraged at having failed to bring about any definite agreement between the two rivals. And Raymond Daniell wired the New York *Times* from London that the discord was greater than ever.

At this moment what was the subject of—or, rather, the pretext for the conflict? It was still De Gaulle's determination to set up a governmental body in Algiers, while Giraud refused with the contention that in the absence of the government of the Republic, the administration must confine itself to taking care of current matters. Then, it was Giraud's expressed desire to restore republican legality in France, once France was liberated, by applying the Tréveneuc law of 1872.

His memorandum of April 19 was proof of this. And the London *Times,* though pro-De Gaulle, was impelled to write:

The principles of the Giraud memorandum are impeccable. The laws and procedure of the Republic are faithfully observed.

Unfortunately, on April 21, De Gaulle rejected the Giraud memorandum *in toto.* He declared that Giraud could not hold both military and civil power in Algiers, and said:

To hold both the offices of Commander in Chief and of member of the central authority would be contrary to the Constitution and to the 1938 law concerning the organization of the nation in time of war, as well as to the time-honored tradition of France—with the sole exception of the period of the Consulate and of the Napoleonic Empire. Such a regime would certainly be disavowed by the French people after the experience they have had with the personal rule, both civil and military, imposed by Vichy.

To grasp the full irony of this text, one must be aware that a few months later De Gaulle was to take over both civil and military command, while claiming to act in compliance with the desires of the French people and invoking the same law of 1938:

The President of the Committee of Liberation is the head of the armed forces. The powers devolving on the President of the Council of Ministers according to the law of July 11, 1938, are exercised by the President of the Committee of National Liberation.

Now the discussion left the highroad and fell into a rut. By May 3 the two generals were no longer arguing about whether they would meet, but about the place where their meeting should occur. Actually, De Gaulle had sent propaganda agents to Algiers to hand out instructions, badges, pennants and money, and mobilize native and French crowds for a triumphal publicity-producing reception for him. It was important, in his opinion, to excite the popular imagination and to impress American and British observers. Giraud considered such demonstrations out of place in wartime and at a short distance from the battlefield. He therefore sent De Gaulle a note:

General Giraud delivered to General Catroux on April 27 his reply to the note of the National Committee dated April 15. He considers that an agreement ought now to be reached through personal discussion, quickly and without public excitement.

Therefore, in his reply to General de Gaulle dated April 27, he proposed to meet him in a North African city and as soon as the agreement is concluded, to go together with him to Algiers.

De Gaulle immediately replied that he would not go to "a North African city" and that he would see Giraud in Algiers and nowhere else.

On May 6 Giraud repeated that Algiers would not do.

The New York *Times* of May 6 explained that the Allies were siding with Giraud and hoped that the meeting would not take place in Algiers, as they wished to avoid political disturbances at such a particularly critical phase of the North African war.

But, as usual, military considerations left De Gaulle completely cold, and the quarrel continued on the plane of burlesque. De Gaulle let it be known that he was "willing to issue orders against street demonstrations, but that he insisted on Algiers as the meeting place." He refused to go to Biskra or any other isolated spot.

The capture of Tunis (May 9) caused people to forget for the moment the trifling matter of meeting places. And finally, the two generals returned to serious business. On May 11 Giraud published his reply to a letter from De Gaulle dated April 20. He proposed that power in Algiers be turned over to the "Superior Council of the Empire" to which reference has already been made in these pages. He offered to share the presidency with De Gaulle. He made it clear that this council would not be a provisional government. Moreover, he insisted that the Tréveneuc law was to determine, later, the return to republican legality.

According to the Tréveneuc law, which was adopted in 1872 on the morrow of the 1870-71 disaster, the legal procedure in case of invasion and enemy occupation is as follows: As soon as half of the departments are liberated, each General Council * designates two members who meet in the Provisional National Assembly; this Provisional National Assembly appoints a provisional government; the provisional government decrees general elections for a definitive Assembly as soon as circumstances permit.

Obviously, Giraud's position strictly conformed to the constitutional plan and was actually the only one that could be taken by a French general who respected his country's institutions.

A significant incident now took place. Churchill went to Washington for a meeting with Roosevelt. Newspapermen and informed persons say that the British Prime Minister expressed himself to the President in no uncertain terms about De Gaulle, in whom he saw, it is said, a "great adventurer absorbed in his own adventure and not the slightest bit in the safety of his country" (the New York *Times*). Excitement ran high when, on May 19, in his speech before the American Congress, Churchill praised Giraud and failed

* An assembly composed of delegates from each district in the department.

to mention De Gaulle by name, but made a disagreeable reference to him. De Gaullists were immensely distressed and Raymond Daniell wired from London to the New York *Times:*

The Fighting French heard the speech with some foreboding. It seemed to them that it was not a mere incident that the Prime Minister went out of his way to praise General Henri Honoré Giraud but did not mention General Charles de Gaulle. But what was more disturbing to them was his emphasis on the wisdom of the founding fathers in combining the job of President of the United States with that of the Commander in Chief of its armed forces. That is one of the major issues that separates Generals de Gaulle and Giraud. General de Gaulle insists that it is undemocratic to combine the two functions in one man and General Giraud holds that it is essential.

Churchill's hostile attitude had its effect on De Gaulle. The next day, May 20, his spokesmen became optimistic and conciliatory. At this juncture, Giraud offered a compromise according to which:

(1) De Gaulle's plan for a Committee of Liberation would be accepted;

(2) Each of the two generals would name two members to the Committee;

(3) The committee of six members—the two generals and their four appointees—would name three more members;

(4) .The definitive Committee of Liberation, comprising these nine persons would meet in Algiers.

"There is hope!" Milton Bracker wrote from London.

But not for long. On May 22 Drew Middleton reported that a propaganda war had broken out in liberated Tunis where De Gaulle had had the Cross of Lorraine painted on doors, while Giraud responded by putting up posters bearing his own picture. According to the American correspondent, General Catroux declared that he was disgusted.

On May 25—a new shift of scene. De Gaulle accepted Giraud's plan for the Committee. Bracker wired the New York *Times:*

Fighting French Headquarters here . . . was substantially cheered up today.

On May 26 the "cheer" had vanished! De Gaulle had flown into a temper on hearing that Giraud was to keep command of the Army. Eden summoned De Gaulle to the Foreign Office and, for the third time that month, indicated the extreme dissatisfaction of the British government (May 27). The Berlin, Vichy, and Paris radios exercised their wits on the quarrel of the "two Anglo-Saxon mercenaries."

Then, on May 30, De Gaulle announced that he was leaving for Algiers—where his secret police had already gone—to organize demonstrations of "spontaneous" enthusiasm.

He arrived there on May 31 and received a wild welcome at the airport. The populace as well as the police wore in their buttonholes the Cross of Lorraine, which Giraud had been imprudent enough to forbid on the ground that it had "become a form of agitation irreconcilable with war needs."

De Gaulle took up quarters in the *Villa des Oliviers,* a sunny and luxurious setting overlooking the sea.

There he was to remain until France was liberated. There, in peace and comfort, he was to succeed in getting himself recognized as the symbol of those who inside France were suffering, bleeding, and dying, that France might live.

Foreign correspondents gathered at the Villa on the afternoon of the thirty-first. One of them asked him:

"Now that you and General Giraud have joined forces, will the De Gaullist movement continue?"

"The De Gaullist movement," replied De Gaulle, "is the incarnation of France herself."

A newspaperman confided to an American Congressman who was passing through Algiers:

"That's the way Hitler and Mussolini used to talk about their respective parties."

But the Committee which the two generals had agreed on was still to be formed. As we have seen, each was to appoint two members. De Gaulle named General Catroux and M. Massigli. Giraud picked General Georges and M. Monnet.

"It's not fair," cried De Gaulle. "I haven't a majority."

"But we six members are going to elect three more members, as agreed," answered Giraud.

"Never! I insist on one member more whom I shall choose myself."

"No. You accepted the plan before you came here. It's simply a matter of following it."

"Then I shall go back to London," De Gaulle threatened.

"But that would create a scandal," retorted Giraud.

"What do I care? . . . I insist on one member more. I want André Philip."

"Impossible."

"Then, good-bye."

The committee members stared at one another in consternation. What were they to do? What was going to happen?

"All right," said Giraud, "I yield to avoid a situation which would be painful to every Frenchman. I accept André Philip."

The surprise attack, the pressure, the blackmail, had succeeded. De Gaulle had four votes in the Committee of Liberation. Giraud had three, one of them belonging to Monnet who had secretly gone over to De Gaulle. From that day on, De Gaulle was to soar from victory to victory.

It is not within the scope of this book to relate in detail the steps leading to the elimination of Giraud. When they are free to talk, witnesses in Algiers will have fuller and more concrete evidence than could be amassed in far-off America.

The elimination of Giraud was carried out with a cold and meticulous hatred, a fierce and ruthless animosity. He was the rival in De Gaulle's path, the only dangerous rival—for though he had no political ambitions it was thought that on the day of France's liberation he could count on the backing of the French Army and the help of American authorities.

Step by step he was driven from his "co-presidency of the Committee of Liberation"—he was demoted from his position as head of the Army—a Commissioner of War was set over him—he was

supervised by civil inspectors and by commissions—his close associates were attacked—he was humiliated, threatened, watched by the
police—he was ignominiously kicked out of the Army—and finally
an attempt was made to assassinate him.

In July, 1943, Giraud came to America to complete arrangements
of prime importance for the rearming of a huge French-African
army. The Americans gave him everything he asked for. How could
the Americans—who supplied arms to so many countries and even
to many adventurers, provided only they were fighting Germany
and Japan—have refused them to the most heroic of French generals?

I had a long talk with General Giraud at Blair House, in Washington. This is the first time I have ever repeated the essential parts
of our dramatic conversation.

"General," I said, "I know many things about the De Gaullist
movement. It is my duty to warn you that your life is in danger."

"I have nothing to fear. I have absolutely no political intentions.
I am only a general who wants to fight the Germans. . . . I have
but one ambition: to enter liberated Metz at the head of my troops."

"That is precisely what De Gaulle does not want to happen. He
will use every means to prevent it."

"I should not like to think that. You must be exaggerating."

"You are spoiling all of De Gaulle's plans. Your strictly military
attitude and your courage both condemn him. He sees your reputation and your friendship with the Americans as a menace. . . . To
get rid of you he will stop at nothing."

"He would never dare. . . . And, well, I have faith in my
baraka. . . ." *

"Your *baraka* against fanatical De Gaullists? A plane breaks up
in flight . . . an automobile is attacked out in the country . . . a
pistol shot fired from who knows where. . . . Do you think your
baraka will protect you?"

"I've always been lucky. I escaped so many dangers in my long
life. . . . Even the Germans didn't get me."

* An Arabian cane supposed to protect one against bad luck.

"The De Gaullists will get you, General. You will never enter Metz at the head of the French Army. . . . And if you don't watch out, you will go back there in a coffin. . . ."

Giraud burst out laughing and repeated: "I have faith in my *baraka!*" *

To expel him from the Army De Gaulle resorted to a classical trick: he retired Giraud from active service and offered him an honorary post, in compensation. He asked him to take over the "general inspection of the armed forces." Giraud, knowing that there was, unfortunately, almost nothing to inspect and realizing the reasons for his disgrace and the meaning of it, rejected the offer with dignity. For that matter, he had learned of the decree ordering his retirement from the newspapers. De Gaulle had not deigned to inform him of it himself.

It was reported that the incident caused a certain amount of friction in the Committee of Liberation. M. Jacquinot is said to have refused to put his signature to the decree. The commissioners' courage seems, however, to have been short-lived. To hold out against De Gaulle meant the loss of their portfolios.

The only ones to speak out openly were the Communist leaders in Algiers. We mention this because it is a fact, that in this matter the Communists showed the most courageous, most chivalrous and most patriotic attitude. Communist Fernand Grenier, Commissioner of Aviation, protested very firmly.

To break down the resistance of the Communists, De Gaulle made use of subterfuge: he led the Communists to believe that Giraud had finally accepted the post of inspector. The Communists decided that there was no need for them to be more "Giraudist" than Giraud. But when they realized that they had been taken in, they published a manifesto which exposed the whole maneuver (April 10).

Giraud had in fact accepted nothing. His career in the French Army was at an end—that army whose most distinguished leader he was, the army to which he had returned after so many trials and

---

* Less than three months later Giraud sent word to the American authorities that his life was in danger in Algiers.

at the sacrifice of happiness, freedom, the safety of his wife and
daughters, and even the life of the daughter who died at the hands
of the Gestapo—the army which he had led into the glory of the
Tunisian battles. His farewell to his soldiers was full of nobility
and grandeur.

> Listen to one voice and to one call only, the voice of France, the voice
> of your families who are hoping, suffering and dying. Men pass on but
> France will live forever. . . .

He went into retirement. But De Gaulle wished to add a further
insult. He ostentatiously suppressed the precious post of inspector-
general, the bone he had tossed to Giraud, thus inspiring the following comment from an American correspondent:

> Some observers thought that this proved that the post was unimpor-
> tant, as General Giraud had said in his letter refusing it (the New York
> Times, April 24, 1944).

On May 6, in the Consultative Assembly, the Communist Deputy
Fajon protested against Giraud's dismissal and supported his position on the separation of military and civil power. The same day,
the Communist Commissioner Grenier declared:

> We must put a stop to these purges which are demolishing the army.
> The past is dead and what matters is the conduct of officers in front of
> the Germans (the New York Times, May 6, 1944).

Magnificent words! Taking them literally, one could not help
wondering what De Gaulle's attitude towards the Germans really
was. Was he indeed fighting them? No. Were his political intrigues
and his campaign against Giraud an aid to the enemy? Yes.

The last act of the drama verges on the tragic.

In July, 1944, in Algiers, General Giraud was shot in the head.
The news was suppressed for a week. Nothing was done. A three-
line communiqué (which attracted little notice) announced that a
drunken Senegalese sentry had fired on the former Commander in
Chief of the French Army and had broken his jaw. The sound of
the shot was drowned in the uproar of the American victory in

France. Not a single newspaper mentioned it. No one asked embarrassing questions. It was the first time in French colonial history that a colored *tirailleur* had fired on a general. What had actually happened? What became of the Senegalese soldier? Was he questioned? Was he tried? Executed? Not a word. The time of the attack was marvelously well-chosen! Who could possibly take an interest in the fate of a poor retired general at the moment when France was being liberated? All the American correspondents and newspapermen had just hurried from Algeria to France, where the outcome of the greatest battle in history was being decided.

The only information I have comes from an Allied report. As I cannot give its source, I shall withhold any passages that do not check with information I have managed to gather on my own account. I shall also refrain from drawing conclusions which point plainly to the more serious responsibilities for the event.

The following details will complete the information already given:

The corps of guards whose duty it was to watch General Giraud's home was under direct orders of General Koeltz. It was supposed to be a guard of honor for the general's protection. . . .

There had been numerous attempts to enter General Giraud's house previous to this attack. They were made by soldiers stationed at Rivoli. A few weeks before, on a date we have been unable to determine, a soldier asked the guard to let him pass under the pretext that he was on a "special mission." He declared that this mission came from "high up" and that he was under the direct orders of a Lieutenant Lehmann who had supplied the jeep that had brought him there. After some hesitation, the guard refused to let him pass. It would be interesting to find that man again. And it would be easy to identify him by three teeth he has covered with platinum. . . .

General Giraud, who knew that he was in danger, had given strict orders to his guard to arrest and, if necessary, to shoot anyone who tried to get into his house. No one can explain how this particular soldier was able to leave in his jeep without being either arrested or questioned. . . .

We have already referred to earlier attempts against General Giraud's life. But we must mention a very revealing fact. After one of those attempts, War Commissioner Diethelm ordered an investigation. It seems that General de Gaulle himself requested this investigation in order to put a stop to current rumors concerning the attitude of his personal entourage toward General Giraud. At a dinner at the home of Mme. Barril (the widow of Colonel Barril), an officer on the staff of the War Commissariat, declared: "We shall kill the traitor Giraud either here or in France." The remark was reported by two witnesses. . . .*

It has not been possible to establish exactly the date of the previous attempt on Giraud's life. Frenchmen are unwilling to aid these investigations for fear of police reprisals. But one incident in connection with that attempt is worth mentioning. An army judge was chosen to conduct the investigation. He started proceedings at once. But scarcely had he begun than he was summoned to Algiers by M. Diethelm's officer. He was kept there four days under various pretexts. When he returned to resume his investigation, all the witnesses had disappeared, some sent to Italy, others to Equatorial Africa. . . .

The soldier who shot General Giraud is not a black Senegalese, as reported. He is part Arab, part Jew, and is a member of a sect known as Derkoua. He belonged to a contingent of twelve new guards who had been brought in on an exchange ten days before the attempt (twelve out of thirty). It has been noted that this soldier telephoned frequently to Oran, which is very unusual for a native. In the course of those telephone conversations there was often talk of money. . . .

The assassin did not shoot General Giraud from a distance, as has been stated, but from up close. The General was saved from certain death by an unexpected movement he made as he leaned towards his daughter-in-law. . . .

The murderer escaped without difficulty. Shortly afterwards, however, he was caught and arrested near the road just where the jeep had picked up the men who made the previous attempt against General Giraud's life. Later, the murderer was released. . . .

Colonel Allégret, of General de Gaulle's staff, was the officer who checked every day for De Gaulle on what was going on at Giraud's. M. Gorion, secretary-general of the government of Algeria makes no secret of the fact that the order to drop the investigation came from the same source as in the previous case. . . .

The information contained in this report was known to many Frenchmen who lived in North Africa. In addition, De Gaulle's hatred for Giraud had been displayed on the international scene for

* The author feels that he must withhold the names of these witnesses.

two years. At the moment of liberation, therefore, De Gaulle, in Paris, was facing a real danger—that the truth would come to light. Besides, the Resistance forces, made up of elements from all the groups that fought Germany (including many officers of the regular army), knew very little about the real character of the struggle between the two generals. On all sides people were asking De Gaulle:

"Look here! Precisely what has happened to Giraud? . . . Why isn't that grand old soldier at the head of the French Army? Is it true you've kicked him out? . . . And, by the way, where is he?"

De Gaulle did not know what to answer. However, a few days after the liberation of Paris, rumors began to circulate about the attempted assassination in Algiers. De Gaullist propaganda agents then spread the story that De Gaulle had a high regard for Giraud; that he had been obliged, much against his will, to retire him temporarily in order to prevent any crystallization about him of the Pétainist spirit; and that, besides, De Gaulle knew nothing of what had happened in Algiers. But the explanation did not satisfy everyone. The rumors multiplied. Then, General de Gaulle resorted to a subterfuge. He published in the press and had broadcasted over the Paris radio a telegram overflowing with friendly sentiments, which he had sent to the man he regarded as his mortal enemy more than ten days after the attempted assassination:

I am deeply outraged at the attempt on your life. I have ordered the most thorough investigation and have recommended that the guilty man be punished to the limit. I shall follow this matter with the greatest attention.

Meanwhile, General Catroux will be at your service to assure your return to France wherever and whenever you wish, as soon as your health permits. My thoughts are with you today as the Allied forces approach Metz. With best wishes for a rapid recovery and assurances of my sincere and respectful friendship,

(Signed)   C. De Gaulle

Reading those lines and hearing them over the radio, the French naturally said to themselves:

"All the same, De Gaulle is a good fellow! How nice he is to Giraud!"

De Gaulle, however, thought it wise to take other precautions: he quickly got out of Paris everyone, even friends, who knew too much about affairs in Algeria—about the Giraud drama as well as those of Darlan, and many others. Emmanuel d'Astier de la Vigerie, Minister of the Interior, at Algiers, was removed from government office. His brother the general was shipped off to Brazil. General Catroux was dispatched to Moscow. As for Colonel Passy, he was sent to London; then, as London was too near Paris, he was given a mission to South America. The more notorious Cagoulards were likewise sent to the four corners of the globe.

The earth lacked room in which to scatter and disperse all the embarrassing witnesses.

Nevertheless, General de Gaulle breathed more easily.

10. The Destruction of the Army

In the next war, Morocco, Algeria, Tunisia, French West Africa and Madagascar will have to furnish the homeland with the largest Colonial army the world has ever seen, from one to two million men. If they don't, the Empire will have to be declared bankrupt.

MARSHAL LYAUTEY
(July 2, 1924)

When they are not using armies to establish tyranny, tyrants destroy armies in order not to be destroyed by them.

GUGLIELMO FERRERO

WHEN the Americans landed in North Africa in November, 1942, they found there eleven divisions of reduced strength, in all about 70,000 French and native soldiers allowed by the Germans and Italians. From this force General Giraud was able to construct a fighting unit of about 60,000 men.

Almost two years later, when the Americans landed in France, in June, 1944, the effective force of French troops from Algeria available for the battle of liberation had been reduced to seven normal divisions with a total of fighting men lower than Berlin and Vichy had left the French.

The battle of Normandy began without the participation of a single French fighting unit, except for two small battalions of parachutists. Later, after the victory, the Leclerc motorized division was landed in the Calvados and placed in the reserve of American

146

troops. According to reports, this division was not actually engaged before the entrance into Paris. Composed for the most part of soldiers from the Foreign Legion, mercenaries and native Algerians, and strangely reminiscent of the special corps created by Franco in Spain, the sole mission of the Leclerc division was to occupy Paris and to make De Gaulle's authority secure there. Much later five divisions under the command of General Delattre de Tassigny were hurled against the Riviera, far from the fronts where the final outcome of the Battle of France was being decided. Afterward they followed the American armies into Alsace, where they fought gloriously.

When these facts came to light, Frenchmen all over the world, who had kept their heads in the midst of the general excitement, were stunned. How did it happen that after two years in Africa, that inexhaustible reservoir of warriors, De Gaulle had been unable to line up more soldiers than the handful he had found upon his arrival? How did it happen that neither the general himself nor any French units figured, if only symbolically, in the decisive battle of Normandy?

Any explanation must begin with the conception which De Gaulle has formed regarding his own duty. A general who finds good reasons for stepping out of his role as a soldier in a great, long-drawn-out, and dramatic struggle in which the fate of his own country is at stake, cannot feel any deep and ardent desire to raise an army. On the contrary, the larger the fighting army he raised, the more clearly would he expose the fact that he himself was not in the fight.

In Russia a politician, Stalin, made himself into a Soviet marshal—to the great good fortune of the Russian Army. In Germany a former corporal, Hitler, also made himself Commander in Chief of the German Army—to its great misfortune. In Jugoslavia a rough, hard man without any military background, the famous Tito, became first the leader of a partisan band, then a general, and finally a marshal; and whatever one may think of Marshal Tito, it cannot be denied that he has displayed admirable energy in raising and leading his heroic army. In France peasants, workers, clerks, enrolled in the Resistance forces, have risen to high ranks and proved to be excellent leaders. The history of France shows also a Napoleon, political head and emperor, who never quit the battlefield; and a Joan of Arc, a simple peasant maid who, donning a suit of armor, unfurled her standard and led the knights of France into the fight for Freedom.

De Gaulle did not emulate Stalin, Hitler, Tito, Napoleon, Joan of Arc, or the leaders of the F.F.I.—all of whom insisted on being soldiers to the last. De Gaulle insisted upon being a civilian.

On August 2, 1943, in Algiers, he took leave of the little army he had gathered together after June, 1940—that army which still looked upon him as its Commander in Chief, though he had never led it into battle. In his order of the day he said:

As for me, upon whom you have bestowed the highest honor a man can know—that of following him of your own free will through stress and sacrifice—I shall remain at the post to which I am called, more closely bound to you than ever.

Thus he was assuming, from then on, a purely civilian mission. He was terminating unilaterally the De Gaulle-Churchill agreement on the "French military force" of which he was to take personal command.

The dispatches of American correspondents in Algiers showed a certain amazement:

General de Gaulle insists on being considered a civilian leader and not a soldier. It is true that he is still wearing his general's uniform, but that is undoubtedly for propaganda purposes since his profile in his present uniform has been well publicized. Furthermore, of late, he has been receiving his friends in civilian clothes, at the *Villa des Oliviers*.

It was indeed paradoxical for a man to wish to be the incarnation of the fight to the finish, to set himself up as the symbol of resistance, and at the same time to pretend a total lack of interest in military action. Yet that is exactly what happened. The accepted theory among De Gaullists was that De Gaulle had so heavy a task of governing to accomplish that he ought to devote himself to it to the exclusion of everything else. And those who ventured to observe above a whisper that Marshal Stalin's job of governing an empire that covers one-fifth of the globe was a heavier task than that of governing Algeria and Morocco were looked upon as troublemakers and traitors. The same troublemakers and traitors recognized that De Gaulle's example would be repeated on every level of the movement, creating various degrees of apathy and indifference to the Army, and resulting in demoralization.

Unfortunately, things went even further. Having become the leader of a revolutionary political party, De Gaulle suffered the inevitable fate of all such leaders—the fate of all usurpers confronted by regular troops—he developed a fear of the Army. Everyone was aware of Hitler's fear of Germany's standing Army and the many-sided and often tragic struggle that went on incessantly between that army and Nazism. De Gaulle hypnotized himself with the same fear and saw in the regular army a natural enemy of De Gaullism.

An officer wrote to me from Algiers in July, 1943:

General de Gaulle has not the slightest consideration for us. He does not like our generals, whom he doubtless sees as future competitors. To find an excuse for himself he accuses them of "Pétainism." What a joke! They all know perfectly well—Giraud best of all—that Pétain would have them shot if he caught them. Besides, even if they were "Pétainists," isn't it the only important thing to know whether they are willing to kill the Boches? Strange, but the Communists have a much fairer and more patriotic attitude. They say openly that we must support Giraud and Juin because Giraud and Juin are good fighters.

When De Gaulle came to Algeria he first intended to separate the regular army from the De Gaullist army, much as Hitler had separated the S.S. from the German Army and Mussolini the Fascist militia from the Italian Army. But his plan met with so much opposition—it so deeply shocked refugees and officers who had seen the German system functioning in France—that he finally gave it up. No sooner had he done so, however, than he let it be known that he had no intention of mobilizing a large French Army. One of the officers in the group around him wrote:

The general does not think it an opportune moment to raise a large army in North Africa. According to him the chief obstacle is the lack of French officers and noncommissioned officers. He also thinks that the mobilization of too large a number of officers would hinder economic recovery. In sum, he stresses the fact that France has suffered such severe losses that to ask more of her would be to imperil her future.

The pretext of the lack of officers and noncommissioned officers was not valid. Throughout the entire war, there were in England and in America a great many French officers, drawing enormous salaries in pounds sterling and in dollars, who had nothing whatever to do—often to the disgust of our Allies. The same was true in Algiers. These countless unemployed officers could have been given intensive training and promoted in rank, and, with native officers recruited for the lower ranks, would have furnished the cadres for a large number of divisions. Furthermore, the De Gaullists undertook to "purge" the Army and in so doing got rid of some excellent officers who were only too eager to fight; and this was done with the obvious intent of weakening the Army.

The result was that Giraud's plan, which he laid before President Roosevelt during his visit to Washington, could never be carried out. The thirty or forty divisions which he hoped to muster in North Africa, West Africa and Madagascar, and which would have provided France with an impressive military force on D-Day and a ten-times greater prestige at the peace conference, never came into being.

It is only fair to say that the Americans soon showed themselves in no hurry to equip the French troops. Why? Because the agitation and the *coup d'état* atmosphere prevailing in Algiers for two years made them fear that they might be furnishing the weapon for a future civil war. With uneasiness and often with vexation the Americans were following the fratricidal strife taking place in Jugoslavia between Tito and Mikhailovitch and in Greece between Generals Sarafis and Zernas. In the De Gaulle-Giraud quarrel they recognized the germ of a similar phenomenon. They also had certain scruples for which the French people can only be grateful to them; watching De Gaullism develop, the Americans began to fear the formation of a praetorian army that would impose its will on the French people after France had been freed.

These fears of the Americans were not their only ones. American diplomatic reports stressed the increasing violence of De Gaullist anti-American campaigns. The continual demands and the bitter reproaches against Roosevelt and America which De Gaulle voiced in the Algiers press and elsewhere at length presented a most serious political problem. Further, the elimination of Giraud, whom the Washington government had long hoped to see in command of the French armed forces—for the simple reason that Giraud had apparently not the slightest political aspirations and was thinking only of winning the war—the progressive elimination of Giraud worked at every step as a kind of danger signal. Thus the Americans quickly reached the conclusion that it would be unwise in wartime to furnish any great amount of guns and ammunition to a party leader with whom they were unable to establish normal friendly relations. The attitudes, acts, plans, and ambitions of De Gaulle and the men around him impelled the Americans to hold back the arming of French North Africa, though at the same time they were stepping up their delivery of weapons to the Russians, the Chinese, the British, the Jugoslavs, to anyone who would use them for war purposes.

A fact less well-known is that the political activities of De Gaullism not only led the Americans to stop furnishing arms to the French Army, but also resulted in their refusal to supply them to the Resistance forces as well. De Gaulle covered up the work of disintegration he was carrying on in the African army by pretending to devote all his efforts to building up an army inside of France. The Americans knew, however, that the general's intentions and ulterior motives were the same in both cases. They frankly feared that he would hand out guns and ammunition in France only to his own partisans. They did not want to arm the De Gaullist Resistance forces without arming the others. They did not want to favor one political faction to the detriment of the rest.

Thus De Gaulle, generally regarded by world opinion as the symbolic leader of the fight to the finish, was during most of the war the chief obstacle to the organization of a French army abroad and a French army at home for such a fight to the finish. This explains the complete bankruptcy of the French Army and its failure to join in the Battle of Normandy.

If we refer, as we did above, to the dispatches of American correspondents in Algiers, we can trace fairly easily the progress of military disorganization in Algeria.

As we saw, De Gaulle arrived in Algiers on May 31, 1943, after eight months of quarreling with Giraud. From the very first day, he announced that De Gaullist troops could not be mixed with other French troops returning from battle covered with glory and wearing the laurels they had won at Pont du Fahs and Tunis. At that moment one of the most fabulous exaggerations of De Gaullist propaganda was exposed. That propaganda had consistently given the impression that De Gaulle had an army of 110,000. Now it came out that the De Gaullist troops numbered in all around 15,000. General Leclerc's division (the story of whose crossing of the desert from Tchad to Tripoli has been told many times) then contained only about 1,800 men, all, except for 300 whites, native Africans. No one would think of disparaging Leclerc's heroes or those under General Koenig, but to falsify their numbers adds nothing to their glory.

To cover up their propaganda lie, and in order to pad the strength of their forces, and make the Allies and the French in Algeria think they were stronger than they actually were, the De Gaullists resorted to a queer operation. They induced mass desertions from the Giraud ranks to De Gaullist units. In other words, they applied the same technique to the African army that they had used with the sailors of the *Richelieu* in New York.

There is a document which presents crushing evidence on this subject. It is a report of the General Staff of the African Army

(July, 1943) expressing alarm at the desertions being induced by De Gaulle's agents. The facts are of the same character as those I had observed in New York at the time of the *Richelieu* desertions: promises of bonuses to deserting soldiers, offers of promotion, use of recruiting agents and of society ladies and fast women, etc. . . .

Here are the principal parts of the report:

Measures Taken by the C.F.L.N. Against Desertions

De Gaullist propaganda was being carried on by every means, following the technique described below. As a result the Commander in Chief was compelled to adopt a series of preventive and repressive measures. Organization of barriers and guardposts at certain highway crossroads, police search of clandestine recruiting centers, etc. . . . During those operations, a mobilization camp of 600 deserters was discovered on June 17 in a well-camouflaged farmhouse near Algiers; it was used by De Gaullist soldiers as an irregular depot. The camp was surrounded and the deserters were sent back to their own regiments.

On orders from Admiral Muselier, General Giraud's adjutant, the same measures have been extended progressively to all of North Africa, with the result that the wave of desertions, which was growing by leaps and bounds, has subsided. But there has been no slackening in the zeal of De Gaullist agents nor the illegal activities of Free French officers—which proves General de Gaulle's firm determination not to keep his agreements.

In addition, legal steps have been taken against recruiting agents acting in violation of French law.

Propaganda Technique Inducing Soldiers to Desert to the Free French Forces

This extremely active and insidious propaganda is carried on, on the one hand, by elements of Free French Forces; on the other, by civilian recruiting agents (men and women) under orders of recruiting offices that are mostly secret.

A. Direct Activity of Free French Forces

Quite some time before the end of operations in the Tunisian theatre, Free French Forces had tried to induce soldiers of the regular army to come over to their ranks. Certain elements in the Leclerc army who worked in liaison with the troops of General Delay, commanding the

East Sahara front, had especially received orders to bring about as many desertions as possible. As a result on April 30, 1943, several soldiers from the Leclerc army on leave and a De Gaullist officer who had come for that purpose by truck from Metlaoui, took along with them six European soldiers of the I/13 R.T.S., stationed near Metlaoui.

A large number of Free French Forces—enlisted men, non-commissioned officers and officers—have been sent on leave since May to the most important garrisons in Algerian territory, with instructions to maintain close contact with members of the regular land, sea and air forces, for the purpose of winning them over to the Free French. These men on false leave, who were actually recruiting agents, were in a position, thanks to the many motor vehicles they brought with them, to send the deserters rapidly on to Tunisia. There they were, very likely, regrouped in one of several secret recruiting depots, given clothing and provided with false identification papers.

Taking advantage of the fact that the regular army had been ordered to lodge and feed them and give them the best of treatment, the Free French soldiery used every means in their power to induce the regular troops to desert.

On several occasions it was reported that members of the Free French Forces on General Catroux's staff had brought about desertions among the Senegalese *tirailleurs* of the XIII R.T.S. who were guarding the mission.

Furthermore, De Gaullist officers or agents who have organized desertions are usually exempt from search and summons by the regular authorities either because they belong to the General Staff or to General de Gaulle's services and live in special quarters.

B. Activities of Civilian Recruiting Agents

A network of clandestine recruiting offices, set up long in advance, was discovered on North African territory, notably in Tunisia and in the department of Algiers.

A great many civilian agents, among them women, tried to impel regular army men to join the Free French Forces. Mobilization points, changed each day, were designated where deserters could be secretly picked up in trucks at a time agreed upon. On June 7, 1943, the police arrested, just as they were about to entrain, some sixty soldiers of all branches of the service gathered in Algiers near the Bois de Boulogne.

Among the secret recruiting centers, one of the choicest was the service club "Combat," on the Place de l'Opéra in Algiers. This canteen, theoretically reserved for the exclusive use of men on leave from the

Free French Forces, actually served as a main recruiting office. Almost all the deserters arrested referred to it as the place where their desertion was brought about.

Recruiting agents were reported to have pursued their activities in all places frequented by soldiers, on the streets as well as in bars, to say nothing of the *foyer* or Catholic club open to the regular army men. Women of all classes of society also launched an intensive campaign among both soldiers and officers, picking up men on the street or working on them at clubs or canteens.

C. Procedure and Propaganda Methods Employed

Every conceivable method and argument was used with much skill and psychological acumen by the Free French Forces and their male and female recruiting agents to win over European and native officers and men to the Free French Forces.

   a. Material Arguments:

     Large bonuses for enlistment—25,000 to 30,000 francs.

     Increased pay.

     Rapid advancement, even immediate promotion.

   b. Moral Arguments:

     Prospect of serving in units outfitted with modern weapons and soon to be called into combat.

     Promises made to Senegalese *tirailleurs* that they would be sent back home promptly (an argument well calculated to touch the natives of the A.E.F.).

     Promise that no penalty need be feared as the result of desertion.

RESULTS OBTAINED BY DE GAULLIST PROPAGANDA

To date the number of desertions induced by Free French Forces or their civilian recruiting agents in Algeria alone totals approximately 2,750, as follows:

          Army 2,000
          Navy 250
          Air Force 500

Despite all its efforts, De Gaullist propaganda now obtains only mediocre results among the soldiers and is therefore aiming at the officers' groups. Recently a French general was promised immediate promotion if he would come over to the Free French Forces—he refused. Moreover, many officers and corps commanders have found their letter boxes stuffed with leaflets violently attacking the regular army and its commanding officers and making threats against those who refuse to rally to the only possible leader, General de Gaulle.

CONCLUSION

The situation to date, July 1, 1943, may be summed up as follows:

. . . The measures—strictly defensive in character—taken by General Giraud have been effective in preventing men from leaving, and the curve of desertions is now very definitely downwards. However, there is great unrest in the army and a keen anxiety about the future, since the press, which is practically controlled by General de Gaulle, daily extols the Fighting French Movement, its leader and the exploits of its troops, leaving the deeds of the regular army in Tunisia completely in the shade.

If the De Gaullist efforts were to succeed, the inevitable result would be civil war between the two armies. Indeed the moment the effectives of one army dropped to the rising level of the other, two forces of equal size would be confronting each other: first, the regular army, deprived of its most ardently anti-German elements, but still constituting a solid anti-De Gaullist force and pushed toward Pétainism by its reaction against De Gaullist extremism; second, an ultra De Gaullist nucleus polarizing the elements that came over from the regular army, under a leader determined to win by any means.

It is obvious that such a situation would have catastrophic consequences for France and the Allies.

This amazing document indicates the tremendous moral crisis stirred up by De Gaullism in the Army. It gives, however, a very incomplete notion of the results obtained by the De Gaullists through their organized desertions, since it was prepared at a time when desertions were still taking place. Yet the figures quoted are extremely significant: 2,000 desertions, largely among officers and non-commissioned officers, from an army of 60,000 at combat strength, is enough to weaken it appreciably, disorganize its combat units, and create indescribable material and moral disorder. Two hundred and fifty sailors jumping ship—many of them gunners, torpedomen and radio operators—are enough to cripple the fighting power of naval craft and leave them at the mercy of the enemy (to recall Secretary of the Navy Knox's accusation that a ship had been sunk because its De Gaullist gunners had deserted). The desertion of 500 pilots, mechanics and specialists from an air force already weak in effectives is enough to paralyze it completely. But the most striking accusation in the report is that concerning the Senegalese *tirailleurs* who were pulled out of their regiments and sent back to Equatorial Africa, three thousand miles away from the Germans, out of fear that, knowing nothing of political ideologies, they might repent their desertions and return to their outfits. It is therefore no exaggeration to say that in North Africa, behind the back of the French Army which was fighting against the Germans, De Gaullism devoted itself to a terrible program of systematic destruction and sabotage which was to the advantage only of the Germans. The degree of dejection caused by such facts among Allied observers, the High Command and Allied governments can be easily imagined.

But to go back to other aspects of De Gaulle's great struggle against the French regular Army.

On May 30, 1943, De Gaulle arrived in Algeria. On June 14, he proposed to the Committee of Liberation that a five-man commission take over the control and reorganization of the Army. On June 17 Giraud rejected De Gaulle's proposals as useless and dangerous. He felt himself to be capable of reorganizing the army he had led to victory in Tunisia, without the help of any committee of politicians from London. Furthermore, as we have seen above, De Gaulle had shown every intention of maintaining a De Gaullist army side by side with the regular army. "To have two armies," Giraud declared, "is to have two Frances." Actually, to have two armies was to allow De Gaulle to build up a praetorian army with which to conquer Paris and establish him in power there.

On June 21 the New York *Times* reported a serious crisis in Algiers. Drew Middleton wrote that De Gaulle had decided to withdraw to Brazzaville or to Beirut unless his demands, notably those concerning the Army, were granted.

This latest act in the tragi-comedy of the past three weeks appears to be "only a gesture." . . .

De Gaulle had grown accustomed to intimidating his enemies by threats and outbursts of temper. Sometimes he would storm out of the committee meetings, leaving his colleagues sitting in dismay around the green table. Other times he would announce his departure for Brazzaville. Then again he would threaten to dissolve the De Gaullist organization throughout the world and retire from the arena. In the end everyone yielded to this pressure.

This time the first round in the fight over the reorganization of the Army wound up in a compromise. On June 23, 1943, it was decided that De Gaulle would retain command of all French military forces outside of North Africa, while Giraud remained at the head of the forces in Algeria, Tunisia, and Morocco.

But on June 24 Drew Middleton reported from Algiers to the New York *Times:*

> Some De Gaullists call today's compromise "a settlement that settles nothing."

On June 22 Harold Callender had already wired to the same newspaper that American circles were more and more disturbed by De Gaulle's doings and by his "dictatorial intentions" (sic) and that they were considering intervening in the French crisis. Two days later Callender learned that De Gaulle was putting forward a new project: he would "retire" a large number of officers of the Giraud army.

> General de Gaulle's demand for the dismissal of 150 or more army officers who had served under the Vichy regime [wrote Callender] was regarded as likely to impair the immediate military efficiency of the French forces. Moreover it seemed to the American military men unreasonable to suggest dropping officers who had fought well and successfully, even when badly equipped, in the Battle of Tunisia, where the French suffered heavy losses and won the acclaim of the American authorities.
>
> The rejuvenation as well as the re-equipment of the French army is regarded as highly desirable but a sudden purge of its commissioned personnel is disapproved. The new units being formed and equipped in the expansion, which may reach 400,000 men, will be able to use all

the officers that there are, military men point out, especially those tested in Tunisia.

It is not believed here that in making these observations Allied authorities were interfering unduly in French affairs, for the view is that the Allies have a vital military interest in North Africa that justifies the Allied Commander in Chief in taking so much interest in the French forces under his command.

Actually, De Gaulle let it be known that he would begin by dismissing 108 generals over sixty years of age. Giraud immediately shot back that (1) the public campaign of the De Gaullists picturing the French Army as senile was dangerous for the morale of the troops and disastrous in its repercussions throughout the Arab world; (2) all French officers, old and young, now in Africa, were needed to mobilize and train several hundreds of thousands of natives.

But De Gaulle stood fast. By dismissing generals and other high-ranking officers, he was destroying the cadres of the Giraud army and at the same time winning popularity among the younger officers who foresaw a dazzling prospect of lightning promotions.

Excitement ran high in Algiers. On June 27 Giraud's censor banned an article in the De Gaullist paper *Combat*. The article in question accused Giraud of being a "puppet of the Americans" and the Americans of interfering in the internal affairs of the French Army. As we have seen, an anti-Giraud campaign always tended to become an anti-American campaign and, likewise, an anti-American campaign always turned into an anti-Giraud campaign. It is to the credit of Giraud's followers that they did not retaliate by presenting De Gaulle as a tool of England. But German propaganda had a field day with the De Gaullist accusations.

On July 1 De Gaulle persuaded the Committee to order Giraud to hand over his authority as Commander in Chief in Algeria to General Catroux. On July 2 *L'Echo d'Alger* published a resolution signed by ten French groups expressing the general uneasiness in France at so-called American and British limitation of French sovereignty in North Africa. Drew Middleton cabled the New York

Times that "Some observers were inclined to regard the statement as a political maneuver by the De Gaullists." The obvious cause of this demonstration was a statement by Churchill, in the House of Commons, pointing out that the two governments had requested assurances from both Giraud and De Gaulle that they would respect the status of the French Army and avoid anything that might interfere with it.

Thus for months and months—with regard to desertions, interminable political wrangles, De Gaulle's military demands—American, and sometimes British, observers, cabinet ministers and even Roosevelt and Churchill themselves kept repeating in more or less veiled terms that De Gaullist scheming was hindering the war effort. And the impression grew stronger in London and in Washington that De Gaulle was too much concerned with his own political career. On July 7, 1943, the New York *Times* reported from Washington that official circles were displeased with De Gaulle's attitude:

In the opinion of high United States officials De Gaulle is less interested in helping to win the war than in advancing his personal political fortune on the assumption that the war will be won in any case; to this end he had made difficulties for the British in Syria and has sought to play Britain and the United States against each other according to high authoritative British testimony. In both London and Washington General de Gaulle is regarded by some who have known him as animated by dictatorial tendencies.

On July 21 De Gaulle presented a new demand. This time it was not 150 generals and high-ranking officers he wanted to retire on account of age, but 400. The Committee of Liberation, which blindly obeyed, voted to dismiss the 400.

The New York *Times* again reported from Washington:

Some here thought that the dismissal of 400 officers in an army of 75,000 might be called "wholesale."

Having retired these officers for "reasons of age," at a time when they were badly needed to mobilize and lead hundreds of thousands of native Africans who might have been thrown against the Germans, the general then ordered expulsions on political charges—in his eyes, service in the old regular army was in itself an ineradicable disgrace. Purges and man-hunts now began. On a mere accusation, for having once made a "Pétainist" remark—had not millions of Frenchmen in their despair and ignorance believed in Pétain in June, 1940?—for having the Marshal's picture in his room, an officer was sent to a concentration camp. Courage in the face of the enemy, hatred for Germany, citations won in battle, bloodshed—none of these counted. Hundreds of officers vanished into prison or into the Sahara, which had become the "Siberia of De Gaullism." Until a tragic incident put an end to the purges. One day, on the Italian front, General Montsabert received an order to hand over a Captain Carré to the De Gaullist police for deportation. He replied: "I shall not be able to carry out this order. This very morning I decorated that heroic officer on his deathbed. He was struck in the chest yesterday by a German bullet."

Though constantly being cut down, the French North African Army remained De Gaulle's nightmare, for it was practically the only organized force that might eventually oppose his seizure of power. How could he reduce it still further? How eliminate once and for all its cadres, officers, and top commanders?

General de Gaulle had a brilliant idea. He asked the American General Staff to send the six hapless divisions of the French Army to fight in Italy, in order, he said, to "increase French prestige."

The Americans did not hide their surprise.

In substance, they said to De Gaulle: we have considerably slowed down the arming of French African contingents because of political unrest in Algeria and Morocco. To our extreme regret we have renounced the terms of the agreement we had concluded with Giraud for the arming of more than 400,000 French colonial troops, for the reason that Giraud, our sole guarantee that politics would not overshadow military considerations, has gradually been stripped of all power and authority. France, therefore, has now no more than the embryo of an army. Would it not be reasonable to keep it intact so that it may take part, at least symbolically, in the liberation of France, the day our soldiers land on her shores?

That was precisely what De Gaulle did not want.

"I insist," he cried, "that the French Army fight in Italy. If you refuse, you do so because you intend to exclude France from the victory over the common enemy."

Thus was the French Army thrown into the savage battle of Monte Cassino. It won glory there under the command of Generals Juin and Montsabert. But it also suffered many casualties. German guns completed the work of the retirements, desertions and purges.

"I should like," said De Gaulle another time, "to have the taking of Elba left to French forces. That will be excellent for French prestige. The island of Elba is a reminder of the Napoleonic epic."

Accordingly, General de Tassigny's army corps was thrown against the island of Elba. And the rest of the available French troops, with the exception of the Leclerc division, was still clinging to the rocky blood-drenched slopes of the Italian mountains when the American armies were mustering for the great battle of the liberation of France.

De Gaulle had one thing left to do: to decapitate these remnants of the French Army. It was then that he dismissed Giraud under the circumstances described above.

But General Juin had also acquired considerable prestige in the battles of Tunisia and Italy. De Gaulle deprived him of his command; and officially and pompously bestowed upon him the title of "Chief of the General Staff"—of an army which, in reality, did not exist. A general without troops, tucked away in an office, can never be very dangerous.

The Americans landed in Normandy, defeated the Germans, and took Paris. . . . And France was absent from the great battle for her freedom.

After he had taken power in Paris, however, De Gaulle urged the Americans quickly to bring into the Battle of France the French contingents in Italy. "I wish them to be landed on the shores of Provence," he said.

As the final precaution, he reckoned that he had better have the regular French troops engaged as far as possible from the capital of France—and there was no place farther than Marseilles.

Meanwhile, to top everything, De Gaullist propaganda in Paris began to accuse the Americans of having refused to equip a great French army and of being responsible for the fact that France had not been restored as a great military power.

Such is the story of the destruction of the French Army during the period of exile. To measure the extent of the tragedy, we must imagine how another general—a real general—another liberator—a real liberator—would have envisaged his task. A Marshal Lyautey, a General Joffre, a General Mangin, finding himself in De Gaulle's situation, would have run to Algiers at the sound of American guns on November 8, 1942, flung himself into battle shoulder to shoulder with General Giraud, ordered universal conscription in Morocco, Algeria, Tunisia, Madagascar, West Africa, the Congo; he would have taken advantage of any lull in battle to rush by plane to all the corners of the Empire to kindle the fighting spirit and preach the holy war of the colored peoples against the slave-driving Germans; he would have flown to Washington and asked for arms and more arms, and if necessary, for officers and more officers; for experts. As a result, the atmosphere of Algiers would have glowed with the fervor of martial glory. Then, the exiles would have been worthy of France. Then, France would have had an army. Then, everything would have been different.

11. The Violation of Legitimacy

> *If, in civilized times, a principle of legitimacy is sud-*
> *denly violated and power is conquered by a coup de*
> *force, a nation will at once revert to barbarism.*
>
> TAINE

A<small>N</small> American newspaperman said that on the day Paris was liberated, a member of the Resistance told him:

"We are not afraid of the future. What we are afraid of is a return to the past."

These words are significant. They express the contempt felt by the French for the institutions of the Third Republic which, on the eve of the war, had reached the last stages of deterioration, lax-ness, and incompetence. They express, too, the revolutionary reaction which belongs specifically to French historical tradition. In 1814, after the capture of Paris by the Coalition and the fall of Napoleon, the French voiced with as much vehemence and passion as in 1944 their desire to break with the past.

In my book *Français, Voici la Vérité*, written in New York in 1942, I myself showed how creaky French democratic institutions had become in the prewar period. And the systematic opposition which I maintained in Parliament, sometimes alone against all other members—as on the Munich vote, the debates on armaments, foreign policy, or treason—was, as it were, my permanent protest before the country.

Long before me, Jean Jaurès, the renowned apostle of French

Socialism, said at Montauban in a prophetic speech: "Our institutions appear to me to have been long since surpassed by time and defeated by progress. We are moving on a sailing vessel which . . . will soon be outdistanced by faster ships driven by steam. . . . I see in Socialism not the suppression of democracy, but a means of saving it from the certain death that awaits it if it is left to its archaic methods and its slow-paced life." And he had already warned of the consequences of "the enriching of the ruling classes; the weakening of their patriotism, the lowering of the parliamentary standard, electoral demagogy and the wretched techniques used at meetings."

Unfortunately, the reformist spirit of Jaurès—that great sincere man who did not always choose the best paths, who occasionally took the worst—was abandoned by French political parties in the thirty years preceding the war, despite the warning contained in the catastrophe of 1914.

It is therefore both logical and extremely fortunate that the tragic lesson of 1939-44 should have been of some use and that the French should have emerged from their appalling ordeal determined to make far-reaching changes in their political institutions and even in their social system, to revolutionize them and accommodate them to the needs of a new world. The discoveries of science—which have shaken up human existence from top to bottom and which are doubtless the indirect and underlying cause of present-day upheavals— are bound to reverberate throughout the whole machinery of social and political life. If everything else changes, the way societies are governed must change too. And the vast sufferings of this war are without question the pangs of the prodigious birth of a new order which none will be able to resist.

To condemn the institutions of the Third Republic does not, however, mean that one must destroy them and reduce them to dust without knowing exactly what will take their place. There was in them, indeed, one element of incalculable value which ought to be preserved at all costs—the thread of legality, the principle of legitimacy. For that principle of legitimacy was desperately needed in the period of transition and political reconstruction upon which we were entering.

It might be well to define here what we mean by the principle of legitimacy. The exact meaning is unknown to most Frenchmen, though it is the most fundamental principle of political life in human societies; and it is still less known to Americans, who have experienced but one ephemeral crisis of legitimacy in their own history—the Civil War.

The principle of legitimacy is the conventional factor accepted in a country at any given moment which gives certain men the right to govern and others the duty to obey.

A case in point would be Guglielmo Ferrero's favorite example. If we were to stop an inhabitant of Tibet somewhere along the rugged slopes of his mountains and ask him: "Who rules you? And from whom does that ruler derive his authority?" the inhabitant of Tibet, were he a poor peasant, a shepherd or a gentleman, would reply: "Buddha is reincarnated periodically in the body of a newborn child. When that child grows up to be a man, he is proclaimed king. When he dies, it is the duty of the priests to discover the Buddha's new incarnation among other newborn babes. Hidden away in a secret dwelling at the bottom of a deep valley surrounded by snow-capped mountains and visited only by omen-bearing vultures, they instruct the child in philosophy, theology and politics. And in his turn that child becomes the absolute, indisputable and uncontested ruler of our people. And so it has been for ages on ages." This answer defines the principle of legitimacy as accepted by the Tibetans.

If in the eighteenth century a citizen of Venice had been questioned on the same subject, he would have replied: "Each year the Grand Council, made up of the four hundred noble families named in the Golden Book of the City, meets and chooses the Doge who becomes the head of the Republic. So it has been for centuries." Here we have the definition of the principle of legitimacy accepted by the Venetians down to the time of the Austrian conquest.

Now, let us suppose that we were to stop a modern American

somewhere in this vast country and ask him our question: "Who governs you? And from whom does that man derive his authority?" The American, whether farmer, businessman, cowboy or banker, workingman or millionaire, New Yorker, Chicagoan, Texan or Californian, would answer: "The President of the United States is the head of the American government. He derives his authority from the will of the people. Every four years we choose a president according to an electoral method accepted by the whole nation. And the nation abides by the result of that poll." This defines the principle of legitimacy as recognized by Americans since the beginning of their history.

With the French the principle of legitimacy has changed frequently. As long ago as the Gallo-Roman epoch, Clovis was recognized as king only because he could claim in his favor the old Roman legitimacy firmly rooted in the public consciousness for centuries. He had himself appointed Patrician and Consul by the Emperor and had the insignia conferred on him with great pomp at Tours by Anastasius' ambassadors. He turned Christian not because he was converted by Clothilde, as popular legend has it, but because the Emperor was a Christian. "Ever since," said Gregory of Tours, "he has been addressed as one would address a Consul or an Emperor." After him the legitimacy of the Merovingians, entrusted with the authority of that amazing imperial legitimacy, lasted for two hundred and fifty years.

Gradually, as the memory of ancient Rome gave way before the new power of the papacy, the principle of legitimacy ceased to be applied. When a mayor of the palace, Charles Martel, of the Héristal family, won a victory over the Arabs at Poitiers, Pope Boniface seized that opportunity to anoint him King of Gaul. In this the Pope revived an old Jewish rite. The prophet Samuel had anointed Saul in the name of Jehovah by pouring consecrated oil on his forehead. Boniface poured holy oil on the forehead of the new king.

From that time on it became a firm belief of the French that to rule them it was necessary to be consecrated by the Pope, God's deputy on earth. The coronation became the ceremony that established the legitimacy of power by a sort of indestructible sacrament. The coronation created the "divine right," in other words, the right of the king to rule by the "grace of God." Even when the Carolingian dynasty came to an end two hundred and thirty-five years later, the custom of the coronation persisted under the Capets. Frenchmen obeyed the king, "the Anointed of the Lord," crowned by the Pope, who was in turn the appointed of God. To rebel against the king, therefore, was to rebel against the Pope, and, consequently, to rebel against God.

We find it difficult in this present age of doubt and unbelief to conceive the irresistible hold upon the popular consciousness of this principle of the divine quality of the legitimacy of power. The greatest and most extraordinary events in the history of France have centered around it.

Out of loyalty to legitimacy the French refused to depose King Charles VI for madness, since insanity could not annul the effect of the coronation and it had to be interpreted as a mysterious intent of God. The case was further complicated when Charles VI died suddenly and was succeeded by the Dauphin: a legitimate king must first be a legitimate son, and there was universal doubt regarding the mad king's fatherhood. It was necessary that Joan of Arc "hear voices" assuring her that Charles VII was "the true king." The intrigues subsided; for Heaven had spoken. In the famous conversation at Chinon, the Maid reassured the noble Dauphin, who was tormented by uncertainty. She led him to Rheims, where he was crowned on July 16, 1429. Then, French legitimacy having been recognized, she felt that her mission was over, but she begged Charles VII, in vain, to allow her to return to Domrémy.

We know that Henry IV's accession to the throne very nearly resulted in a drama of royal legitimacy. The legitimate Protestant king could not be consecrated. The League thought it could snatch the power from him. It looked as though French monarchy and French legitimacy were to perish together. A foreign Catholic king, Philip II, presented the Infanta Isabella as a candidate. The Pope accepted her. Henry IV saved his throne and the monarchial legitimacy by foreswearing the Protestant faith in the Church of Saint-Denis.

Not till the seventeenth century were there any signs of a fundamental change.

The "mental and moral crisis," which Paul Hazard has analyzed so penetratingly, brought about an attack upon mystical feeling, which was growing lukewarm. The spirit of criticism awoke, the prestige of theology declined, agnosticism gained ground. Gradually, the view prevailed that the "divine right" to govern men was a debatable matter. The ferment increased throughout the eighteenth century; new ideas darted across the general upheaval like shooting stars. And suddenly a fire-ball flashed past those stars and plummeted down upon a decadent and skeptical society—Rousseau's *Social Contract*. The Genevan denounced the hereditary and monarchial principle based on "divine right." Being a foreigner and not daring to speak openly of France, he condemned the old principle of legitimacy in general. The king was "legitimate" only if crowned, not by the Pope, but by the will of the people.

A day was to come when this revolutionary thesis would find expression in a gesture at once insolent, theatrical, and sacrilegious: having received the holy oil of the coronation, Napoleon I snatched the imperial crown from the Pope's hands and placed it on his own head. That day France applauded wildly the fusion of two principles of legitimacy, one emanating from God, the other from the people, the principle of Tradition and the principle of Revolution. France did not suspect that they are irreconcilable and that one of the two would have to perish. The nineteenth century, with its endless series of revolutions, was but one long struggle between a declining monarchic legitimacy of divine right and a rising popular legitimacy. Finally, for seventy years the Third Republic was to impose a new legitimacy unquestioned by nine-tenths of the French people—that of popular sovereignty determined by election and a majority of votes.

The legitimacy of the Third Republic was destroyed by the victorious Germans in June, 1940. It was to this end that they put

Marshal Pétain in power; it was his job to raze the foundations of the republican regime and to prepare the way for nazism. The duty of every Frenchman fighting Germany and its monstrous revolutionary ideology, and determined to defeat Nazi plans to degrade France, should therefore have been to restore first of all the principle of French legitimacy and so wipe out the harm done by Pétain.

General de Gaulle realized this so well that even while he was planning to seize power, he constantly promised in his speeches to restore republican legitimacy. On January 9, 1941, at the "Literary Foyle Luncheon," he declared:

The Free French are careful to make no encroaching claims. It is not they who are destroying rights and liberties under the pretext of a national revolution.

On September 23, 1941, in his radio speech from London, he said to the French:

The constitution and the laws of the Republic have been and are being violated daily by the invader and his accomplices. We do not recognize any of these violations.

His manifesto of June 23, 1943, entitled "What We Want," declared again:

Any usurpation, whether from within or from without, must be swept away. . . . The day the French are liberated from enemy oppression, all their domestic liberties will be restored.

None of those solemn promises has been kept. Pétain's usurpation of power has been succeeded by De Gaulle's. The constitution violated by the marshal was next violated by the general. The domestic liberties abolished by the marshal have not been restored by the general.

This amounts to saying that in truth De Gaulle has continued the marshal's work and has allowed the German plan to be carried out.

We shall examine later the political machinery which De Gaulle built in Algiers—after the model of the Vichy government—and which he afterwards moved to Paris. But a preliminary question arises: Was it possible to spare France the crisis of legitimacy sought by the Germans and let loose by them? In the condition France was in during the occupation, was it possible to save, not the old and discredited regime which fell in 1940, but—and this is something quite different—the principle of legality and legitimacy that was indispensable if order and the republican spirit were to be restored as the basis for an immediate transition to a new political system?

Had De Gaulle, on his arrival in Algeria, not tried to capture the New Power for himself, but behaved like a soldier, faithful to his duty and his officer's oath, had he worked in harmony with Giraud to repair the damage done by the Germans, he would have had three possible solutions before him, all three legal, regular, and respectful of legitimacy. Mindful of circumstances and possibilities, he could in all good faith have made a choice among them:

(1) He could have considered the colonies and territories of liberated Algeria as military zones, provisionally entrusted to French military administration, pending the liberation of France.

(2) He could have applied in Algeria Article II of the Tréveneuc law of 1872, enacted in anticipation of a possible invasion and occupation of France by an enemy power, until that law could be applied in liberated France.

(3) He could have convened in Algiers those French deputies and senators—qualified representatives of the National Assembly—who had escaped from France, and entrusted them with the task of forming a provisional government endowed with plenary power until the liberation of France and the convening of the regular National Assembly.

De Gaulle promptly rejected the first solution: it eliminated any chance of establishing his New Power and left him only his military function—in which he was not interested.

Let us now examine the possibility of the second solution—the application of the Tréveneuc law, which, as I have pointed out elsewhere, was enacted on February 15, 1872, for the express purpose of avoiding a crisis of legitimacy.

The text of the law follows:

LAW OF FEBRUARY 15TH RELATIVE TO THE FUTURE ROLE OF THE GENERAL COUNCILS UNDER EXCEPTIONAL CIRCUMSTANCES

Art. 1. Should the National Assembly or the assemblies which shall succeed it be illegally dissolved or prevented from convening, the General Councils shall assemble immediately, with full rights and without need of special summons, in the chief town of each department. They may assemble elsewhere in the department if the place where they regularly hold their sessions does not appear sufficiently to guarantee freedom in their deliberations.

The Councils are validly constituted only when a majority of their members are present.

2. Until the day when the Assembly, to which reference will be made in Article 3, shall have announced that it is properly constituted, the General Council will provide in emergency for the maintenance of public tranquillity and law and order.

3. An Assembly composed of two delegates chosen by each General Council in secret session shall meet in the place to which have come such members of the lawful government and deputies as have been able to escape.

The Assembly of delegates is not validly constituted unless at least one half of the departments are represented.

4. This Assembly is instructed to take such emergency measures for the whole of France as may be necessary to the maintenance of order and in particular such measures which aim to restore to the National Assembly its complete independence and the full exercise of its powers.

It will provide temporarily for the general administration of the country.

5. It must be dissolved as soon as the National Assembly shall be reconstituted by the meeting of a majority of its members at some spot on French soil.

If such reconstitution cannot be accomplished within one month after the occurrence, the Assembly of delegates must summon the nation to general elections.

The powers are terminated on the day the new National Assembly is set up.

6. The decisions of the Assembly of delegates must be executed,

under penalty of dismissal, by all officials, agents of the law and commanding officers.

Such is the categorical text binding a general loyal to the Republic.

Oddly enough, in his "Fundamental Declaration" of November 16, 1940, De Gaulle explicitly pledged his allegiance to that law. At that time he blamed the Vichy government for having forbidden the assembling of the General Councils when he said that:

In default of a free parliament functioning lawfully, France could have expressed her will through the great voice of her General Councils; the General Councils could even have provided for the administration of the country by *virtue of the law of February 15, 1872*, and in view of the illegality of the Vichy organization.

And he added that:

In spite of Vichy's efforts to destroy it, the Constitution is still legally in force.

On February 9, 1943, in the course of a press conference at his London headquarters, De Gaulle again referred to the Tréveneuc law—in precise terms. He declared:

The General Councils are qualified, in a situation like the present, to decide on the general administration of Algeria. This is a primary and very important point.

During his interminable correspondence with Giraud, De Gaulle referred to the stipulations of the Tréveneuc law, in which he saw, he declared, the only legal means of safeguarding the rights of the people and of opposing the Vichy regime already established in Algeria.

On April 20, 1943, in his speech, "The Future of France," he stated:

The nation which acknowledges no ruler other than herself, demands that, as she is being liberated, her former laws shall be put into effect.

Now the only French law that provides for restoring the constitutional machinery in relation to eventual liberation is the Tréveneuc law.

Finally, on June 3, 1943, the organic law of the Committee of National Liberation, in Algiers, which was drawn up and signed by De Gaulle—thus sanctioning his seizure of political power—provided in Article IV that the Committee should exercise its functions until the evacuation of France allowed the formation of a government to which he (De Gaulle) would hand over his powers "in conformance with the laws of the Republic"—in other words, with the Tréveneuc law.

In 1940, De Gaulle invoked the Tréveneuc law to oppose and condemn Marshal Pétain; in 1942-43, he used it to oppose Giraud—whom he accused of remaining loyal to the Vichy constitution and of violating the laws of the Republic—and to lull minds to rest and cover his seizure of power in Algeria. Once firmly established in office, he then denounced the Tréveneuc law, declared it inapplicable, and decided to force himself on Paris by means of General Leclerc's tanks. In his first report on "the establishment of the government of the Republic as soon as the country is liberated," De Menthon, De Gaulle's Commissioner of Justice in Algiers, coolly announced:

We are not in the situation provided for by the Tréveneuc law, the situation of an illegal dissolution.

Therefore:

The French Committee of National Liberation will immediately exercise power in the liberated territories. This assumption of power meets the need for public order.

De Menthon's statement was false and intended solely to justify that seizure of political power which De Gaulle had so often sworn before all of France never to attempt.

If we refer to the *Official Journal of the Republic* of February 6, 1872, for the discussion of the Tréveneuc law, we find the following statement by its sponsor, M. Fournier:

The purpose of the law is first and foremost to affirm the principle of national sovereignty exercised by the elected representatives of the country. It is our desire to render the representative system indestructible by seeing to it that if ever the representative body is overthrown in any given place, it can immediately begin to function on some part of our territory. . . .

We feel instinctively that even if the national representation is no longer in existence, nevertheless, below it, as a second line of defense, another assembly, recruited from among the councils on a lower level than the legislative body, but like it chosen by universal suffrage, will be able to establish itself or should at least try to do so. . . .

There is nothing left—neither law nor legal government in France. Therefore only the Nation will make itself heard; only the Nation will have the right to rise up. We call on the Nation for help, and in such circumstances even if the General Councils should exceed the limits of the mandate we have outlined, the Nation will have the final decision.

The De Gaullists defended themselves against the charge of violating the Tréveneuc law by arguing that since the establishment of the Committee of Liberation in Algiers, circumstances were so different from anything the legislators of the Tréveneuc law could have foreseen that the provisions of the law did not apply. The texts give them the lie. The *Official Journal* recording the debates of 1872 refutes them further. On February 7, 1872, Léonce de Guerdan, President of the Commission, stated:

Application of the law is undoubtedly difficult since we cannot foresee what vicissitudes future revolutions may bring. We cannot specify such and such a case. We are obliged to be uncertain, indefinite.

And on the day the vote was taken, the sponsor, Fournier, contributed this conclusive explanation:

I am asked how many deputies there must be in a town in order that the delegates (of the General Councils) join them there. My answer is that the number is unimportant. The purpose and the spirit of the law are clear: the delegates will go wherever there is an element of resistance. . . . This law is written for the purpose of giving men who respect the law *a weapon which they will use according to circumstances* and as directed by their patriotism.

If, therefore, De Gaulle had been "directed by his patriotism" instead of his personal interest, he would have left each General Council free to fulfill its constitutional duty—in other words, to maintain law and order in the departments of Algiers, Oran, and Constantine, until such time as an Assembly of delegates from the General Councils (in which at least half of the departments would be represented) could be convened. As soon as France was liberated, there was nothing to prevent the Tréveneuc law from going into full operation. But, as we have already seen, De Gaulle was determined to destroy the republican machinery; and we shall see farther on how he replaced the legal assembly with an extraordinary assembly—appointed by him and placed at the service of his *coup d'état.*

We come now to the third possibility formulated above: instead of invoking the Tréveneuc law, to convene provisionally in Algiers the remnants of the National Assembly (about seventy deputies and senators who had fled to Algiers or gone into exile) until the return to Paris permitted the convening of the National Assembly representing republican legality.

To avoid that eventuality, De Gaulle declared: (1) that the powers of the National Assembly had expired; (2) that its members were disqualified because they had voted plenary powers to Marshal Pétain in July, 1940.

The powers of the National Assembly could not be said to have expired since the deputies and senators chosen by the people had not come up for re-election solely on account of the presence of the enemy. In 1918 the French Chamber, which had been elected in 1914, continued in office after its powers had expired, until peace was signed. In 1939 the Chamber elected in 1936, following this precedent, extended its life for two years and would have extended its term until the end of hostilities even had the German victory not taken place. England also presented a splendid example of loyalty to the rules of popular representation. The British Parliament elected in 1935 was to have lasted until 1940, but it continued to function for the duration of the war. De Gaulle, however, for the sake of his cause, violated French precedents and ignored the British example of democratic procedure in a state of national emergency.

As for members of Parliament being disqualified, it was not for
a brigadier general to decide that point. Psychological errors and
political mistakes, no matter how serious, are not grounds for dis-
qualifying a popular assembly. The vote of confidence given Marshal
Pétain at Vichy in an hour of catastrophe and despair was extorted
under such pressure and in such circumstances that only a few particularly well-informed deputies and senators were able to detect
the danger. In June, 1940, most Frenchmen, having no idea of
Pétain's innate defeatism, secret ambitions, and former intrigues,
thought of him as the only man who could take the lead in France
and save the remnants of the dying constitution. Though Pétain
misused, and even criminally abused, the authority legally bestowed
upon him on July 10, 1940, it does not follow that the deputies and
senators who trusted him before the offense are criminals, nor that
all of France that followed him is guilty. In the same way De Gaulle
also abused the trust of those Frenchmen who hastened to answer
his call on June 18, 1940, with never a thought that instead of going
to do their duty on the battlefield they were plunging into a political adventure for personal power, which history may perhaps stamp
as criminal—yet it does not follow that these Frenchmen are responsible for that criminal adventure.

To stress the gravity of the responsibility incurred by De Gaulle,
we must refer to a significant incident which took place the summer
of 1944 between the Germans and Pétain. At that time the marshal,
vaguely conscious of his mistakes and his responsibilities, was anx-
ous (for reasons difficult for us in exile to determine) to restore
some of the powers of the National Assembly, trustee of France's
principle of legitimacy. The German government, however, was
violently opposed to this plan. The *Journal de Genève* of April 11,
1944, published *in extenso* the indignant letter von Ribbentrop then
sent to Marshal Pétain. It contains the following passage:

The project for the revision of the Constitution which has been sub-
mitted to us seems to entrust the designation of the future French Head
of State, even in wartime, to an organization of bygone days: the French
National Assembly. It seems, *Monsieur le Maréchal,* that in so doing

you have completely failed to take into account the fact that this National Assembly is the very one which, in September 1939, declared war on Germany without the slightest justification and in spite of the solemn assurances of peace exchanged between Germany and France as late as December 6th, 1938. You seem to forget, too, that a portion of the membership of this Assembly—and their number is not negligible— once again violating in a flagrant manner the agreement reached between our two countries by the Armistice, has taken up arms once more against Germany. The government of the Reich must reject with indignation, and as an impossible suggestion, the plan of the French Head of State to restore such an Assembly to its functions by the projected Constitutional Act, thus giving legal sanction to the activities of traitors and criminals.

Today, the former National Assembly is no longer in any way the legal representative of the will of the French people. During the war, elections are impossible in France as in other states. And a National Assembly formed in any other manner could not represent the will of the French people. Consequently, at this time there exists no legal assembly capable of exercising the functions anticipated by the speech broadcast on the radio, and therefore no assembly can be recognized by Germany.

Pétain was forced to yield. And after him, De Gaulle's actions followed the exact pattern desired by von Ribbentrop, who knew exactly what he wanted and why he wanted it. Having brushed aside all legal solutions in North Africa, any solution that would have made possible an immediate and thoroughgoing reform of the institutions of the Third Republic, De Gaulle had the field free to draw up in Algiers, and later to transfer to Paris, a constitution created by his imagination—or, rather, by that of the Cagoulards— a Bonapartist and Hitlerian type of constitution, intended to establish his New Power.

12. The De Gaullist Constitution

It is not a constitution, it's a joke.

HENRI ROCHEFORT

O Dieu! Si vous avez la France sous vos ailes
Ne souffrez pas, Seigneur, ces luttes éternelles,
Ces trônes qu'on élève et qu'on brise en courant;
Ces tristes libertés qu'on donne et qu'on reprend;
Ce noir torrent de lois, de passions, d'idées,
Qui répand sur les moeurs ses vagues débordées;
Ces tribuns opposant, lorsqu'on les réunit,
Une charte de plâtre aux abus de granit;
Ces flux et ces reflux de l'onde contre l'onde;
Cette guerre, toujours plus sombre et plus profonde,
Des partis au pouvoir, du pouvoir aux partis;
L'aversion des grands qui ronge les petits;
Et toutes ces rumeurs, ces chocs, ces cris sans nombre,
Ces systèmes affreux échafaudés dans l'ombre . . .

VICTOR HUGO

DURING the seven months between the American landing in Algiers (November 8, 1942) and General de Gaulle's arrival there on May 30, 1943, the campaign to restore the laws of the Republic

---

* O Lord, if you have France under your wing,
  Do not suffer, Lord, this eternal strife,
  These thrones raised and dashed to bits,
  These sad freedoms won then lost again;
  That black flood of laws and passions and ideas
  That overflows the ways of man;

had dominated the desperate uproar of the De Gaulle-Giraud controversy. De Gaulle's memoranda, his radio speeches, the articles published in his press, the statements of his followers—all harped incessantly on the same theme: "General de Gaulle is a Republican, returning to Algiers for the sole purpose of restoring the institutions of the Republic."

The fundamental institutions of the Republic are based, as we know, on parliamentary assemblies. And the very functioning of parliamentary assemblies presupposes freedom of the press, freedom of speech, and freedom of public assembly.

Now, on arriving in Algiers, the first thing De Gaulle did was to abolish freedom of the press, freedom of speech, freedom of assembly, and, of course, secure exclusive control of the radio.

After this he set up his dictatorial political machinery—which strangely resembled that set up in Vichy by Pétain. Executive power was lodged in the Committee of National Liberation, over which De Gaulle presided—and whose members, after the elimination of Giraud, were practically all picked by him. The Committee of Liberation promulgated decrees that had the force of laws. There was no redress against these decrees. The French State was De Gaulle in Algiers, as it was Pétain in Vichy.

Side by side with the Committee of Liberation there was a "Provisional Consultative Assembly" with eighty members—later increased to one hundred and twenty. In composition and powers, the Consultative Assembly was an exact reproduction of the National Council which Marshal Pétain formed in Vichy in 1941. It could not enact laws. The Committee of National Liberation was not responsible to it. It was a registry office. An anecdote that appeared in *La Gazette de France* in Paris the day after the proclamation of

---

Leaders who quarrel when they meet;
A charter inscribed on plaster not on granite;
This war, always growing darker and more intense,
Of parties for power, of power for parties;
The hatred for the great that consumes the small;
And all these countless clamors, shocks and screams
And hideous systems built behind the scenes . . .

the Consulate might have been repeated in Algiers. "What's in this constitution?" a woman asked her neighbor. "There's Bonaparte!" the latter replied. "The representatives of the people get 15,000 francs for talking. That's too much. The members of the Legislative Body get 10,000 francs for keeping quiet. That's not enough." Thus in the Algiers constitution there was only General de Gaulle —and the members of the Assembly were paid too much for talking. . . .

That, nevertheless, was what De Gaulle called "restoring the Republic." In vain I wrote to him that such a gross caricature of parliamentary institutions was dangerous for the Republic, for "ridicule kills." I also told him that he was creating "a dangerous precedent" and a source of permanent misunderstanding with Allied Anglo-Saxon countries, who "do not like to have democracy jeered at." And above all, that this Hitlerian innovation (so welcome to the brain of a brigadier general dreaming of the glory of the First Consul) had nothing to do with the liberation of France— the only mission proper to a soldier in time of war.

When I received in New York an invitation to go to Algiers and take part in forming that Assembly, I promptly replied with a categorical refusal, and at the same time addressed the following open letter to M. Gouin, the president of the parliamentary party in Algiers:

My dear President and friend:

On Thursday, October 14, 1943, I was informed in Washington of a telegram from M. Philip, Commissioner of the Interior, summoning members of Parliament now in America to Algiers on November 3 for the purpose of choosing deputies and senators to take part in the Consultative Assembly provided for in the De Gaullist constitution.

This summons left me only twenty-six days in which to get ready, whereas medical examinations and government regulations normally require four weeks, barring exceptional cases, and the journey alone takes two or three, except for unusually favorable circumstances.

It seems to me that this procedure with respect to members of Parliament not only shows a lack of consideration but, above all, a deliberate determination to prevent them from carrying out the mission for which they are, supposedly, being convened.

Permit me therefore to make this formal protest.

I have every reason to fear that the measures taken to prevent French members of Parliament in exile in America from getting to Algiers is part of a systematic campaign to exclude from French politics any influence favorable to the United States. As you can see for yourself, most of the Algiers Committee are now carrying on in many respects the anti-Anglo-Saxon propaganda of the Vichy government, with perhaps greater subtlety but no less effectively.

Apart from this, my dear colleague, I also wish to protest against the purpose of the summons sent us.

I recognize the right of no one but the French people themselves to destroy the Constitution of the Republic which they have created of their own free will and which they themselves will certainly wish to amend in order to adapt it to the new era.

But the creation of a Consultative Assembly is tantamount to the destruction of the legislative power, just as the creation of the Committee of Liberation is equivalent to the destruction of the executive power as defined in the Constitution of the Third Republic.

The Assembly in which the deputies are asked to participate—in the humiliating proportion of twenty members to eighty—will have only advisory powers. The executive authority will have the right to override its decisions. We are reverting to the darkest ages of absolute monarchy, when the King, in assembling the States-General, reserved the right to disregard their advice and invoked his famous: "Such is our good pleasure." Moreover, the King represented a power recognized as legitimate in those days.

Again, the deputies of the States-General were elected by the three Orders [the clergy, the nobility, and the third estate], whereas practically fifty-two out of eighty members of the Consultative Assembly will be chosen by the executive power.

Let us have the courage to recognize and proclaim the fact. that the new Algiers constitution is the most dictatorial that France has ever seen. How could I, for my part, approve of it when one of the main goals of this war is to save Democracy and crush personal rule. I share the opinion expressed by President Roosevelt on September 17, 1943, before the American Congress, when he declared that the war would not be won if only the forms of fascism, or only its evil forms, were eradicated.

I may add that I consider unacceptable the resolution set forth in M.

Philip's letter against the deputies who voted on July 10, 1940, in favor of Marshal Pétain. Those deputies are damned *en bloc*. And they are invited to seek absolution before being allowed to join in the work of their colleagues. You know how much opposed I am to Marshal Pétain (who, incidentally, has taken away my French citizenship) because of the part he played before the armistice, then in concluding the armistice, and later in collaborating with Laval and the Germans. But the deputies who voted for Pétain on July 10, 1940, were merely interpreting the will of the French people, who, helpless and overwhelmed by the disaster, fell into the arms of the man in whom they saw the "Hero of Verdun." Besides, their vote was formally subordinated to the consent of the people when it could be freely expressed after the war. With few exceptions, the deputies are guilty only of having participated in a mistake common to all Frenchmen. Many of them have since suffered cruelly at the hands of the Germans. Some of them are in prison or being hunted. Some are resisting heroically and are sacrificing themselves for the nation. Members of the Committee of Liberation who have not known the enemy yoke, who have been fortunate enough to shield their families from the hardships of the invasion, have no right to declare these deputies outcasts. The National Committee of London and afterwards the Algiers Committee of Liberation have, furthermore, brought notorious "Pétainist" officials into the Administration. On the other hand, "Pétainist" officers and soldiers have died in great numbers on the battlefields of Tunisia. Would one dare to brand them as infamous? And if not, why bear down on these particular deputies and precisely when the unity and reconciliation of all Frenchmen in opposition to the Germans is our most sacred duty?

The ulterior motive seems clear. In the Washington and London governments there are friends of France, staunch democrats, who want the liberating countries to restore France, after victory, to the same political condition she was in when Germany defeated her. They do not intend to prevent her from amending a constitution which has proved to be lamentably deficient. But they want her to have time to bring back her prisoners and her sons scattered in exile, to rid herself of the deadly poisons that German propaganda injected into hearts and minds, and finally to know what is going on in the outside world hidden from them for years by their prison walls. They want all this to save France from civil war and disastrous adventures. It is to prevent the good friends of France, who advocate this solution, from being heard that efforts are being made to discredit Parliament, which is the only legitimate trustee of the will of the French people. And that is the spirit in which the Committee of Liberation wrote the letter summoning the deputies in terms that amount to an affront.

If, therefore, I had been able to answer the call, it would have been to raise a formal protest in Algiers and to vote both against the establishment of the Consultative Assembly and against the manner in which the representatives of the French people have been treated.

The French people, moreover, charged us with a clear and sacred mission—that of defending our country and the Republic. We have no right to abdicate. The nation has entrusted us with control over the executive power and with the authority to enact laws. It expected us to be judges, and we have no right to turn defendants. We shall be held responsible by the nation and by posterity, until the people are called in full freedom to elect our successors. If the people must suffer new trials in the future through the fault of masters who, taking advantage of the defeat, picked up the political power cast down by the armies of the enemy, we should be guilty in their eyes and this time cast out forever by the people themselves.

Let me remind you that when the Vichy government, under pressure from the Germans, browbeat, humiliated, and dissolved the Parliament, the Presidents of the Chamber and of the Senate protested vigorously and gave voice to the cry of reprobation that rose from the French conscience.

Today, the Algiers government is imitating the Vichy government—in its turn suppressing parliamentary assemblies, replacing them by a servile assembly, outraging and humiliating the nation's representatives; it would certainly draw down on its head the same indignant protest if those two great Frenchmen were not prevented by the enemy from doing so.

In their absence, it is our duty to interpret their thought, which is the thought of the people.

I ask you to be so kind as to read this letter to my colleagues so that it may appear in the *Official Journal*. If they try to prevent you by force from doing so, I should like you to give each one a copy. I am greatly distressed that I cannot be with you in these dramatic moments. At least I have the consolation of thinking that now, as on the day when Pétain seized power, one can do more for France on the outside, as a free man, than inside, as a prisoner, under the dark shadow of a military dictatorship.

Rest assured, my dear President and friend, that I have unfailing faith in the future of France and that I shall work to the very end, with all the strength of my being, for her deliverance and her greatness.

That was the spirit in which on June 17, 1940, in London, I rallied enthusiastically to General de Gaulle's cause, when that cause stood for a refusal to accept the armistice, for loyalty to the British alliance, and for the fight to the finish. In those days I believed that General de Gaulle would go from battle to battle at the head of the heroes who had responded to his call from all parts of the world, and that with his own hands he would unfurl our flag on the battlefields of liberation. In that same spirit I cannot approve of the conditions under which the Algiers government was formed, or of the measures it is taking—measures contrary to our democratic ideal—or of certain general lines of policy which it assumes the right to lay out and which can involve the future of France for years to come, against her will, and even without her knowledge.

I send you my protest from an anguished heart. In the night of exile and grief for our martyrs, I hope soon to be able to fling across the Atlantic a shout of faith and enthusiasm at the announcement that France has found again the bright road of her destiny.

With affectionate greetings to you and to my dear colleagues,

Henri de Kerillis

My protest, of course, had not the slightest effect, and the "Rump Assembly" was formed.

Its members were recruited from three sources: (1) about sixty members were so-called delegates of the Resistance; (2) twenty were appointed by the seventy deputies and senators who had escaped from France; (3) the rest represented Frenchmen in exile.

Let us first consider the delegates of the Resistance. It is certain that there were among the delegates of the Resistance in Algiers authentic and even heroic underground fighters who had come from France. But they had no authority—for two reasons: on the one hand, many of them were concealing their identities under false names and thus lost their prestige; and on the other, no one could check on the validity of their mandate. It soon got around that three-quarters of the delegates of the Resistance movement had been appointed by Frenay, De Menthon, and Philip—fanatical De Gaullists—and that they had not been chosen in France by the heroes of the underground. This news created a feeling of profound uneasiness.

It must be remembered that the Resistance was a secret institution, and it would have been extremely rash to bring its members— whose families were still in France—into the limelight in Algiers. An example of the danger involved was the tragedy of Jean Moulin, who was made a member of the London Committee under the name of M. X., allowed to appear openly in the British capital, and then was sent to France, where he was denounced, captured, tortured and executed by the Germans. And was it not easy to foresee the fate that awaited M. Médéric, that member of the Algiers Consultative Assembly, who went back to France, was caught by the Germans in Paris and killed on the spot?

I said to M. Hoppenot, De Gaulle's representative in Washington: "Either the members of the Algiers assembly are not authentic representatives of the Resistance, and a deception is taking place; or they are, and the Germans are going to seize their families, torture them and get hold of the threads of the underground organizations in the homeland. In either case, reason rejects such representation."

But there was, as we have seen, another category of members in the Algiers assembly—the twenty members who represented the old parliament. The people of France will some day indicate whether they approve of those deputies and senators who accepted their abdication and became part and parcel of the illegal assembly. My letter to the president of that assembly sufficiently expresses my own opinion.

As for the third category—the deputies in exile—it formed the most unexpected, most comical, and most absurd innovation of what is called the "De Gaullist constitution" of Algiers.

De Gaulle, who had promoted the De Gaullists of New York, London, Buenos Aires and other parts of the world to be "members of the Resistance in exile," authorized them to appoint deputies to Algiers, like the "members of the Resistance in the homeland."

Exile has its sufferings, to be sure, sometimes cruel sufferings. Uprooted Frenchmen flung by the great shipwreck of war onto the shores of hospitable lands have mourned for years their lost country and their absent relatives, and have endured silent griefs;

not to mention the extreme material poverty of some of them. But in no way do they deserve to be placed on the same footing with the martyrs and heroes of the underground. The moral atmosphere of exile, as Lamartine, Chateaubriand, and Victor Hugo have described it, is always depressing, always productive of violent passions and fanaticisms and all sorts of mental disturbances. De Gaulle may have found it useful for his personal publicity in Algiers to be able to show that deputies came to him from all over the world. But from the political point of view, from the French point of view, to have the exile represented could be nothing but ridiculous and detrimental. And in any case, how could the exiles choose their deputies?

In Quebec, De Gaulle nominated a Madame Simard, a friend of his former personal secretary, the overexcitable Mademoiselle de Miribel, as the "deputy from Canada." Immediately the presidents of the French associations of Montreal, which represent the material and moral interests of France in French Canada—*l'Union Nationale Française,* the French Chamber of Commerce, the Veterans' Association, *l'Alliance Française, l'Assistance aux Œuvres Françaises de Guerre*—protested against the impression created through the press that this nomination had been proposed by the French in Canada, whereas in truth none of the directors of these associations had been consulted.

In Buenos Aires, De Gaulle appointed as delegate a certain Guérin, a newspaperman without distinction, who was editor of *La France Nouvelle,* the De Gaullist organ which specialized in abusive attacks on the United States. This nomination raised a storm of protest among the French in South America.

In New York the appointment of the deputy to the Consultative Assembly led to ludicrous consequences. De Gaulle asked the executive committee of the De Gaullist society France Forever to appoint the delegate. Now, France Forever was an American organization, and its members were largely Americans. The De Gaullist "French deputy" was therefore to be elected, if instructions were followed literally, by Americans. And that is not all. The executive whereas in New York alone there were about 6,000 French exiles and 100,000 French residents, besides a Chamber of Commerce, representing important interests, groups of war veterans, and corporative groups of all sorts, which were not consulted.

However, the executive committee of France Forever, meeting in special session, elected by some thirty votes M. Henry Torrès, the well-known Paris lawyer, as the deputy from America. This choice immediately raised a tumult in Algiers.

Greatly embarrassed, De Gaulle asked France Forever to name two other candidates, so that he might choose among the three. Count d'Ornano and M. Perrin were elected. General de Gaulle took M. Perrin who departed to represent America in Algiers. It is not difficult to imagine the impression such incidents created in American political circles.

Many of the Algiers De Gaullists were outraged because the United States did not quickly recognize the De Gaulle government. They should at least have refrained from deriding democratic institutions right in New York and from openly showing the world what they thought of popular representation.

To get back to the Consultative Assembly in Algiers—what was its real function?

In Algiers, under the existing circumstances, there should have been generals and other officers working to build up a great French colonial army which, on the day of the invasion, would have contributed to the liberation of France, side by side with the Allied armies, fighting its way from Normandy to Paris, thus becoming the foundation of France's renewed prestige.

The rebirth of political life in the first liberated territories could not fail to be disastrous in itself, for before all else the French needed to forget politics and to rebuild the unity of all hearts in an atmosphere of fraternity and military glory. The Consultative Assembly, formed under such unusual conditions, could only supply material for dissension and turmoil. Having but the role of resembling a representative body and of serving De Gaullist propaganda, the Assembly's only signs of life were its oratorical and spectacular meetings, useless and childish, and its so-called works of legislative preparation, even more useless and childish. It helped to bring forth collections of projected laws for the future France, as if France would accept wholesale legislation which bore the stamp of ignorance, haphazardness, and all the sterile excitements of exile.

It was noteworthy that all strong personalities had either been side-tracked or had refused to serve. There were no men of talent in the Assembly. The mediocrity and servility of the membership added to the anomaly and impotence of that chamber whose function was to acclaim De Gaulle periodically and to fool the world about his republicanism.

In the end, almost all of the laws voted by the Algiers Consultative Assembly were brushed aside, in a mass, by the representatives of the F.F.I., when the government moved to Paris. The Resistance rejected disdainfully what is called, amusingly enough, the "laws of the *casbah*." *

With the passage of time, we might have tried, therefore, to forget the Algerian institution as the harmless nonsense of a brigadier general doing his lessons in politics. Unfortunately, De Gaulle doomed himself in advance to transfer to Paris his antirepublican, Consular, dictatorial and Cagoulard-inspired political machine.

What would have happened had he made his entry into the capital as a soldier, without trying to impose a political system? That, obviously, we do not know. It was inevitable that France should emerge from her trials with a revolutionary mentality and should become the scene of political upheavals. One may, however, assume that the entry into Paris of a triumphant French army, led by men who were the incarnation of unselfishness, courage and heroism, might have provided the necessary counterbalance to the violence of unleashed passions. To inaugurate the greatest day of her history in purity and in glory, to mark her return to greatness, France needed to have pass under the Arc de Triomphe a Joffre or a Foch, symbols of an army loyal to its country and government —or even Joan of Arc as she made her entry into Rheims, beside the Dauphin, to consecrate there the legitimacy of power.

* Algerian citadel surrounded by restricted quarter.

Now, the "liberator" who did appear was a soldier who never fought a battle throughout the four years of the tragedy. All he had done was to quarrel with the magnificent soldiers who were fighting the Germans in Africa and with the Allied nations who were saving France. He entered Paris behind General Leclerc's tanks, dragging with him his political machine. He brought not unselfishness and glory, but usurpation of power, with all the immorality that implies under such circumstances, and illegality pompously adorned with the name of the Fourth Republic.

Why a Fourth Republic? Everything in the institutions of France could have been changed without departing from the path of legality.

There was the famous precedent of the National Assembly convened at Versailles in 1881 under the Jules Ferry cabinet, which profoundly altered the constitution of 1875 by doing away with life membership in the Senate.

The National Assembly of the Third Republic could have purged itself in a minute by voting in August, 1944, in freed Paris, to exclude its collaborationist members and, if need be, by handing them over to the High Court. In another minute, it could have elected De Gaulle President of the Republic, since he was so set upon it. In one day it could have reformed the Constitution and voted a new provisional one for the duration of the war. It could have settled all problems, including that very new and delicate one of the representation of the Forces of the Interior. It could have made the Senate the High Assembly of the Resistance or decreed the formation of a third assembly to be called Assembly of the Resistance. (The Constitution of the Year VIII of the French Revolution actually provided for three assemblies.) *

Why, then, that Fourth Republic, since all necessary changes could have been effected through reforms, within the framework of the Third Republic? The republican Constitution of the United

---

* The author, who is still in exile, cannot judge whether the integration of the forces of the Resistance in the new provisional constitution was justified by the facts.

States has been altered nineteen or twenty times since it was drawn up, but that has been done through the normal channel of amendments; and it has never occurred to the Americans—not even after their tragic Civil War—that with each change the Republic should bear a new number.

In order to formulate an answer to the above question it is necessary to refer back to the movement in favor of a Fourth Republic with plebiscitary tendencies, which was launched between the two world wars by Jean de Granvillers, as well as to the articles and speeches of the sinister Marcel Déat and Jacques Doriot, both of whom were the apologists of an authoritarian and antidemocratic Fourth Republic. This Fourth Republic, without ties of any sort with the Third, without legal foundation, fascist in form and in spirit, is the solution which, under German pressure, the National Revolution of Vichy and the Cagoulards were approaching. Ever since the days of London and Algiers, General de Gaulle and the Cagoulard Passy had been preparing for the establishment of the New Power and for their control of France by way of a regime bearing the misleading title of "Fourth Republic."

At the moment when these lines are being written the scheme is being put into effect, and the elections, which were held in October 1945, are its most essential step. Dubious elections, indeed, held in ignorance and darkness, with an electoral body divided and decomposed by the dramas of the war and the climate of usurpation—an electoral body separated from the free world for six years, completely ignorant of the general's conduct while in exile, misled by a systematic propaganda campaign that harped on one chord only—an electoral body which includes ten million women who are voting for the first time in their lives.

All men and all political parties with any background of experience have condemned these elections. The Consultative Assembly has registered a unanimous protest. But General de Gaulle had overridden all objections. It is in this atmosphere that the Fourth Republic will be born. The very act of its birth condemns it.

13. "Liberator" versus Liberators

Go hang thyself, brave Crillon, we have won without thee!

HENRY IV

NOW comes the Allied invasion of France. In that critical phase of history, to what extent did General de Gaulle fulfill the first and most sacred of duties—that of aiding the Allies who were about to free his country? We shall let facts and documents speak for themselves.

Let us go back to the beginning of March, 1944, *just three months* before the offensive that was to lead to liberation. At that moment tension between De Gaulle and America was at its height. And why? Because Roosevelt still refused to recognize the Committee of Liberation in Algiers, as the legitimate government of France. His position may be summed up as follows: The Committee of Liberation is not a duly authorized government. It has no legal foundation. General de Gaulle, its head, is self-appointed. We do not know to what extent he has, and will have, the backing of the French people. We do not know who remains of the former representatives of the Third Republic. We shall therefore suspend our decision until we have seen what is happening in France. General Eisenhower will be the first on the spot and, taking account of the actual state of affairs, he will make the arrangements he deems best for the prosecution of the war. For the present he will have authority to negotiate with anyone in France who can be of value to his military operations. Such is our policy. It is governed both by the demands of the war and by the admiration I feel for the French people, whose desires I wish to respect and who must not be confronted with a *fait accompli*.

This was a reasonable and highly politic attitude and it deserved the understanding and gratitude of the French—but, naturally, it did not suit De Gaulle. If he could not seize power by virtual surprise the first day in Paris; if time were allowed for "people in the know" to come from London, Algiers, and New York; if the patriots and republicans inside France were alerted and given the facts, the gains of a four-year struggle for power would be lost. Consequently, when he saw that the Allied offensive in France was near at hand, De Gaulle decided to hasten events and force the decision of the President·of the United States. Since Teheran he had been counting on British help. Though definitely not highly regarded in London, De Gaulle was looked upon there as a person over whom the British "held the upper hand," because of services they had rendered him and the innumerable mistakes or scandals committed in his name which they had witnessed. De Gaulle was also counting on the anxiety the American De Gaullists might cause Roosevelt in 1944, the election year. Tremendous opposition had been organized in America against the President. Pro-French Americans of unquestionable integrity were conducting a passionate campaign on behalf of De Gaulle, in whom, like many Frenchmen, they saw the symbol of reborn France. Liberals and left-wing Democrats sided with them for ideological reasons, because they saw in De Gaulle the future creator of a Socialist planned economy. Great numbers of pro-Germans and isolationists favored De Gaulle out of sheer hatred for Roosevelt. Then, too, a strange and unhealthy mental phenomenon caused De Gaullism, as an element of unrest, to spread in America as, for that matter, in all countries. In a world that is sick and topsy-turvy, frontiers no longer keep men apart, and mysterious contagions spread on planes which lie above countries.

In March, 1944, therefore, De Gaulle launched a great psychological and political offensive against Roosevelt. On March 11

Sonia Tomara, the extremely pro-De Gaulle correspondent of the New York *Herald Tribune,* struck a significant note from Algiers:

> I have heard the most moderate members of the High Council of Resistance here say: "If the Allies try to rule us we shall have a revolution. We have had enough of one occupying power."

On March 18 De Gaulle made a threatening speech before the Consultative Assembly. He declared:

> Any artificial creation of power alongside mine would be intolerable. I assert emphatically that any effort to maintain the power of Vichy, be it even partly or under disguise, is doomed in advance.

General de Gaulle spoke of *his* power as Hitler spoke of his. And in addition, he again denounced Roosevelt and accused him of having an understanding with Laval, Darnand, or their accomplices.

On March 19 the correspondent of the New York *Times* wrote that the minister D'Astier de la Vigerie had recently given a statement to the press in which he said that ". . . Vichy officials hoped for the support of the Americans and Canadians after France had been liberated."

In Washington, De Gaulle's speech and D'Astier de la Vigerie's statement roused strong feeling. The State Department promptly issued a statement:

> The absurd reports and rumors periodically occurring, and which are evidently inspired, endeavoring to create the impression that this Government, upon the liberation of France, intends to deal with the Vichy regime or with certain individuals directly or indirectly supporting the policy of collaboration with Germany, are false on their face. The fact that this Government kept representation at Vichy for some time for such vital purposes as combatting Nazi designs, the preservation of the French fleet from German hands and the prevention of Nazi occupation of French North Africa or the establishment of military bases there has been most amazingly and falsely represented as founded upon a sympathetic relationship between the American Government and pro-Axis supporters at Vichy. Every person at all informed knew that throughout the entire period just the opposite was true.

No loyal supporter of the Allied cause would make the ridiculous charge that the United States Government, while sending its military forces and vast military supplies to the most distant battlefields to prosecute the war against the Axis powers, would at the same time have any dealings or relations with the Vichy regime except for the purpose of abolishing it.

In plain terms, in an explanation obviously truthful and sincere, Secretary Hull accused General de Gaulle of not being a "loyal supporter" of the Allied cause.

De Gaulle, however, turned loose his machine of lying propaganda. The next day the New York *Times* wrote:

The report that the United States has been in contact with Georges Bonnet and Anatole de Monzie through Spain was widely repeated in Algiers, and not in irresponsible circles.
Even General Charles de Gaulle reflected these doubts about American policy.

Then a dramatic and particularly significant incident occurred. A wire from Algiers stated that M. Bret of the news agency France-Afrique and his close associates had resigned in protest against what they called "government control" of their organization. The attempt was actually being made to force newspaper men to transmit false news for De Gaullist purposes! The conscientious revolt of the France-Afrique agency does honor to French journalism.

The De Gaullists thereupon dropped the theme of Roosevelt's collusion with Vichy, which had made the rounds of the anti-Roosevelt press in America and throughout the world.

On March 26 the New York *Times* printed a wireless from Algiers under the headline: "French Blame U. S. on Economic Impasse." It contained an incredible piece of news: negotiations on food supplies for France had been interrupted.

Negotiations regarding French stockpiles to be created in North Africa for the relief of France on her liberation have been stalled by French inquiries as to the Allies' plan for supplying the French with food and other necessaries—inquiries to which there has been as yet no definite answer. Pending an answer, the Committee of National Liberation is unwilling to proceed.

Thus, during the last days of March, 1944, while the Americans were feverishly carrying on their preparations for the liberation of France, De Gaulle was threatening to stop all participation in plans for supplying France with food! Once liberated, the unhappy French people were to suffer further and wait still longer for Allied aid—so that their misery might force America to yield to De Gaulle. That was only the beginning of a piece of blackmail which—as we shall see later—stopped at nothing.

On March 27, 1944, De Gaulle again addressed the Assembly—this time to launch a new attack against America:

> Our government need not take lessons from anyone. . . . France, which gave liberty to the world and still is the champion of liberty, need pay no attention to remarks beyond her frontiers regarding her destiny.

On March 30 the correspondent of the New York *Times* gloomily wired his paper from Algiers:

> There has been a marked recrudescence of anti-American feeling. . . . Many Frenchmen consider this an ominous augury for the future, since they consider it represents the tendency towards xenophobia, which runs counter to the interests of France.

For a long time the interests of France had been superseded by those of De Gaulle, and the former were being deliberately sacrificed to the latter.

The correspondent continued:

> In influential French circles here there is a feeling that the differences between Washington and General Charles de Gaulle go far deeper than a diplomatic or personal plane. . . .
> The view is expressed here that between President Roosevelt and General de Gaulle there is this gulf: That De Gaulle espouses today social conceptions that Mr. Roosevelt espoused a decade ago. That General de Gaulle proposes a kind of New Deal for France long after Mr. Roosevelt had been induced by the circumstances of war to abandon some phases of his New Deal.

A few months later Roosevelt was elected with the support of all the Left forces in the United States, including the Communists, but

De Gaullist propaganda continued to accuse Roosevelt of being a Fascist with Nazi sympathies.

On April 2 De Gaulle "notified" the Allies of the administrative and political arrangements he had made for the liberation of France without asking their advice—as much as to say that he was not considering their wishes and that he was openly defying them.

April 3 marked the beginning of a new attack. It was learned that 600 delegates from "Resistance groups in Algeria" were demanding the abolition of the Clark-Darlan agreement.

This agreement regulated the relations between the French administration and the American Army in Africa. The conditions were harsh, it is true, because in November, 1942, the American Army had many reasons to distrust pro-Vichy French authorities in North Africa, beginning with Darlan himself. But now the war in Africa was over. The Battle of France was about to begin. Why argue about old agreements that had terminated? De Gaulle, however, used any weapon he could against Roosevelt. It reminded one of the time when Hitler left no stone unturned to attack Benes. The technique of agitation was the same: the important thing was to mobilize hatreds. De Gaulle was determined to make the liberator of France hated.

On April 4 came the outrageous expulsion of General Giraud, who had been backed by America. It was obvious that Giraud could not fight against the methods and techniques of the new "Man of Brumaire." * The Americans left him to his fate.

On April 29 De Gaullist propaganda made an unexpected discovery. It protested against American policy in Iraq. The New York *Times* published a wireless from Algiers:

> The Committee expresses concern for "the defense of French rights and interests" in the Irak Petroleum Company, which is Allied-owned. . . . The fact that the French describe the negotiations with the Allies on this subject as a defense of French rights is eloquent of the diplomatic situation today.

* Napoleon.

While De Gaulle was worrying about the oil wells of Iraq, President Roosevelt was busy with the invasion of the Normandy shores. It was now one month from the great day!

Suddenly De Gaulle dropped the attack against Roosevelt and turned on Churchill who, however, was backing him quite strongly against American diplomacy. The pretext for the Churchill attack: on May 1 the British, in view of the imminence of the attack on France, prohibited any communications save in British code. In that way they would get hold of instructions De Gaulle was giving his agents.

"It is a blow at French sovereignty," D'Astier de la Vigerie declared at his press conference on May 3.

On May 6 De Gaulle decided that he would refuse to continue conversations with the Allies on the subject of the liberation of France. The New York *Times* said:

The Committee takes note that the necessary conversations . . . cannot be usefully pursued, and that the Commissioner from the Administration of Liberated Metropolitan Territories cannot himself go to London as long as communications between the Committee and its representatives in Great Britain are interrupted.

On the eve of the offensive, De Gaulle therefore broke off diplomatic and military conversations with the Allies. True, he had no army to offer for the Battle of Normandy, and the only request he did not make was to be allowed to go and fight in person—as a symbol.

On May 12 there was great news—very great news indeed!—which the Algiers propaganda was to make much of: the wicked British had had the effrontery to examine the luggage of the De Gaullist minister André Philip as he was leaving England for Africa. The De Gaullist press waxed indignant.

Four days later the matter of the Clark-Darlan agreements reached the expected end. De Gaulle denounced them unilaterally. Washington replied that it was completely indifferent to the general's impudence and that it regarded the agreements as still valid.

One can imagine the atmosphere of unhealthy excitement that reigned in Algiers. Patriots and republicans followed events with growing anxiety. On May 25 the President of the Algiers General Council, M. Frogier, who at first had been so friendly to De Gaulle, took the floor to accuse him of violating the spirit and the laws of the Republic. He was expelled from the Council.

However, on June 2, Churchill, who saw D-Day approaching, informed De Gaulle that his place was in London. The latter, kept in ignorance of all plans (and for good reason) thought the great day was still some way off. He did not hurry. On June 3 he proclaimed his committee in Algiers the "Provisional Government of France." Once more it was a case of a unilateral diplomatic act. Neither London nor Washington so much as noticed this piece of insolence. British and American officials thereafter received notes from the "Provisional Government of France," but they replied to the "Committee of National Liberation."

Since the end of May, the British and the Americans had been bombing German communication centers in France. Those bombings were terrible—frightful. But how could the battle of France be won without first fighting the dreadful battle of the air? Would a French army planning to attack the Normandy shores have failed to throw its air force at the German supply lines? The author was an aviator-bombardier in 1915 and 1916 on the French front. How many times, with death in his heart, did he bomb the rear of German armies before Verdun, Metz, Bar-le-Duc, Laon, Péronne, and so many other unfortunate French cities! A horrible and tragic necessity of war, made even more horrible and more tragic by the inevitable errors of the bombers who sometimes mistake their objectives and take hamlets for factories, abandoned towns for occupied, and French civilians for German soldiers! What could patriot leaders do in the face of this slaughter but try to relieve French suffering, and explain to the people that a terrific price must be paid for liberation? Vichy, who knew whom it was working for, whipped up anger to the boiling point. And Algiers did the same thing. Press and mouth-to-mouth propaganda seized upon these bombings to stir up resentment and hatred in Algiers against the liberators of France.

American diplomats and newspapermen were dismayed. A correspondent of the New York *Times* wrote on June 3 that he had met a high dignitary in Algiers who said to him:

I read this morning a big headline saying that a thousand Allied planes had raided France. To you that seems good—and, in a sense it is to me, too. But you will forgive me if I winced. For that means maybe a thousand or more Frenchmen killed and perhaps large parts of French towns wiped out.

Even this would be accepted gladly by Frenchmen generally if they knew it was the harbinger of an early landing. But it has gone on and on, and when is the landing?

. . . The French do not understand these bombings. . . .

For instance, the center of Nantes has been wiped out. I do not know what was the technical reason but it was. . . .

At Marseilles the Gare Saint-Charles has been destroyed and with it a large number of people and buildings. . . . Was the strategic gain worth such terrible casualties? The French cannot believe it was.

Orléans is on a branch line, not on a main railway; yet its station has been bombed with similar civilian casualties. The strategic value of that cannot be of the first order. The same goes for the railway station at Angers.

Can you blame Frenchmen for saying that these bombs are falling on the wrong side of the Franco-German border?

In Washington, a prominent official, commenting on similar dispatches sent by American correspondents and diplomats, told me plainly:

"What De Gaulle is doing is terible, Kerillis! Up to now he has been fighting us on the diplomatic field and using the most unfair weapons against us. But this time he is making capital out of the blood of innocent people, the blood that is mingled with our tears and also, don't forget, with our own blood. No, that man, I assure you, is guiltier than Pétain. Pétain is an old man and he is tied hand and foot. De Gaulle, on the contrary, is a young leader and fully responsible for his wicked actions."

But the needle was turning on the dial of history and the solemn hour was drawing near. On June 5, 1944, the eve of the day when General Eisenhower was to launch the invasion, De Gaulle arrived in London from Algiers. He was informed of the decisions taken. He saw General Eisenhower. The meeting was extremely cool. He was received by Churchill. The meeting was stormy and almost tragic.

We shall not know all the details until the diplomatic files are opened. Till then we must rely on a long dispatch from Geoffrey Parsons published in the most pro-De Gaulle paper in America, the New York *Herald Tribune,* a newspaper famous for its honesty and accuracy. That dispatch gives us the third and most dramatic act of the blackmail.

Here is the high point of Mr. Parsons' story on the De Gaulle-Churchill meeting (New York *Herald Tribune,* June 11):

> He [General de Gaulle] threatened not to join with the heads of other exiled governments in broadcasts to Europe on D-Day unless the British and American governments made an effort to settle some of the many outstanding problems that still remain unsettled regarding France.

(We must understand that De Gaulle in speaking of "unsettled problems" was thinking of his personal situation in that stirring moment; for what he meant was his recognition as head of the government—before the Allies could find out in France whether the French people really wanted him.)

> Prime Minister Churchill, however, insisted De Gaulle toe the line. Complete censorship had been imposed on any news of the French general's arrival in England. The Prime Minister offered to send De Gaulle back to Algiers by the next plane and told him that no one would be the wiser since his presence in England, although widely known in newspaper circles, would not be made public. The Prime Minister said he would have to go before the House of Commons on Tuesday, which was D-Day and announce to the world that General de Gaulle had refused to associate himself with the greatest effort yet made to liberate France.

There was nothing left for the general to do but give in. He did. . . .

The accuracy of this report, more complete and more detailed than those of other British and American correspondents, is confirmed by numerous semiofficial sources.

Moreover, De Gaulle himself was to disclose the gravity of the disagreement between himself and General Eisenhower when he was asked to appeal to the French people on the radio immediately after Eisenhower's speech, at the very instant when the liberators were landing on Norman soil. At first De Gaulle flatly refused. In the end he gave his message—but after a delay of five hours and in language that caused an uproar because it contradicted certain statements and orders in Eisenhower's speech.

General Eisenhower said to the French people:

Citizens of France! I am proud to have again under my command the gallant forces of France. Fighting beside their Allies, they will play a worthy part in the liberation of their homeland. Because the initial landing has been made on the soil of your country I repeat to you with even greater emphasis my message to the people of other occupied countries of Western Europe. Follow the instructions of your leaders. A premature uprising of all Frenchmen may prevent you from being of maximum help to your country in the critical hour. Be patient. Prepare.

As supreme commander of the Allied Expeditionary Forces, there is imposed on me the duty and responsibility of taking all measures necessary to the prosecution of the war. Prompt and willing obedience to the orders that I shall issue is essential. Effective civil administration of France must be provided by Frenchmen. All persons must continue in their present duties unless otherwise instructed. Those who have common cause with the enemy and so betrayed their country will be removed. As France is liberated from her oppressors, you yourselves will choose your representatives and the government under which you wish to live.

In the course of this campaign for the final defeat of the enemy you may sustain further losses and damage. Tragic though they may be, they are part of the price of victory. I assure you that I shall do all in my power to mitigate your hardships. I know that I can count on your steadfastness now no less than in the past. The heroic deeds of Frenchmen who have continued their struggle against the Nazis and their Vichy satellites, in France and throughout the French Empire, have been an example and an inspiration to all of us.

This landing is but the opening phase of a campaign in Western Europe. Great battles lie ahead. I call upon all who love freedom to stand with us. Keep your faith staunch—our arms are resolute—together we shall achieve victory.

For his part, General de Gaulle declared:

The final battle has begun. After so much grief and suffering, the decisive clash which we have all been waiting for, is on. It is, of course, the Battle of France, and it is France's battle. Tremendous blows, for us blows of salvation, are being launched from the shores of old England. Not long ago it was on this last bastion of Western Europe that the tide of German oppression spent itself. Today it is the base from which oppression will be smashed.

France, overwhelmed for four years but never conquered, is on her feet to take part in the fight. The clear and sacred duty of her sons, whoever and wherever they may be, is to battle with all the means at their disposal. We must destroy the enemy who is crushing and befouling our country, who is hated and dishonored and who will do everything in his power to escape his doom. The enemy will stubbornly cling to our land as long as he can. But for quite some time he has been but a beast on the run—from Stalingrad to Tarnopol, from the banks of the Nile to Bizerte, from Tunis to Rome. He has now become accustomed to defeat.

France will fight this battle furiously, but she will fight it in good order. And it is thus that we have won all our victories for the past fifteen hundred years. And that is how we shall win this one—in good order. For our Army, Navy and Air Force, this is no problem. They will never be more eager, more capable, more disciplined. Africa, Italy, the oceans and the skies, have beheld the rebirth of their strength and their glory. Tomorrow their motherland will see it.

For a nation which fights bound hand and foot against a fully armed oppressor, battle discipline imposes several conditions. The first is strict obedience to instructions given by the French government and by French leaders named by the national and local resistance.

The second condition is that our action in the rear of the enemy shall be co-ordinated as quickly as possible with the action of the Allied and French armies. We must expect that the struggle of the armies will be hard and long. That means that the work of the forces of resistance must go on and must increase right up to the moment of the German collapse.

The third condition is that all who are able to play an active part, either by taking up arms, or by sabotage or by giving information, or by refusing to do work of use to the enemy, shall not allow themselves to be taken prisoner. They must, whatever the difficulties, take steps to avoid imprisonment or deportation. Anything is better than to be put out of action without fighting.

The Battle of France has begun. In the French nation, in the Empire, in the armies, there is now but a single will, a single hope. From behind the cloud laden with our blood and our tears there reappears the sun of our national greatness.

If we compare the meaning of the two texts we find:

General Eisenhower says: Frenchmen, I am the Commander in Chief. You must obey me.

General de Gaulle says, in substance: You must obey *me*.

General Eisenhower: When you have been freed, you yourselves will choose your government.

General de Gaulle: I am the government.

General Eisenhower: Any premature general uprising of the French might prevent you from being useful to your country. Be patient. Make ready.

General de Gaulle: It is the duty of every Frenchman to fight now.

Thus De Gaulle actually gave instructions and even military orders contrary to those of the commander responsible for the Battle of France.

But there was more, much more.

General Eisenhower paid a chivalrous tribute to the French troops under his orders. Now, in reality, these French troops that were to take part in the decisive Battle of Normandy which was to determine the fate of France were only a tiny handful of men: two battalions of parachutists and twenty liaison officers.

For his part, General de Gaulle did not even mention the Commander in Chief or the Allied officers and men who, at first one million strong, then two million, and then three million, were going to fight on the soil of France. To those heroic sons of England and America, who were in no way to blame for the political-diplomatic difficulties that had arisen between himself, Roosevelt, and Churchill, De Gaulle had nothing to say. Those who were soon to fall and die on the soil of France for the deliverance of France did not rate even the salute of the thanks of the man who called himself the incarnation of the French Resistance. At the time when all of France was vibrant with wild enthusiasm, his lips were sealed, his blood was cold, his heart stood still—because he was thinking of his political career, and it was causing him some uneasiness.

Worse than that. For the great drama which had been unfolding since June 18, 1940, date of that magnificent order of the day which gave birth to De Gaullism, had reached its climax. And not only was De Gaulle not fighting personally by the side of the Allies, not only did he not personally land on the Normandy beaches where the Germans were trying to crush the forces of liberation, but he behaved as if he were trying to spread bewilderment and cause confusion in the battle, and he chose just that solemn occasion to sow once again in the French mind the seeds of distrust and ingratitude towards their liberators.

But to return to the facts: the Normandy attack began on June 6. And on June 10, in London, De Gaulle again hurled reproaches at the Americans. He attacked Eisenhower while the latter was waging a bitter and still undecided battle against the Germans. He declared the situation "unacceptable." In London, at a press conference, he told fifty newspapermen:

At present there is unfortunately no agreement between the French government and the Allies' governments concerning the co-operation of the French administration with the Allies' armies in liberated French metropolitan territories. Furthermore, the proclamation addressed to the French people on June 6 and the one published today seem to foreshadow a sort of taking over of power in France by the Allies' military command.

This situation is obviously not acceptable to us and it could provoke in France itself incidents that, it seems to us, should be avoided. On the other hand, the issuance of a so-called French currency in France without any agreement and without any guarantee from the French authorities can lead only to serious complications. At a moment when the battle is being joined on the soil of France, the French government is eager, in the common interest, to see an end to such confusion and infringement.

This time, among the De Gaullists themselves there were "mixed feelings"—that is to say, some were very sincerely moved. From their Algiers capital, Harold Callender wrote to the New York *Times* on June 10:

General de Gaulle's statement tonight in London was received here with mixed feelings. Some persons . . . thought that he had chosen an inappropriate moment . . . and that the result might be . . . to offend the Allies.

The same day the De Gaullist press in Algiers opened fire on the Americans. And Callender went on:

Armed with the authorization of De Gaulle's statement yesterday, the ultra-nationalist press here gave even fuller rein than usual today to its suspicion of the Allies' motives regarding France. The suspicions expressed in the "Dernières Nouvelles" are that the Allies, for some reason, want to take over the ruling power in France; that the State Department obstinately persists in repeating in France all the errors that it committed in North Africa; that the American secret service may have found isolated individuals in France to co-operate with it but that those individuals if they act against the honor of the nation, will be disavowed by the Resistance movement on which the American military government cannot count for aid.

Was that the moment to accuse the Americans, who were fighting with redoubled courage under the walls of Saint-Lô, of wanting to seize power in France? Was it the moment to denounce and threaten Frenchmen who "collaborated" with their liberators, or to announce that Americans could not count on the help of the Resistance?

The anti-American offensive spread. On June 12 Callender pointed out that his country was now being openly accused of trying to ruin France:

Another fear is that the Allies' currency, that General de Gaulle denounced tonight, might stimulate an inflation for which the United States would be blamed for many years.

In Washington excitement ran high. That very day President Roosevelt held a press conference. He was questioned about this new De Gaullist accusation that the liberators' monetary arrangements bade fair to ruin what the Germans had left of French finance. One newspaperman asked whether De Gaulle had been notified of those measures and whether he had approved them. To this the President replied that the word "approved" was incorrect, but that the Committee of Liberation had been informed and had not offered any objections.

In London, feeling on the subject was no less keen than in Washington. On June 14, in the House of Commons, Churchill was assailed with questions from pro-De Gaulle as well as from anti-De Gaulle members in Parliament. He requested the House not to demand a reply at that time "on the ground that to do so now could be only comforting to the enemy."

Commenting on those words and describing the atmosphere of that meeting, Raymond Daniell wrote to the New York *Times* on June 14:

He made such strong pleas for the indulgence of the House that some members who knew his own mental reservations about General de Gaulle wondered what statements could be worse than this implication.

On June 15, 1944, the New York *Times* published on its front page an even more significant story: it showed that De Gaulle was not satisfied to issue orders of the day and statements injurious to military operations:

The blackest cloud from the international point of view is the deterioration of relations with General de Gaulle. Washington has let it be known that at the last moment he withdrew permission for several hundreds of liaison officers to accompany the invasion forces into France. In other respects the agencies of the Committee of Liberation at Algiers have become much more explicit in their denunciation of President Roosevelt and the United States.

The accusation is couched in moderate terms. But it is a dramatic one. De Gaulle is openly accused by this great American newspaper (which, it cannot be too often repeated, is passionately sympathetic to the De Gaullists and has urged public opinion to recognize De Gaulle) of having withdrawn his liaison officers from the battle of Normandy—in other words, of having sabotaged the battle in so far as he was able.

And to back this up the New York *Times* published a wireless from the Associated Press which, considering the gravity of its content and the fact that it was passed by the censor, takes on an almost official character.

The Allied troops already were moving onto the beaches of Normandy when De Gaulle withdrew all but a handful of the French officers who had been counted on by the Allies' command to act as liaison officers with the French patriots to help take over civil administration. . . .

Angered by non-recognition of the CFLN as the Provisional Government of France and by the refusal of the Allies' command to let him take over the issuing of radio directions to the French people on D-Day, qualified Allied sources said, De Gaulle cancelled arrangements that had been made after weeks of planning between the Supreme Headquarters civil affairs branch and his representative Gen. Koenig, assistant chief of the French General Staff and liaison man with the Allies.

De Gaulle permitted only a token force of twenty out of the hundreds of trained French officers who were ready to go with the troops, it was said.

This news went round the world and aroused strong reactions. What was General de Gaulle's reply?

That same day through his press attaché he issued a denial—a denial that was really a confirmation.

The Associated Press report is simply incredible. We have not broken any such agreement, for we have not signed any. For several months we have been negotiating with the Allies but, as the whole world knows, we have not reached any accord with the Allied governments or with their heads on the subject of the liberated territories or on the question of sending liaison officers with the invasion forces. As to reports stating that co-operation between the French people and the Allied armies has deteriorated, it is possible that they are true, but it is not our fault!

This so-called denial—which was really a public admission, without any expression of regret, that relations between the French people, or rather the De Gaullists, and the soldiers who were liberating them had "deteriorated"—did not, however, deny that only twenty French officers had landed with the Americans. The general confined himself to disputing that there had been an "agreement signed" to land any more.

How many French officers were there in London on June 6, 1944? Several hundreds, or rather several thousands. And could the Allies have thought that they had to get a signed agreement from De Gaulle in order to obtain the services of those officers in the decisive hour of the Battle of France? Could it have occurred to them that those officers would be held back at the last moment? Could they have expected that, after four years of preparation, the participation of the De Gaullists in the first battle of liberation would be limited to twenty officers? And could they have anticipated that De Gaulle's official newspaper, *La Marseillaise*, would go so far as to brand the French who gave General Eisenhower political aid as "traitors"? * That article in *La Marseillaise* confirms the fact that De Gaullist officers were not, and could not have been, sent along with the American Army.

On June 14, Harold Callender sent a dispatch to the New York *Times* which is worth quoting in its entirety—for we must not forget that he was writing from Algiers, chief center of De Gaullism.

American troops are battling in France to drive the Germans out. It is almost entirely American material that has enabled the large French army to strike effective blows against the Germans in Italy. Lend-lease is supplying the French forces in reserve that will form the nucleus of the future army of France yet, since De Gaulle's diplomatic impasse with the Allies, Algiers is not a pleasant place for an American.

The Anglo-American blow for the liberation of France has coincided with a new wave of anti-American sentiment here, stimulated by De Gaulle's fear that the Allies were seizing power in France. The expression of that suspicion was immediately followed by a campaign against the U. S. Government in one newspaper here. It continued today with

* See page 58.

an article in the *Républicain* saying that President Roosevelt had plans for French reconstruction devised by Admiral William Leahy, but that Washington was wrong in thinking that the French needed a guardian. The official radio here attacked American policy last night on the lines that De Gaulle was left out.

All day long Frenchmen ask why Washington insisted on an Allied council in France, why we did not dismiss the mayor of Bayeux, whether Mr. Roosevelt gets his idea about France from Camille Chautemps and Henri de Kerillis. At the end of the day an American driven into a slightly cynical mood said: "There is only one solution. That is for the Allies to withdraw from France."

Many Frenchmen regret that when the long awaited blow was struck to free France, De Gaulle was preoccupied with the mayor of Bayeux and with the suspicion that we would assume undue power over the French. This thesis closely resembles that of Vichy as some Frenchmen here point out, since Vichy has been telling the French that the invasion is just another conquest like that of the Germans. The Vichy radio has a field day with the argument that De Gaulle has broken with the Allies.

Perhaps, after reading these accounts, the reader will appreciate the following words which I jotted down in the diary of my exile:

"I keep wondering what more De Gaulle could have done to hamper the Allies while the Battle of France and the fate of the whole war were being decided. I can think of nothing. . . . Any ordinary Frenchman who had put the slightest obstacle in the bloody path which General Eisenhower and his soldiers followed, would have been arrested, tried, condemned, and stood up against a wall. . . . General de Gaulle is lucky to be a man-symbol!"

14. General de Gaulle and the Allies

The De Gaulle-Giraud quarrel is an aid to the enemy.
FRANKLIN D. ROOSEVELT

Of all the crosses I have borne, the Cross of Lorraine is the heaviest.
WINSTON CHURCHILL

THE preceding pages should have destroyed any existing picture of General de Gaulle as helping the Allies to liberate France. Further details are, however, necessary.

De Gaulle's enmity for the Russians dates back to the period immediately preceding the fall of France and the launching of his amazing adventure. It is not generally known that he was the author of a plan to bring France into the Russian-Finnish war on the side of Finland. According to that plan—which Paul Reynaud outlined to me briefly in a letter I have preserved—a motorized expeditionary force was to arrive in Finland by way of Norway, quickly put to rout the disorganized Russian hordes and march on Leningrad. Even another important cabinet minister, who respected De Gaulle's intelligence, was momentarily influenced by his brilliant reasoning. I was obliged to put up a vigorous fight against the plan. It was all too evident that the Russian-Finnish war was the first episode in the Russian-German war, a vanguard skirmish to win bases in the Baltic and in the Arctic Ocean. On the other hand, to conclude from the setbacks suffered by the Russians that they were incapable of fighting was plainly absurd. Any French army that landed in Finland was doomed to defeat and capture. "We should be running headlong into a super-Beresina," I told this minister, "in the snows of the Great North."

While De Gaulle was pushing his strategic plan in the hope of being immediately promoted to the command of an expeditionary corps in Finland, General Weygand commanding the army in Syria, was assuring the Minister of War that with a few reinforcements and two hundred planes he could seize the Caucasus and "slice through Russia as if it were butter." It is fortunate for France that the proposals of these two generals to plunge France, already at war with Germany, into a war against Russia, were consigned to oblivion.

To be sure, De Gaulle's ideas changed abruptly when Germany attacked Russia. He made several speeches in London along much the same lines as Churchill's. But his anti-Russian sentiments cropped out again when he began to fear that Russian prestige might increase the prestige of the French Communists and interfere with his plans to seize power for himself. At the beginning of 1942 he assured the British that the Communists were gaining ground in France and there was danger of a Russianized France after victory. He therefore insisted that the Foreign Office give him more authority, more importance, in order to increase his prestige in France and, he said, to strengthen pro-British feeling there. His arguments evidently met with strong opposition, for on February 12, 1942, he wrote me a bitter letter saying:

The British and Americans, finding fault with a good bargain, are trying to keep France from rallying round us. One feels that plainly in Paris, in Lille, in Toulouse, as well as in Brazzaville and Beirut. As a result, the only sympathies that are gaining a hold on French minds are all in favor of the Russians. That looks bad for the future.

On February 16 he expressed the fear that German barbarism was only the first wave of Asiatic barbarism and that it would soon be followed by the Russian wave.

Those comments worried me intensely. I thought it strange to bring in the "Russian menace" against the background of the "German menace." In the prewar period the "Russian menace" had been the French Nazis' favorite slogan and the basic theme of Nazi propaganda throughout the world. In 1942 Russian armies were waging a titanic battle against the German hordes, a battle that was to smash the German drive, exhaust their strength and allow the Anglo-American armies to come forward in their turn. It was hardly fitting, therefore, for a French general to pose postwar problems on a pseudohistoric, pseudophilosophic, and fantastic plane that could not fail to interfere with the war spirit. The political problem which the growth of Russian power presented, though serious and certainly disturbing, had to be set aside until after victory.

But at the end of 1942 De Gaulle again switched his position, following the American occupation of North Africa. He forgot the menace of Moscow the better to assert his anti-Americanism. Besides, he was at that time making his first serious contacts with the forces of the French Resistance and learned of the important part the Communists were playing in the movement and the courage they were showing. A change of course therefore seemed essential. That change was the more marked because of the need to set himself up against General Giraud as "a man of the Left." He had to create for the use of Frenchmen and of democrats throughout the world, a simple crude medallion showing a General de Gaulle rallying the democratic and Communist forces against a General Giraud, the hope of Fascists and reactionaries. The former collaborator of the *Action Française* and the *Echo de Paris*, the author of *Au Fil de l'Epée* ("At the Point of the Sword"), which extols the idea of dictatorship, the leader of an organization of exiles dominated by Cagoulards, suddenly became the "red general," the friend of the Soviets. These tendencies became more pronounced in 1943 at the time of the marvelous and almost miraculous series of Russian victories. During the first months of his Algiers reign, De Gaulle, busy demolishing Giraud and building up his propaganda against the Americans, curried favor with the

Communists; seeing through his game, they granted their support "with a medicine dropper." He ordered his press to sing the praises of "dear and mighty Russia"—and chimed in himself.

In February, 1944, however, De Gaulle got wind of the coming offensive in France and had no difficulty in figuring out that in all probability Paris would not be freed by a Russian army, but by an American or British army. He therefore thought it advisable to shift his attack again. Through Massigli, his Commissioner for Foreign Affairs, he assigned to the deputy Viénot, whom he had made his ambassador to London, the job of manipulating the British by waving the Communist scarecrow in front of them. The general lines of his policy may be summed up as follows: The Americans and the British are prisoners of their doctrine of the right of peoples to self-determination. If, when they come to France, they apply their principles, who will have the best of it? The Communists who, without question, have the upper hand in Paris and in all the large cities at a time when the countryside is depopulated. Make it quite clear to the British that if the Communists win out, the immediate result will be to throw France into the Russian orbit. Remind them also of the experience in the war of 1914-18 when, after the downfall of Germany, Bavaria and Hungary fell into the hands of Communist dictators.

After the setback of the Teheran conference, the British government was fully prepared to listen to such language and fell into the trap of the once more anti-Communist and anti-Russian De Gaulle, now proclaiming himself the only person who could prevent France from falling prey to Bolshevism. That was the moment when the British government definitely changed its attitude towards De Gaulle and decided to bring him into France in General Montgomery's wagon-train.

Everything went off according to plan.

But no sooner had De Gaulle taken power in Paris than he began to perceive the difficulties the Communists held in store for him. These difficulties could not be overcome by a motorized division. He had to find other means. Social reforms of too revolutionary a nature would have encountered the bitter resistance of the notoriously conservative French middle classes. Too-drastic purges among the bourgeoisie, who were collectively responsible for "collaborationism," were impossible—for the reason that De Gaullism had welcomed the onslaught of the Vichyites with open arms. De Gaulle therefore conceived the idea of seeking a diversion in foreign policy and neutralizing the Communists by sealing the alliance they were hoping for with the Soviets.

Thus the anti-Russian of the Finnish war, the anti-Russian of 1942, the pro-Russian of 1943, the anti-Russian of the beginning of 1944, turned pro-Russian again in December, 1944, tricked the British and went off to sign the Moscow agreement.

Every Frenchman wanted an alliance with Russia, which had become the dominant power on the Continent. The European war had opened the eyes of the blindest. The fact that Russia is Communist has nothing to do with the needs of French security. And considerations of national interest must prevail over all ideological considerations and over all conceptions of social organization. But before concluding a twenty-year alliance with Russia, one should at least know what the situation in Europe is going to be and what position the Allied powers will take in the peace settlement.

Even the most passionate Russian sympathizers saw tremendous objections to the treaty signed in December, 1944. Here are the principal ones:

(1) At that time German defeat was already inevitable, and all the available forces of Russia and France were engaged in the final battle against Germany. The alliance therefore introduced no new element. It had no meaning, no immediate bearing.

(2) In so far as the Anglo-Saxons were planning to build European peace on the basis of collective security, special alliances conspicuously compromised in advance the chances of the Anglo-Saxon plan.

(3) On that account, the Franco-Russian alliance appeared to be much less an anti-German instrument than an anti-Anglo-Saxon instrument.

(4) The only power that can immediately come to the direct defense of the road to Paris when threatened by a Continental power is not Russia but Britain, making use of the port of Calais and hurling her air force to the aid of France.

(5) Since Russia is not a maritime power, she cannot defend French colonies. The whole De Gaullist policy based on the "primacy of the resurrection of the Empire" was belied by the priority given to the Russia alliance, especially when one considers that the Soviet doctrine is anti-imperialist and anticolonial.

(6) More than ever before, England needs an ally on the Continent. The policy that once led her to seek a *pied-à-terre* or a European ally in Hanover, then in Belgium (British creation in 1830), then in France (*Entente Cordiale* of 1905, alliance of 1914 and 1939), has become a vital necessity for the henceforth weakened Great Britain. If France were to alienate herself from Great Britain by a premature alliance with Russia, Great Britain might some day find herself obliged to seek a counterweight in Germany in order to remain true to her policy of having a Continental ally.

(7) The alliance signed with Russia was to run for twenty years. Now, no one had authorized General de Gaulle, the head of a provisional and illegal government, illegitimate and without democratic roots, to take on such an obligation.

A provisional French government, sincerely well-disposed to Russia and not merely motivated by petty considerations of domestic politics, would immediately have established relations of close friendship with Russia while waiting to conclude with her an alliance, within the framework of future peace treaties, corresponding to the realities of the new Europe emerging from the war. Instead a usurper's government acted hastily, incoherently, and within the unknown quantity of an unpredictable peace and a world in the process of formation, exposing the Russians to the possibility of a bitter disappointment—that of seeing the French people some day disavow a treaty concluded without its consent.

In sum, De Gaulle played the Russian game solely to get rid of his domestic difficulties with the French Communists. He was preoccupied with his own interests. He had lost sight of the interests of France.

The conflict between De Gaulle and the British government continued without interruption throughout the war; it ceased only at the time of the invasion of Normandy then flared up more furiously than ever with the Syrian incidents.

There is no doubt that Churchill disliked De Gaulle intensely. The strife between the two men was one of the permanent factors in the London diplomatic situation from 1940 to 1944. It was marked by violent conversations, exchanges of sharply worded notes, long-lasting ruptures of personal relations, maneuvers of all sorts, and by the anti-British propaganda of Free France. In London, Syria, Egypt, Equatorial Africa, Djibouti, and, to a lesser degree, in Algiers—where it sometimes pretended to be pro-British the better to play up its anti-Americanism—De Gaullism fairly wallowed in hatred for Britain. It would, however, be a mistake to attribute Churchill's sentiments towards De Gaulle to personal animosity, resulting from the inevitable difficulties that always crop up between public figures representing different interests. Churchill had many such inevitable difficulties—with the exiled governments in London, with the heads of Russia and America—but they were never the same as, nor even similar to, those he had with De Gaulle. Nor can one believe that the old conservative leader was shocked by the revolutionary spirit the De Gaullist movement flaunted during a certain period. For twenty years he had defended the Russian Alliance in the House of Commons. He was friendly to Stalin. During the war he supported Marshal Tito, the Jugoslav Communist leader, against a loyalist rival. But throughout the months and years before the liberation of France, he detested De Gaulle simply because he saw in him the adventurer out to build his political fortune on the adversities of his country, the doubtful ally on whom one could not depend for the task of liberation.

One of the most dramatic incidents of the tension between

Churchill and De Gaulle occurred in the summer of 1943, on the occasion of one of Churchill's visits to Washington.

During that time Churchill had urged on President Roosevelt the view that the liquidation of De Gaullism—a phenomenon clearly Fascist in character—had become necessary in order to clear the political atmosphere and get on with the war. He had even drawn up in his own handwriting a very important document which was to prepare public opinion in the Allied countries. The text of that document, however, never got to be fully known, nor was it ever officially handed to anyone—Churchill was restrained by the Foreign Office.

However, strangely enough, there were leaks in both London and Washington.

On July 12, 1943, a well-known correspondent, Ernest Lindley, published a sensational article in the Washington *Post,* in which he disclosed both Mr. Churchill's intentions and the existence of the document. Since that report created quite a stir and gave rise to a discussion in the House of Commons, we consider it necessary to reproduce it here in full:

Copies of a statement of British policy towards General de Gaulle have been placed in the hands of British and American officials in Washington. The statement was originally prepared, it is understood, to acquaint British officials and the British press with the views of the Prime Minister.

To weigh in full its significance, it is necessary to bear in mind that after the fall of France, the British government devoted itself .energetically to building up General de Gaulle. It invested millions of pounds sterling yearly in paying and supplying his armies and his administrative overhead. Except for small revenues from the colonies under Free French control, these were De' Gaulle's only financial resources. Moreover, it was the British broadcasts to France which made his name the symbol of resistance among his conquered countrymen.

The British stuck with De Gaulle through thick and thin, condoning his faults and mistakes. Some months ago the British government began to modify its policy towards De Gaulle. But this was interpreted in some quarters as a reluctant concession to the United States government, which had assumed primary responsibility for the Allied venture in French North Africa.

The British statement now at hand, it is felt here, destroys that hypothesis as well as several others advanced by De Gaulle's American and British supporters. Among its high points are these:

1. De Gaulle can no longer be considered a reliable friend of Britain. In spite of all that he owes to British assistance and support, he has left a "trail of Anglophobia" wherever he has been.

2. From August, 1941, on, he has tried to play Great Britain against the United States, and the United States against Great Britain.

3. He has striven to create friction between the British and French in Syria.

4. He clearly has "Fascist and dictatorial tendencies."

5. In spite of these grounds for complaint, the British government has treated De Gaulle fairly and recognizes the value which his name has come to have in France—chiefly through British publicity. It still hopes that he will cooperate loyally as co-president of the new French National Committee of Liberation. So far, however, he has struggled for complete mastery.

6. Peace and order and smooth communications in the French North African territory are essential to the great military operations now being prepared.* Likewise it is highly important to avoid throwing into turmoil the French forces which the United States is now arming.

This statement alludes to President Roosevelt's strong views on the subject, and to the need for taking care that the differences among the French are not allowed to affect British-American relations. But the reasons given for dissatisfaction with De Gaulle were based on British experience and observation.

In the Syrian difficulties, referred to in the statement, the United States has played no part. The Free French, with British military support, wrested Syria from the Vichyites in August, 1941, to forestall an Axis coup. The Free French assumed civilian and local military control. The British retained overall military control. Syria is an important base of the Middle East Command. Its stability is essential to the conduct of the war. But there, as in North Africa and elsewhere, De Gaulle, according to this statement, has sought to set the French against the British.

It is not difficult to arouse popular support among one's own people by playing up to their nationalist sentiments. This is De Gaulle's tactic, and it may be that it is winning some success. But it is not the way to wage

---

* This statement was written before the invasion of Sicily.

coalition warfare. The restoration of France depends on American and British arms: even the new French army in North Africa is being equipped with American arms.

The United States and Britain are not trying to foist a puppet on the French people. They have given their solemn pledge that the independence of France will be restored and that the French people will be given the opportunity to form a government of their own choosing. They do have a right to expect the full collaboration of patriotic Frenchmen in the vast military effort necessary to liberate France, if it is to be liberated.

But De Gaulle, it is felt in Washington and, as this statement shows, in London, is chiefly concerned with his own political power. He is behaving as an opponent of Britain and the United States, rather than as an ally.

The fact that a statement like the above could be openly published in Washington in July, 1943, is more eloquent than any commentary.

Seven days later, *Newsweek* came out with an extract of the famous Churchill document which contained the following:

De Gaulle owes everything he has to British support, yet he can't be considered a wholly reliable ally. He has "Fascist and dictatorial tendencies." At one moment, he poses as the sole barrier against Communism in France; at another, as a friend of the Communists. It is part of his strategy to gain prestige in France by showing how rough he can be with the British and Americans. As early as 1941 he began playing the French against the British and the British against the Americans.

Upon the publication of this material in America, the British press and Parliament were much perturbed. On July 21, 1943, Mr. Boothby, a Member of Parliament, asked the Prime Minister for an explanation. Churchill replied:

"I assume full responsibility for this document. I myself drew up the text. It is a confidential document. I am not ready to discuss it other than in secret meeting and only if such is the general desire of the House."

After that, there could be no doubt in England as to how Churchill felt about De Gaulle.

This raises a question: Was De Gaulle so ingenious that, though an exile without real authority, an illegal representative of a defeated and occupied country, he was able easily to get the better of both Churchill and Roosevelt?

Let us consider the matter.

Firstly, by gradually creating in London a New Power, an embryo of political power, in the tragic days of 1940, De Gaulle made sure, at the outset, of establishing a considerable lead over any eventual French rival. He had at his disposal not only a small army and a small navy, but a police force and, especially, a tremendous propaganda machine, the two most important cogs of which were the London and Brazzaville radio stations. Consequently, no other Frenchman, soldier or politician, coming before the Anglo-Saxons with empty hands could have a chance against him. He refused to rescue Georges Mandel and the prisoners of Vichy. He got rid of Admiral Muselier, Admiral Darlan, and General Giraud, in a trice. He would have disposed of President Lebrun, Herriot, Jeanneney, or any other possible rival.

The British and the Americans therefore found themselves confronted by a monopoly: De Gaulle was the only real French power in existence outside of France, a power around which an amazing combination of mysticism and morbid fanaticism had crystallized. To oppose him was in effect to oppose all there was of organized power in renascent France. And De Gaulle, well aware of this fact, took advantage of it to blackmail the Allies outrageously. It was as though he were saying to them, "I have founded a New Power. You will accept it and help me, or else I will set you at loggerheads with the France I represent, and I will make trouble in the Allied camp." A score of times De Gaulle threatened Churchill that he would demobilize the Free French Forces, withdraw to Brazzaville and declare his neutrality. And a score of times Churchill partially yielded to his demands—in order to avoid a huge scandal that would have weakened Allied morale and furnished rich material for German propaganda.

Another lucky element for De Gaulle was the support he gained in certain British and American circles hostile to Churchill and Roosevelt. By corruption, propaganda, methodical exploitation of the general ignorance concerning his personality and his actions, by making use of the strong sentimental impulses that were ready to crystallize around any French name at all, he kept up a continual agitation and intrigue in the two Anglo-Saxon countries, and in this way frequently managed to bring heavy pressure to bear on the decisions of the two statesmen.

The decisive factor, however, in De Gaulle's favor was, as noted above, the change in the attitude of the British Foreign Office and British Intelligence Service after the Teheran Conference. At Teheran the British became really alarmed at the multiplicity and complexity of the issues that arose between them and the Russians with respect to Persia, Jugoslavia, Greece, Poland. They saw the shadow of a gigantic Russia stretching over Asia and Europe. They had made war on Hitler to prevent him from ruling the Continent. Now, after so many superhuman efforts and sacrifices, they had come within sight of victory only to discover that Stalin might well become the unifier of Europe. Consequently, one solution flashed momentarily through their minds: to build hastily a powerful federation of western and Mediterranean nations within the zone of Anglo-Saxon influence.

Now, such a West European and Mediterranean federation, comprising Holland, Belgium, France, Spain, Italy, and Greece, could succeed only if France agreed to be its foundation. It followed that General de Gaulle, "made in England," might perhaps be the strong man, the ideal figure to realize the great enterprise.

Learning of the British attitude from M. Viénot, his representative in London, and from conversations with the Right Hon. Duff Cooper, De Gaulle was not slow to take advantage of it. He promptly dropped his anti-British political line and set his propaganda into motion. Through May, June and July, 1944, he became the apostle of the future Western European Federation. If we scan the African newspapers of that period and read the reports of the meetings of the Committee of Liberation and the speeches of the Consultative Assembly, we find the new De Gaullist doctrine amply presented:

> The countries of Western Europe are interdependent in danger, poverty and calamity. In the future they must closely unite to overcome these. France will be the rallying point of the future Western Federation.

Britain fell into the crude trap set for her.

The Foreign Office put heavy pressure on Churchill to change his attitude towards De Gaulle and to support him in Paris. Convinced or not, Churchill in his turn brought pressure on the White House to prevent the Americans from interfering directly with the British plan. The presidential election campaign was on and also the decisive battle of the war—the conquest of Normandy. Thus, busy with other matters, America yielded. And General de Gaulle was free to seize power in Paris.

Shortly after that, he was compelled by public opinion to invite Churchill and Eden to visit Paris. They were welcomed there on November 11, 1944, with wild enthusiasm. Churchill made an appeal to the French:

> Rally around the government of General de Gaulle. In the past I have sometimes disagreed with him. . . . I have forgotten those dissensions in the interest of France. . . . You, too, must forget your dissensions. . . . Follow your new leader. . . .

That same evening he had a conversation with De Gaulle. "It would be a good idea," he said to him, "if we were to draw up on paper, in practical form, all the plans and projects we have outlined these past days." De Gaulle replied evasively. Churchill pressed him for a reply. "I must study those plans more closely," said De Gaulle.

The next day he asked Stalin for an immediate audience in Moscow.

A few days later he set off in haste, and signed at the Kremlin a treaty of alliance to remain in force for twenty years—after having turned down the British offer to transform the Anglo-Russian alliance into a tripartite pact.

On his return to France, De Gaulle published, in his press, observations insulting to England:

The French government considers that alliance with Britain is much less urgent than alliance with Russia, and all the more so because there are still many problems to be settled between France and England.

A little while later the events that occurred in Syria provoked a new explosion of anti-British fury. In order to conceal from the French, who ignored them completely, the faults committed by the De Gaullists, in the Middle East, between 1941 and 1943—faults whose evil consequences were suddenly being brought to light—official propaganda sources kindled a hatred of England.

The gulf between the two countries was deeper then than it had been even during the days of the Vichy regime, until there occurred an event of considerable importance: the Socialist elections in England.

General de Gaulle was quick to discover that the mass of French workers was no longer attracted by Moscow alone. Given a choice between Red Russia and Communism on the one hand, and Red England and Socialism on the other, they might now be expected to swing over in greater numbers to England.

Consequently, the general began another hurried about-face. He sent his Minister for Foreign Affairs to London, and informed the London *Times,* during the course of a well-publicized interview, that he was about ready to fall in love with England.

De Gaulle's differences with Churchill were, however, less serious than those with President Roosevelt. The President's reluctance to recognize him as the head of the government of France without the consent of the French people is well known.

Now, the American government's attitude was dictated in the first place by its firmest diplomatic tradition, a tradition that dates back to Jefferson's letter to Morris, his minister in Paris, when the latter was completely bewildered by the revolutionary course of events developing in France in 1793: "It is our principle to recognize any government which is formed by the clearly expressed will of the people."

The revolutions which broke out later in all the countries of Central and South America confronted the United States with many difficult problems of recognition. Each time, it remained faithful to the Jeffersonian principle. And in a letter sent by the State Department on May 16, 1936, to Representative Tinkham on the subject of the recognition of an illegal government in Paraguay, American policy was defined as follows:

It is the practice of the United States to defer any recognition of an executive government until that government controls the machinery of State; until it governs by consent of the people and without substantial resistance to its authority; and finally until it is in position to fulfill all obligations and responsibilities incumbent on a sovereign state, as provided for by treaties and international law.

Now, one could not say that De Gaulle was governing by "consent of the people," nor that he "controlled the machinery of State," nor that he was in a position "to fulfill the obligations and responsibilities incumbent on a sovereign." Nor was his case similar to those of the "legitimate governments" of other occupied countries established in London, like Holland, Greece, Jugoslavia, and Norway, who were represented by their monarchs; or Belgium, Czechoslovakia and Poland, represented by regular, constitutional powers.

However, De Gaulle did not understand—or did not wish to understand—that America, often confronted with irregular regimes in Latin America, could not reverse its diplomatic practice without creating a precedent dangerous to its own interests. Especially did he not understand—or did not wish to understand—that being still neutral in 1940, the United States had to remain lined up with all the other neutral countries with regard to the Vichy government. Soviet Russia, the Vatican, Sweden, Argentina, Brazil, and even China were recognizing Vichy at that time. Great Britain—the only power then at war with Germany—maintained secret relations with Vichy, notably through M. Dupuy, the Canadian representative, who shuttled back and forth between London and the unoccupied zone in France. There were plenty of practical reasons for this. To pursue an anti-Vichy policy too sharply might perhaps have ended in giving Laval the excuse he needed to hurl the French fleet against the Allies. A too-sharp anti-Vichy policy would have deprived America of her best diplomatic observation post in Europe just when she was feverishly preparing for inevitable war, and would have cut her off entirely from the mass of the French people, at the very time when she felt the need to win their support and weaken the German stranglehold.

Roosevelt, therefore, allowed De Gaulle to come in on lend-lease, agreed to arm and feed the Free French in collaboration with Britain, resigned himself to receiving the general's so-called diplomatic agents—among others the incredible "ambassador," Adrien Tixier, with whom he was surprisingly patient—but he refused to recognize the London Committee of Liberation as a political organism.

In reply—tragicomic as it may seem—General de Gaulle refused to recognize President Roosevelt. From 1940 to 1943, he did not go to Washington to see him. Not till after his landing in France in July, 1944, did he resign himself to crossing the Atlantic. Representatives of occupied and conquered countries were flocking to Washington. The Queen of Holland and her daughter, Princess Juliana, the Kings of Norway, Greece, and Jugoslavia, the Grand Duchess of Luxembourg, the Presidents of the Polish and the Czechoslovak Republics, the Belgian Prime Minister—all were guests, at least once, at the White House. De Gaulle did not put in an appearance. The Americans informed him a dozen times that they would be glad to welcome him. An Assistant Secretary of State authorized me to forward the official invitation of the American government to him myself. De Gaulle declined haughtily. He demanded that he be recognized and received as a chief of state. My beseeching letters were either not answered at all, or he replied in substance that America had committed grave wrongs against him.

When the Committee of Liberation moved from London to Algiers, the conflict with America grew even more bitter. Roosevelt recognized the De Gaulle committee, but only as a body administering the liberated French colonial territories. The official American text read:

> In view of the paramount importance of the common war effort, the relationship with the French Committee of National Liberation must continue to be subject to the military requirements of the Allied commanders.
>
> On these understandings the Government of the United States recognizes the French Committee of National Liberation as administering those French overseas territories which acknowledge its authority.
>
> This statement does not constitute recognition of a government of France, or of the French Empire by the government of the United States. It does constitute recognition of the French Committee of National Liberation as functioning within specific limitations during the war. Later on the people of France, in a free and untrammeled manner, will proceed in due course to select their own government and their own officials to administer them.

On a point of capital importance—namely, the attitude of the United States toward the Committee from the moment when the Allied armies would enter France, the American text said:

> The Government of the United States desires again to make clear its purpose of co-operating with all patriotic Frenchmen, looking to the liberation of the French people and French territory from the oppressions of the enemy. . . .

These last lines clearly indicate the intention to co-operate with all French patriots, including non-De Gaullists—which was perfectly sound and strictly in accordance with the principles of the Atlantic Charter and with American ideals.

Never can Frenchmen be sufficiently grateful to President Roosevelt for showing—in spite of the avalanche of attacks to which he was subjected—how much he respected the rights of the French people who could not speak for themselves, how anxious he was to prevent, in so far as lay in his power, the creation of a state of affairs which would end, on the day of liberation, by putting them completely under the heel of a dictator.

In any event, De Gaulle's hatred for Roosevelt and for America was not brought about solely by the hardships he encountered in obtaining recognition as head of the French government. Had that been the case, that animosity would have ceased automatically the day when, having overcome all difficulties and surmounted all obstacles, he reached his goal in Paris.

The anti-Americanism of De Gaullism is the result of a poison cleverly injected, from the beginning of the movement, by German agents and particularly by the Cagoulards around De Gaulle. It is the natural, instinctive, and violent reaction of a movement inspired by a Fascist ideology and corrupted by personal ambition against the country which headed the anti-German coalition and quickened it with the democratic philosophy. It is one of the forms of the mental sickness from which France and the rest of Europe suffered in the revolutionary era that culminated in the war; of a dark madness marked by amazing, complicated outbursts which, at certain moments, led every country to hate its natural allies, its benefactors and saviors, while granting its indulgence to, and pinning its hopes on its hangmen and assassins.

Throughout the war, as we have already seen, De Gaullist propaganda—in the press, in leaflets, and by word of mouth—was bitter against America, against President Roosevelt, against General Eisenhower, taking advantage of every pretext, every deceptive appearance, every susceptibility of saddened and anguished French minds.

Far from slowing down anti-American propaganda, the landing of the Americans in France, their victories, the freeing of Paris, the magnanimity with which they promptly allowed full liberty to a government they knew to be unlawful, Fascist, and deeply hostile to them, furnished the De Gaullists with new material. That the Americans were sometimes clumsy and even made mistakes in their contacts with the French, no one can dream of denying. But those clumsy gestures and mistakes, so pardonable, so insignificant by contrast with the gigantic act of liberation, were used against them by the De Gaullists treacherously and in bad faith, and also with incomparable psychological skill.

Let us look at dispatches of the Associated Press, the United Press, and American newspaper correspondents after Normandy had been freed. Let us look at the French newspapers. Let us look at facts. They eloquently tell the story and reveal the diversity of that formidable anti-American campaign.

On July 5, 1944, De Gaulle attacked the invasion currency the Americans had introduced into France.

On August 10, we have the De Gaullists' accusation that America was going to cause inflation in France. On August 27, Henry Morgenthau, Jr., Secretary of the Treasury, said:

The French who were concerned that the arrival of American troops might cause inflation, are now complaining that they are not spending enough money.

On September 18, the De Gaullists demonstrated because the French had not been invited to the Quebec conference.

On October 6 M. Bidault, Minister for Foreign Affairs, declared to the press: "I haven't the slightest doubt that President Roosevelt is a true friend of France. But . . ." And Anne O'Hare McCormick stressed that: "M. Bidault diplomatically left the sentence unfinished."

On October 9 Callender reported in the New York *Times* that one of De Gaulle's close associates had delivered a diatribe against Roosevelt.

On October 14, at the very moment when he was making repeated appeals to America for arms, ammunition, foodstuffs, pharmaceutical products, chemical fertilizer, and all sorts of supplies, De Gaulle declared that the French must depend on themselves and "not on the benevolence of others." The Associated Press noted that his speech had been bitter.

On October 15 the arrival in Paris of the American ambassador to France, Jefferson McCaffery, let loose a campaign in the French press for a "juster comprehension of the needs of France."

On October 17 the Paris paper *Franc-Tireur* accused the Americans of treating German prisoners too well. That was the beginning of a perfidious attack which was to continue for months.

On October 21 the De Gaullists were in a rage because, they said, General Holmes had announced a plan for the occupation of Germany without informing them.

At his press conference on October 25 De Gaulle accused the Allies of delay in arming the French. He declared that the enormous needs of the Allied armies explained that delay only "to a certain extent." A correspondent asked him what those words "to a certain extent" meant. He replied that there were other reasons and hinted at Roosevelt's ill will.

On October 27 American correspondents reported the Allies' astonishment at the disagreeable tone of De Gaulle's speech delivered the day after he had been officially recognized by the American government.

On November 4 a dispatch announced the arrival in Paris of a French politician who had been on a trip to the colonies. "Will America return North Africa and West Africa?" he asked bluntly. Callender wired that America's alleged designs on the French Empire formed one of the points of propaganda common to Vichyites and De Gaullists alike.

On November 26 came a new wave of propaganda on the good treatment the Americans were giving German prisoners, who were getting cigarettes and orange juice. American authorities in Paris felt obliged to explain that America was fighting for the upholding of international agreements and that she followed the Geneva convention, although she had learned that her own prisoners were tortured by the Germans. The French press refused to accept this explanation. The De Gaullist deputy Jacques Debu-Bridel brought up the matter in the Consultative Assembly.

On December 19 De Gaulle gave out the results of a so-called poll conducted by the "French Institute of Public Opinion." That poll showed that 53 per cent of the French considered the attitude of Americans in France unsatisfactory, that 33 per cent found it satisfactory, that 14 per cent had no opinion. That outrageous release—which the German press rapturously reprinted—appeared at the very moment when Americans were being killed by the thousands on the road to Paris, in the last great push of the Germans against France.

Regarding this new German offensive, the whispering campaign in France ran as follows: "The Germans attacked the Americans after having made a deal with them. The 'boys' have had enough of war and want to go home. They will accept defeat to prove that they cannot win this war and that they ought to go home." On January 5 Marc Blancpain, a radio commentator, was moved to protest in *Le Parisien Libéré* about the whispering campaign directed against the Americans.

But on January 17 De Gaulle made a radio speech in which he denounced "imprudent ideas as to German means of resisting the Allies" and blamed part of France's sufferings on the mistaken judgment of the Allies. Callender sent a wireless to the New York *Times:*

> This apparently unrelieved resentment towards the Allies on the part of General de Gaulle is reflected among his official associates and spreads, aided by his speeches, among the French population.

On January 26 the De Gaullist paper *Combat* complained that the Americans were punishing too severely soldiers who dealt on the Black Market. Earlier the newspapers had complained that the Americans were tolerating the exploitation of the French through their Black Market.

On February 7 the De Gaullist newspaper *L'Ordre* declared that the State Department had continually deceived President Roosevelt and the American people on the situation in France. It attacked Roosevelt's two confidential advisors, Admiral Leahy and Robert Murphy.

On February 11, the De Gaullist paper *L'Aube* published an article by a Mr. Schumann accusing the State Department of being hostile to De Gaulle's advanced social reforms.

On February 12 American correspondents in Paris pointed out that General Eisenhower's message congratulating the French Army on the liberation of Colmar had been suppressed by the French censor.

On February 15 the De Gaullist minister Paul Ramadier, yielding to the demand of the American and British embassies in Paris, denied the whispering campaign in France according to which the Americans and the British requisitioned French butter and shipped it to their own countries. American newspapermen in Paris considered that this incident threw a revealing light on propaganda "made in France."

The next day the De Gaullist paper in Toulouse, *Le Patriote,* wrote: "We had more to eat when the Germans were here." On February 18 representatives of the American government in Paris issued official figures to the French press on American deliveries to France of locomotives, trucks and freight. American correspondents reported, however, that only five out of twenty-four Paris newspapers published them.

On February 21 the ultra-De Gaullist papers *La Monde* and *Le Figaro* attacked the American press, accusing it of indiscretions in connection with French affairs.

On March 14 De Gaulle made a speech in which he accused the Allies of failing to help the French effort in Indo-China: "It is not the fault of France," he said, "if the plans for Indo-China which she has been preparing for so long do not coincide with those of the Allies." On March 20 he complained to the Consultative Assembly that his suggestions to parachute help to the French fighting in Laos had not been heeded. On the 21st *L'Aurore* declared that the United States had supported against France Chinese demands on Indo-China.

On March 24 American correspondents reported that there were rumors in France to the effect that the Americans were giving twice as much meat to the Germans on the left bank of the Rhine as the French were receiving.

On March 27 the deputy Lapie announced in the Consultative

Assembly that the Americans intended to seize New Caledonia. Far from giving Lapie the lie, Bidault, Minister for Foreign Affairs, supported his attacks by declaring that France would never yield an inch of territory. On March 28 Harold Callender wrote that De Gaulle was making no effort to allay the suspicions being aroused among the French.

On the same day, March 28, a wireless to the New York *Times* reported that the French were annoyed because the American Army was occupying too many hotels in Paris.

On April 4 anti-American rumors in Paris spread the news that the Americans were requisitioning as much food as the Germans had. Upon protest from the United States embassy, the government agreed to issue a denial.

On April 11 the newspaper *Combat* discovered that the Americans "were just beginning" to ration meat, and demanded that the liberated French people be given the right to eat the crumbs that fell from American tables.

On April 16 Philippe Barrès—who used to praise the work of Hitler in *Le Matin,* and was now De Gaulle's enthusiastic biographer—hinted in *Paris-Presse* that the arrest of von Papen, in Germany, had been arranged by Anglo-American financial groups.

On April 23 Adrien Tixier, Minister of the Interior, refused the Paris City Council the right to hold a special session to commemorate the death of President Roosevelt.

This recital of facts known to all Frenchmen, since they occurred after the liberation, gives a quite incomplete impression of the character of De Gaullist propaganda. It fails in particular to mention such prominent subjects of controversy as the peace plans, the Dumbarton Oaks Conference, the Yalta Conference, the San Francisco Conference, De Gaulle's incessant and often childish claims regarding France's place among the Great Powers, and the quarrels that sprang up when Stuttgart, Ulm, Frankfort, Cologne, and Coblenz were occupied. But it does throw some light on the clever, systematic, all-embracing, totalitarian technique of De Gaullism and its anti-Americanism.

The high point of that propaganda—alas, often effective—was reached when General de Gaulle refused to meet President Roosevelt on French territory, when the President, sick, fighting off death, stopped in Algiers on his way home from the Crimea. This insult to the Commander in Chief of the liberating army was an insult to the entire American Army; this insult to the leader recently elected by the people of the United States was an insult to the American people as a whole. Nobody but a brutal soldier could have been guilty of an act so contrary to France's tradition of chivalry and courtesy, to the deep feeling of gratitude France will always have for America, and also to the interests of France, which for long and difficult years to come must depend on American aid, generosity, and friendship.

It is fortunate, for the sake of historic clarity, that relations between Franklin Delano Roosevelt, one of the greatest citizens of humanity, and Charles de Gaulle were brought to a close by this act of amazing ingratitude.

However, the insult to President Roosevelt was followed by an abrupt switch in De Gaullist foreign policy. In August, 1945, to the amazement of international diplomatic circles, De Gaulle paid a visit to President Truman and set about extolling the Franco-American alliance, to which he had for so long been obstinately opposed. He placed a wreath on the tomb of President Roosevelt at Hyde Park, and calmly declared to Mrs. Roosevelt:

"I have always had the greatest admiration for your husband."

When American newspapermen spoke to him about the anti-Americanism of the French press, he replied by placing the responsibility upon those of his countrymen to whom he had always supplied the directives and materials for anti-American propaganda.

"Don't be too hard on the French journalists," he said. "Most of them are young and completely lacking in political experience."

Actually, the motives for De Gaulle's provisional quick change with regard to America were:

(1) To try to wipe out the bad impression made on the French public by the gross insult to President Roosevelt.

(2) To cover up the crying failure of a foreign policy that had resulted in the total isolation of France. (The Russians had not supported any of the French demands at San Francisco. When the uprising occurred in Syria and Lebanon, De Gaulle tried to avoid his own responsibility by blaming the British.)

(3) To win a diplomatic victory, or at least the appearance of one, on the eve of the French elections in October, and to present this victory to the French people as a reinforcement of his electoral campaign.

(4) To neutralize American public opinion while proceeding with those elections in a form that was arousing strong protest from all French political parties.

Once again the foreign policy of France was made to serve the special interests of General de Gaulle.

15. The De Gaullist Doctrine

The doctrine of tyrants is dictated by their stomachs.
VICTOR HUGO

THERE is no De Gaullist doctrine.

By turns, General de Gaulle has appeared as the hero of the fight to the finish and the destroyer of the army; as the savior of the Third Republic and the grave-digger of the Third Republic; as the hope of the Leftists and the hope of the reactionaries; as the leader of a great social revolution and the leader of the conservatives; as the representative of the Resistance and the "breaker" of the Resistance; as the implacable enemy of Vichy and the continuator, in many respects, of Marshal Pétain; as the opponent, and then the friend of, the Russians, the Americans, the British.

It was as if one were watching, transferred to the stage of public affairs, that clever artist, Frégoli, who for nearly half a century drew wondering audiences to the circuses of France and all Europe by the lightning speed with which he changed into altogether different disguises.

De Gaulle, however, is trying to create a touchy and suspicious neo-nationalism. He poses as a super-patriot. He preaches a doctrine which saddened and humiliated Frenchmen like to hear. He maintains that France, defeated, broken, ruined, without an army or navy, her population decimated, her factories destroyed, her towns a mass of rubble, has in no wise lost her position as a great power. He forgets too easily that France must first become a great

236

moral power and also a great power of the mind, bringing ideas, plans, systems and enlightenment to a world which has gone adrift. But De Gaullism has offered nothing, proposed nothing. In exile it wallowed in intrigue and represented the total absence of French genius.

Dictators need excitement, diversions, constant demands, in order to turn dissatisfaction aside and canalize it. When they cannot achieve real glory, they must have sham glory. The drive to win laurels, real or illusory, is the tragic fatality of their destiny—it led Napoleon I into his mad ride to Moscow, Napoleon III toward the distant shores of Mexico, Mussolini to the depths of savage Ethiopia, Hitler to the foot of the Caucasus mountains. General de Gaulle is forced to limit his ambitions, for romantic and glorious adventures are not within his reach. He is the leader of a poor, exhausted country struggling back from the edge of the grave. He governs a people that has turned into a phantom of hunger and misery. He reigns over ruins and devastation. He must therefore confine himself to gestures in the diplomatic wings. To build his reputation as the defender of "French sovereignty" he can only indulge in insults and defiance hurled at London and Washington.

As a super-nationalistic movement, De Gaullism has oriented itself in opposition to all modern solutions, in a direction which is in reverse to the evolution of the world. The future belongs to economic, social and political solidarity. The future belongs to internationalism. The astounding revolution that is upsetting the entire globe is determined by the development of science, which is radically transforming the way of life of individuals, nations and continents, and the relations between them. Nations can no longer draw back into themselves when radio broadcasts of other nations cross their frontiers and bring them all through the day currents of ideas from all over the world. The laws governing the relations of neighbors cannot overlook the possibilities presented by the tank, amphibious craft, planes traveling at 500 miles an hour, and the devastating robot, to say nothing of the atomic bomb, which opens up such revolutionary perspectives with regard to the intercourse among nations that our imaginations cannot yet grasp them. Countries lacking oil, rubber, nickel, must depend upon the countries that have those products, indispensable to life in present-day civilization. Natural obstacles have ceased to exist. Distances have vanished. The world is shrinking day by day. Civilizations are becoming more and more intermingled. The races are no longer separated by oceans, deserts, mountains. At the same instant, the war has introduced modern armies among the cannibals of New Guinea, the Eskimos of Greenland, and the Europeans. It has brought all these people into contact with the same bombs, the same machines of death, and also the same machines of progress. It has confronted them with a common future. One feels that one is dreaming when, in the midst of the din of these transformations that are destroying the past, fossil voices continue to propound outdated theories and to claim rights which the march of events has canceled. The revival of the nationalism of a Charles Maurras, a Léon Daudet, or a Pierre Taittinger, the men who opened the way to fascism in France, is an insult to the intelligence. And one feels defenseless when, upon the ruins and vast poverty of the defeat, the isolationism of De Gaulle cries out to France that "she must rely only upon herself for her recovery."

It was clear that, the day after victory, France would have to choose between communism, socialism and democracy.

We have seen that De Gaullism rambled around without making a choice.

On the other hand, it was equally clear that, after victory, France would have to decide between joining an Anglo-Saxon bloc or a Russian bloc, at least during the transition to an internationalized world, and for the long period that France will remain a second-class power.

Obviously, an honest man with France's interest at heart might hesitate. There are arguments for and against both policies—both have their attractions and their fearful risks. France belongs to the Eurasian continent, but she also belongs to the Mediterranean-

Atlantic world. If she dissolves into the Russian mass, she becomes a small province within a vast empire; she loses her physiognomy, her intellectual and political independence, her historical characteristics. If she amalgamates with the Anglo-Saxon world, she runs an even greater danger of becoming the battlefield between England and Russia. One path leads her into the Soviet Union where she will always feel herself to be a stranger and, moreover, reduced to a standard of living far below that to which her workers and her peasants have been accustomed for centuries. Britain and America offer her a place in another commonwealth—in it the natural isolationism of these two countries will always be a source of instability but, on the other hand, the living conditions, comfort and the well-being of the masses are much superior, and there is greater harmony of intellect and culture. Furthermore, France, like Britain, is a colonial power. And on that ground she is bound up with the Anglo-Saxon maritime powers, as are Belgium, Holland, Spain, Portugal, and Italy.

Hence, it was probably difficult to choose, since politics is but the investigation of the greater or lesser evil. The most patriotic Frenchman might turn in all good faith toward communism and toward Russia. But he might also, in equal good faith, turn toward democracy and the Anglo-Saxon powers.

Now, General de Gaulle has gone neither to the one side nor the other. Despite his uncertain and confused shiftings in accordance with circumstances and his momentary interests, he has distinctly avoided both combinations. To each he has displayed defiance, disdain, fear, hatred.

To be able to follow unhampered so fantastic and extravagant a line of domestic and foreign policy, one so contrary to the obvious interests of France, De Gaulle had to surround himself with complacent and gullible people. The beginning of this book told how he managed to create such a group in London. Later he took them to Algiers, then from Algiers to Paris. When he seized power, upon the liberation of France, he provoked a confusion favorable to his plans. In the Ministry of the Interior—to which should have been appointed men who had lived in France during the occupation and who knew the problems of the country and all the details of the tragic situation in which the Germans had left it—he placed completely uninformed exiles. Adrien Tixier became Minister of the Interior, and M. Pelabon, a confidant of the Cagoulard Passy, was made Chief of Police. On the other hand, a man was needed at the Quai d'Orsay who had lived in exile in Moscow, London, or Washington and had been in contact with world realities; here De Gaulle placed Georges Bidault, one who had spent four years in the catacombs of the underground. In sum, a man from inside France was put in charge of foreign affairs, while a man from outside the country was given control of internal matters. As a result there were blind men in every post.

But that monstrous confusion was not enough. De Gaulle undertook to destroy the diplomatic cadres. To the embassy in Washington he sent a gentle professor, Henri Bonnet. At Rio de Janeiro he installed General d'Astier de la Vigerie. To Moscow, where he should have had a young, well-trained diplomat, capable of penetrating the mysteries of the Kremlin, he promoted ageing General Catroux. General Petchkoff, a White Russian, went to China. And to Rome he dispatched the philosopher Maritain, who came down from the clouds for the occasion. Every one of these was elevated to an ambassadorship—and that in a time of international turmoil, when France needed not amateurs but well-tried Talleyrands to represent her abroad.

The San Francisco Conference brought to light the tragedy of French diplomatic incoherence. Since General de Gaulle had insisted that France be treated as one of the Great Powers, the Allies named her an "Inviting Power." But once appointed an "Inviting Power," France refused to invite anyone and did not join the Big Four. That was the moment when the small powers thought that France might perhaps become their leader. De Gaulle discovered, however, that to accept this role was to acknowledge the secondary status of France. He therefore declined. The result was that France was neither a "great" power nor a small power. She remained isolated and silent.

Moreover, her delegation contributed not the shadow of a constructive idea.

To justify De Gaullism, the movement has been depicted as the embodiment of all the anti-German feelings of the French. But that image is too simple. We may say that, on the contrary, it often acted in a manner that could not fail to please the Germans.

As a particularly disturbing instance, we might mention De Gaulle's reaction when Churchill and Lord Vansittart, supported by Americans like Secretary Morgenthau, undertook to influence international public opinion in favor of a ruthless punishment and dismemberment of Germany.

Such a suggestion was of incalculable value to France, for it allowed the question of the left bank of the Rhine to be raised.

What did General de Gaulle do?

He came out openly as an adversary of the dismemberment of Germany. He first expressed his views in London during private conversations in diplomatic circles. Then, all at once he described his attitude in an interview with Drew Middleton—which was widely publicized. On July 21, 1943, Middleton wired the New York *Times* a summary of their long conversation:

As for post-war problems, General de Gaulle declares that it is obviously impossible to destroy Germany and that it is "too late" to break it up and recreate the small states as they existed before Bismarck united them in the German Empire. "There will always be Prussia, the heart of Germany," he said, "and the other provinces have become accustomed to unity."

This statement caused surprise, commotion, and distress in Allied political circles. With the exception of a few well-informed individuals, everyone still thought of De Gaulle as the champion not only of a fight to the finish against Germany but of punishment to the finish. And yet, at the moment when the Allied Powers were beginning to catch the first faint gleams of the dawn of victory on the distant horizon, General de Gaulle suddenly formulated the discouraging theory that Germany could never be destroyed, that the victory could never be a total one; and he presented it unexpectedly in the terms of a statement of historical fact, without expressing the slightest regret, as if he himself acquiesced in what he claimed to be inevitable.

I had no sooner seen the text of that interview than I sent General de Gaulle a cable in which I said:

AS A MEMBER OF THE COMMITTEE ON FOREIGN AFFAIRS OF THE CHAMBER OF DEPUTIES, I WAS DEEPLY PERTURBED BY YOUR INTERVIEW WITH MR. MIDDLETON, PUBLISHED IN THE TIMES OF JULY 21. IN IT YOU COME OUT FRANKLY AGAINST DISMEMBERMENT OF GERMANY AND YOU STATE THAT PRUSSIAN HEGEMONY IS AN ACCOMPLISHED FACT. I TRUST THAT THIS IS AN ERROR ON THE PART OF THE AMERICAN CORRESPONDENT. PLEASE SEND YOUR OFFICIAL DENIAL AS QUICKLY AS POSSIBLE. IN MAKING THIS URGENT DEMAND, I AM CONFIDENT THAT I AM EXPRESSING THE UNANIMOUS VIEW OF THE MARTYRED FRENCH PEOPLE.

No confirmation or denial ever arrived. There is no doubt that the foreign service in Algiers and his mission in Washington informed De Gaulle of the excitement aroused by his interview. In addition, I published it in *Pour la Victoire,* hoping to force him, by my insistence, to counteract the impression he had created. Nothing had any effect. He could not deny the views he had expressed so often before so many Frenchmen and so many foreigners.

This defense by De Gaulle of Prussian rights and German unity, made against England at a moment when Prussia was occupying and torturing France, deeply colored the policy of De Gaullism in exile. In London, in New York, the New York *Times* interview immediately became an article of faith for the party. Always on the lookout for their master's line, the De Gaullists suddenly discovered that they were partisans of German unity against the wicked British and the wicked Americans, whose "unconditional surrender" concealed an abominable plot to carve up Germany. De Gaullist thinking and propaganda never came closer to Vichy propaganda than at this moment.

The amazing thing is that it even spread for a time to the ranks of certain heroes of the Resistance. Magnificent De Gaullists, who had come out of the *maquis,* their hands bloody and their guns still smoking, adopted the same point of view almost instantly. The most extraordinary example is General de Gaulle's own Foreign Minister, Georges Bidault, a splendid fighter of the Paris Resistance. Loyal disciple of his master, he used almost exactly the same words to express the same ideas, and he chose the same vehicle to broadcast them to the world. He, too, gave an interview to the New York *Times,* on November 11, 1944. John McCormack interviewed him and furnished us with what amounted to a slightly amplified version of the general's conversation with Drew Middleton.

General de Gaulle says that he favors neither any "artificial" dismemberment of Germany nor French participation in any exclusive Western European agreement. "There must be a Germany," he said. "Not an enslaved Germany. . . . The peace with Germany should not be one of vengeance; it must be just and human. Germany will have to be controlled for years to come but I am not for trying to make her harmless by dismembering her artificially. . . . We do not want any German minority within our borders. Our greatest interest lies in the control of the Rhineland because it represents our very own frontier. International control has been suggested. We would not object to that, but there are different kinds of international control and, if such are set up, France, as a direct neighbor, ought perhaps to have a privileged position in this control. . . .

"I do not believe it would do any good to convert Germany into an agricultural country."

Why make this amazing statement? Why make it to America? Why feed the pro-German propaganda of German refugees and pro-Germans in America? Why protest against the dismemberment of Germany at a time when the British and the Russians were accepting the principle of it? Why miss a historic opportunity, a solemn opportunity—which was appearing only for the second time since the treaties of 1815—to assert France's right to her natural borders, as Clémenceau and Foch had done in vain in 1918? Why burden France with the job of protecting German industry—this is the real meaning of the phrase referring to an agricultural Germany—when German industry, geared to war production, was the

gang! The Cagoulards belonged for the most part to the upper middle class. Many had attended the leading schools. They were engineers, financiers, executives, technicians, men who were qualified for leadership. One could hand over to them the operation of a revolutionary political machine intended to take hold some day of the administration of the French State. Thus, bit by bit, an alliance, no doubt regarded by De Gaulle as a temporary one, was formed for the seizure of the New Power.

There is still a third hypothesis. People began to wonder—the British in particular—whether the Cagoulards' hold over De Gaulle might not be ascribed to the fact that he had formerly more or less compromised himself with them, in all sincerity, because of hatred for democratic institutions and the fear of communism.

There is no doubt that, before the war, De Gaulle held antirepublican views that invariably tended toward a romantic conception of dictatorship. His writings of that period contain odds and ends of political musings which show hopes, inclinations, and, above all, exalted ambitions hardly to be expected in a French officer. In his book *Au Fil de l'Epée* there are significant statements like these:

Confronted by the issue, man embraces action with the pride of a master, for if he enters into it, he takes possession of it.

Prestige is not a matter of virtue, and evangelical perfection does not lead to Empire. The man of action is scarcely conceivable without a strong dose of egoism, pride, hardness, cunning. But he is forgiven all that, and it even adds to his stature, if he uses it as the means to accomplish great things.

At the same time that he was setting down ideas that seem uncomfortably like a germ of the theory of *Mein Kampf*, De Gaulle was taking a strange delight in political intrigue. Between 1933 and 1939 he established contacts with newspapermen, deputies, politicians. I myself made his acquaintance in the corridors of the *Echo de Paris*. He ran after ministers and members of parliament and offered to do odd jobs for them in connection with their military interpellations and debates. He knew Paul Reynaud—gave him the idea for a pamphlet and so prepared the way for his future career. He frequented the *Action Française,* which swarmed with Cagoulards. It is well known that at that time he was close friends with Marshal Pétain and that he hung about the lobbies of the Boulevard des Invalides.* Now it was precisely in Pétain's circle of acquaintances that the Cagoulards installed the center of their military setup, and it seems highly probable that De Gaulle fell into a cleverly prepared trap—a trap which may have been set by the Germans themselves. For their treachery succeeded in ensnaring so many good men.

The last book that De Gaulle published before the war—*Vers l'Armée de Métier* ("Towards a Professional Army")—was widely circulated in Germany, in a German translation. This technical work, written by an officer who was practically unknown, was at that time completely ignored by the French public. We can understand that German military circles would be interested in analyzing and studying it, but it is less easy to see why Nazi political circles should have found it useful to circulate the book among the German public. Apparently, Herr Abetz's propaganda services took charge of De Gaulle's book, for the translation and publication were announced by the *Revue France-Allemagne,* edited by Count de Brinon, and printed by Herr Abetz on his press in Karlsruhe. This announcement was made at a time when it was public knowledge that the German propaganda services were trying to win over many French writers and intellectuals by offering them contracts for the translation of their works. Henri Bordeaux, Georges Suarez, Count de Brinon, Paul Ferdonnet, Doriot, Abel Bonnard, Louis Bertrand —all figured on the list in question, along with the name of Charles de Gaulle and various good Frenchmen whom the Germans were seeking to compromise and involve in a mechanism of whose existence they had no idea.

Yet the facts above are bewildering. It has often been said that De Gaulle should never have presented his military theories to the French public at a time when Europe was filled with rumors of war,

---

* Headquarters of the French General Staff.

but that these theories should have been kept restricted to military and government circles. That is an open question. But a French officer who believed that he held the secret of future strategy and victory should certainly not have agreed to circulate it to the Nazi public.

Once the mistake had been made, under conditions which are but dimly discernible, the "dark forces" had the means with which to blackmail General de Gaulle. And that can explain a great deal.

16. Conclusion

THIS book is the fourth of a series.

In 1936 I published *Français, voici la Guerre!* ("Frenchmen, Here Is the War!")—a cry of alarm. I implored the French to prepare morally and materially for the inevitable war and to strengthen their natural alliance with Britain and Russia.

In 1938, after the abominable Munich Pact, I issued a new, more urgent and more beseeching appeal. That book was called *Laisserons nous démembrer la France?* ("Shall We Let France Be Carved Up?").

In 1942, in exile in New York, I published a work, *Français, voici la Vérité!* ("Frenchmen, Here Is the Truth!"), intended to supply Frenchmen who had escaped from the German hell with an analysis of the causes of the disaster, and to turn them from the shameful policy of Pétainism.

Here, in *I Accuse De Gaulle,* I am trying to expose one of the most fantastic impostures in history.

De Gaullism was born out of the mental turmoil and derangement of a tremendous moral and political earthquake. But it is also the fruit of ignorance.

When De Gaulle arrived in London in 1940, he was known neither to the French nor to the British. All they knew about him was his name and his rank. Only a few specialists had heard of his books.

That a man should suddenly spring from nowhere and play a leading role on the world stage is in itself an amazing and frightening anomaly. The origins, background, failures, successes, ideas

talents, defects, blemishes, behavior—the whole personal life of
public men is supposed to be public property. The more difficult
and painful the time, the more thoroughly familiar should the
people be with those who lead them. Especially since revolutionary
periods are marked by the violence of intemperate and abnormal
natures amid mass excitement and madness.

Nothing was known, then, about Charles de Gaulle, about his
really remarkable intelligence, nor about his dark and melancholy
temperament, his fits of raving fury, his fierce obstinacy coupled
with an astounding egocentric instability.

In addition, the De Gaullist phenomenon developed among extravagant circumstances and in places separated by enormous distances or by the impenetrable barriers raised by the war. When De
Gaulle had already begun to be known to the French and British
in London, and to arouse fanatical devotion there as well as growing apprehensions, he was still unknown in New York, Cairo,
Beirut, Brazzaville, and Buenos Aires. He was even less well-known
in France. When the Americans landed in Algiers, they knew very
little about him. His fame was the result of mass infatuation created
by propaganda and kept alive through ignorance. This ignorance
set him almost above the human plane. In certain circles—among
women and very young people—De Gaullism had already taken
on the delirious and morbid forms characteristic of ideological and
religious revolutions. A subtle historian wrote: "It is a revival of
the convulsionaries of Saint Médard." *

Later, when De Gaulle arrived in Paris in the Allied train, the
forty million liberated Frenchmen were steeped in similar ignorance
and some were smitten by the mystical madness. The more reasonable mistook De Gaulle for a reincarnation of Bayard and Du
Guesclin, for the man who had caused liberating armies to come
forth from exile, who had been the faithful friend of the Allies, who
would root out in France the last vestiges of collaborationism, the

* Well known in the seventeenth century for their mystic fanaticism.

Cagoulards and fascism. Still later, when Germany was invaded and the French captives were freed, they emerged from the dark ness of their prisons acclaiming a man whom they did not know. The first exclamation of a Léon Blum, of an Edouard Herriot, of a Paul Reynaud, of hundreds of thousands of captives and slaves loosed from their chains, was: "Long live De Gaulle!"—addressed to the supposed author of their liberation, the supposed savior of France. Clouds of ignorance followed upon each other, mingling with the growing clouds of fanaticism. Borne by them, the false legend continued on its way. And General de Gaulle continued his incredible career of adventurer, plundering the prestige and the glory of other men's heroism, in the midst of the staggering reversals of fortune brought by the liberation of France.

Let us examine the facts with the cold, austere glance of the historian. He delivered a speech and performed an admirable deed on June 17, 1940. That is all. To the sound of cheers he entered Brazzaville—where a handful of colonial office-holders and soldiers had seized power before his arrival. Later, in 1941, he entered Beirut in triumph—after the English and a small group of Frenchmen commanded by De Larminat had won without him. Still later, he entered Tunis as a conqueror—after the Americans and Giraud had liberated North Africa without him. Later yet, he entered Ajaccio under a rain of flowers—after some contingents of the African army had freed Corsica without him. Following that, he landed in Normandy—after the Americans had taken the beaches, the villages and the towns by storm, still without him. A swarm of propagandists and unprincipled politicians preceded or accompanied him. He had himself welcomed with applause by the wretched populace and ordered a banquet at Bayeux—where the American dead still lay unburied. Later, he entered Paris—behind the tanks of Eisenhower and the Leclerc division. There he had himself proclaimed as "France's First Resister," and paraded under the Arc de Triomphe, erected in honor of Napoleon, the giant of France's military epics. The defeat of France, the victories of the Allies, and the heroism

of a handful of Frenchmen had given him a miraculous opportunity
to create a legend and to build an astonishing political career.

In June, 1940, I was the only French political figure in exile who
had really known Charles de Gaulle before the war.

I had a feeling of friendliness toward him mixed with fear. I
enthusiastically applauded his first moves. I sent him frequent reports from New York. I was the chief founder of *Pour la Victoire*,
the French exiles' newspaper in New York, and its political head,
from January, 1942, to November, 1944. For a long time I was an
ardent De Gaullist.

But when I discovered the Cagoulard character of De Gaullism,
when, beyond the shadow of a doubt, I had taken the measure of
De Gaulle's plans, when I clearly saw the dangers he implied for
France and for America, I became anti-De Gaullist. And I tried
to open the eyes of the French and American publics. *Pour la Victoire* was quite a small newspaper. But it was the most important
of all those published in exile. It penetrated everywhere in the countries at war.

Soon De Gaulle banned it in Algeria and in the liberated colonies.
And the Cagoulards began a fierce struggle to prevent me from
telling the truth and breaking down the wall of ignorance which
was indispensable to their seizure of power. They threatened me
with all sorts of vengeance, encircled me with slanders, lies, rumor
campaigns, tried to start a financial scandal about the funds I had
brought from France—which I have already mentioned—accused me
of "being in the pay of the State Department," of having turned
over names of patriots to the Germans—in sum, of being a traitor.
On the day of the liberation of Paris, they induced a French minister to threaten me with the fate of Laval and Déat—the firing
squad.

Naturally, I refused to be intimidated. Throughout all of 1943 and
1944, *Pour la Victoire* denounced the De Gaullist menace.

Unfortunately, I was not the owner of the paper. Here is the essential provision in the contract that bound me to the trustee—that is to say, to Geneviève Tabouis:

> In consideration of the moral and material contribution of M. Henri de Kerillis to the society since its organization, and in view of the exceptional advantages derived by the society from the collaboration of M. de Kerillis with the newspaper, *Pour la Victoire*, the society agrees to publish immediately upon their receipt the articles of M. de Kerillis, just as they are sent in, without any change to which he does not consent, on the first page of each number of the paper, *Pour la Victoire*, with the same introduction as those previously published. It is clearly understood that M. de Kerillis remains, and will remain, the sole judge of the contents of his articles for the duration of the present contract, which is to run for three years from this date.

With such a contract in my hands, I felt it unnecessary to start another newspaper. The "exceptional" position I had held in launching this one had been recognized. My independence had been proclaimed. I was "sole judge" of all that I might write, and, in addition, I thought I had a moral pledge that Mme. Tabouis would scrupulously respect the spirit and the letter of our contract.

However, no sooner was the success of De Gaulle assured in Paris than Geneviève Tabouis undertook to convince me that I ought to stop criticizing him, even though in the past she had herself published violently anti-De Gaullist articles in several small papers to which she contributed. In this she was supported by her managing editor, one Poberesky, who chose to call himself Michel Pobers.

This undercover battle took place inside the only paper that could publish the truth. The De Gaullists knew that. In October-November of 1944 De Gaulle sent the Cagoulard leader, Passy, to New York for the purpose of exploring every means by which he could get rid of my campaigns, which were becoming more formidable since numerous Frenchmen in France had established contact with America.

Then—by a coincidence which is, to say the least, extraordinary—the following events took place:

—On November 25, 1944, Mme. Tabouis followed my weekly

anti-De Gaullist article with a criticism of the paper's management.

—On December 2 she rejected my reply to her criticism, although I was recognized by contract as the "sole judge" of my articles.

—In the following issues she praised De Gaulle, declaring that "he has deserved well of the country."

A few days later, to replace me, she appointed Jules Romains, former associate of the Count de Brinon, former signer of the "plan of the 9th of July," in 1937.

After that, she left happily for Paris and paid visits to the leaders of De Gaullism.

My voice was silenced.

I wish to express no rancor in saying these things, and I should have refrained from mentioning so personal an incident in a book devoted to so serious a subject were it not that the strong-arm tactics of *Pour la Victoire* had profound repercussions in the history of De Gaullism.

If, during the year preceding the French elections I had been in a position to publish, in New York, what I knew about the De Gaullist adventure, had I been able to display the facts and the evidence before the many travelers who came to America from France in 1945, the French would not have gone to the ballot boxes blindfolded, in total ignorance of the events that took place during their captivity. From the shores of America, a tiny flame of truth flickering beside the Statue of Liberty would have filtered through to them.

Now it will be difficult, terribly difficult, to root out De Gaullism from French minds and, above all, to remove De Gaulle from the position of power which he usurped when France was liberated.

Thanks to the progress of science, thanks to the technique of propaganda, thanks to the crisis created by extreme specialization at the expense of culture among the top layers of society, modern tyrants possess unlimited means to enslave the people. Whoever can get control of the radio through seizing the State apparatus, whoever has the opportunity to organize a force of political police and set up concentration and torture camps, becomes virtually ineradicable. Philosophers who announced that the twentieth century would see the emancipation of the masses were wrong. The twentieth century is the century of the enslavement of the masses. In former times, the people could readily revolt against the forces, armed with pikes and breechloaders, which guarded the positions of power. To fight for freedom, all the people had to do was to find some pikes and breechloaders of their own. Ragged women dragged a King of France from the palace at Versailles and led him a prisoner to Paris. But one cannot fight on equal terms with a police force equipped with rocket guns, poison gas, supertanks, to say nothing of the limitless resources of lying propaganda. How can ragged women, how can revolutionary crowds, readily pluck De Gaulle from the *Palais de l'Elysée?*

Consider the examples of Germany and Italy. The German and Italian peoples were at no time able to shake off the chains that bound them to their tyrants. They were forced to follow their bewitched, defeated, and hunted hangmen into the depths of misery, into the depths of the grave. It was finally necessary for Hitler and his gangsters to commit suicide, since seventy million Germans did not succeed in putting them to death.

De Gaulle, too, is on a psychological slope that condemns him to embark upon the most extravagant enterprises rather than risk a failure. For a failure might mean that he would have to render an account, a personal account and an account of his party.

But a dictatorship freely employs devices quite as effective as the weapons invented by scientists. The old adage "Divide and Rule" always holds good. The classical method used by all tyrants is to create and to maintain situations that are at once ambiguous and confused, bordering upon disorder and anarchy.

And it was inevitable that De Gaulle should devise means of complicating and corrupting the political life of France. Instead of creating a party of his own, his followers infiltrated existing parties. There were De Gaullists among the conservatives and the liberals, the Christian-socialists and the socialists. This boring from within is similar to the prewar tactics of the Cagoulards and the Hitlerites; in the old parliament such men as Philippe Henriot, Xavier Vallat, and Tixier-Vignancourt were conservative or clerical Hitlerites, Montigny was a radical Hitlerite, Déat and Marquet socialist Hitlerites, Bergery a Hitlerite of the extreme left, and Doriot a convert from communism to Hitlerism.

The tactics used by De Gaulle during the elections of October 21, 1945, throw fresh light upon his ability to confuse the issue.

First, he insisted upon Proportional Representation, which has been repudiated by the democracies in Great Britain and America because it inevitably tends to foster the growth of minorities and prevents the formation of stable majorities.

Then at the polls voters found upon their ballots a number of technical questions specially designed to cover up an indirect plebiscite. They were not asked whether they wished to elect General de Gaulle, but whether they wanted to revert to the Constitution of 1875 (which had been abolished), and their reply, which could easily be anticipated, was then interpreted as a triumph for the general. Frenchmen weren't given a clear-cut choice between two candidates as the Americans were when they chose between Roosevelt and Dewey, or the English between Churchill and Attlee: De Gaulle had no opponent; he wasn't even supposed to be a candidate . . . but he was, and everyone knew it.

In these elections the electorate was asked to vote for deputies without knowing whether they would be "constituent" deputies elected for seven months, or "legislative" deputies elected for four years.

In all history there is no record in any country of such well organized electoral intricacies.

In the end, the elected Chamber of Deputies found itself to be a constituent, not a legislative, chamber. Divided into four groups— communist, socialist, MRP, and moderate—the Chamber elected De Gaulle by the unanimous vote of its 555 members, for it was powerless to select as head of the government a member of any one of the four groups. . . . And everything had gone according to plan.

After these elections the tragic situation in which France found herself became immediately apparent.

It was all too clear that the task of fashioning a new constitution had been entrusted to an assembly split into irreconcilable factions, composed of new men devoid of political experience, incapable of seeing this tremendous undertaking through to a successful conclusion. And this General de Gaulle must have foreseen.

With such an assembly any number of possibilities now lie before him.

He can allow the assembly to moulder in its own powerlessness.

He can use its lack of power to maneuver it hither and yon; he can frighten it and play up its dissensions.

He can discredit it and rouse the people against it, thus reinforcing his personal authority.

And, in last analysis, having used and discredited it, he can force the assembly to accept a constitution of his own devising.

The inevitable conflict between the general and the Communists is now out in the open. That this conflict should have arisen is not surprising, for the sequence of events today is astonishingly reminiscent of events that occurred during the French Revolution of 1793. At that time the king, Louis XVI, had been condemned to death for having collaborated with the Austrians, and the monarchy had been abolished. Today Marshal Pétain has been condemned to death for having collaborated with the Germans (though his sentence was commuted to life imprisonment because of his great age), and the Third Republic has been abolished. In 1793 two factions, the Girondins and the Montagnards, made common cause to accomplish their destructive and bloody mission, but afterward the Montagnards drew away from the Girondins and a merciless struggle for power ensued. The same pattern is being followed today by the De Gaullists and the Communists.

Nonetheless, a large majority of public opinion in France and abroad turns toward De Gaulle in the belief that he represents the only salvation from communism. The reverse is closer to the truth: De Gaulle has created and perpetuated conditions propitious to the spread of communism. Instead of entrusting the reform of the constitution to the old, legally constituted Chambers, composed of experienced men whose tone was relatively moderate, he has entrusted the reform to an assembly elected in an atmosphere of fever and revolutionary violence, and the assembly is dominated by the Communists, for their group is numerically the strongest party. Furthermore, De Gaulle is responsible for the opening of the breach through which the Communists are now rushing, for they are profiting by the dissensions and the disorders, the confusion and the instability, which he created and expected to use to his own advantage.

The argument which attempts to present De Gaulle as the protector of France against communism is exactly the same argument which was used to present Hitler and Mussolini as the saviors of Germany and Italy from communism. And it is impossible for an adventurer masquerading as the Indispensable, the Providential Man, to check the tremendous ideological, social and revolutionary drive of communism.

The concept of the Indispensable, Providential Man is the last recourse of societies which have lost faith in great ideas; the last recourse of decadent and foundering societies: it is the barbarous vision of a Man-God who must be blindly followed, whose presence does away with the need for independent thought, the need to understand or to struggle; behind this symbol faltering leaders hide.

Can a Miracle-Man, alone out of forty millions, save France? If so, doesn't this imply that these forty millions are incompetent and politically bankrupt? And what would their fate be if this unique individual were to die?

This, certainly, is a Fascist concept in all its amplitude. This is the concept which World War II sought to abolish; a concept which, if it persists, might well lead to dramatic deceptions and to catastrophe.

In order to overcome communism it is necessary first of all to restore faith in order, in legality, in morality—and this faith De Gaulle has destroyed.

In order to combat communism one must have reason on one's side.

The Communists were reasonable when, before the war, they demanded a Franco-Russian alliance and maintained that the only continental power capable of smashing the German war machine was the USSR. And the irreparable error of the French bourgeoisie was that it left to the Communists the privilege of proclaiming this self-evident truth.

The Communists are right today when they denounce General de Gaulle as the supporter of the Cagoulards and of fascism. And the *bourgeois* will be committing another irreparable blunder if they allow the Communists alone to proclaim this truth (this, in a sense, is why this book is being written by a *bourgeois*, who is anything but a Communist).

De Gaulle is far from being the protector of France against communism. At first he may score a few successes, he may organize ephemeral anti-communist coalitions, but in the end he will plunge France into communism.

A public man examining the development of events resembles a physician diagnosing a disease of the human body. He explores, he analyzes, he looks as deeply as he can. Then he reflects, and makes his diagnosis.

Now, it seems to me beyond doubt that De Gaullism is a phenomenon originating in fascism. It is a political movement born at a time when Nazi ideology was victorious in France and in the rest of Europe. It is the Pétainism of the exile. The German armies have been defeated. But German ideas have not. They are adapting themselves to the new situation. Under many guises they have found a lodgement in the Allied victory.

De Gaullism is a form of fascism that placed its stakes on the winning side. It is a fascism that glibly uses the language of Democracy, while despising and hating it. It is a fascism that digs into the structure of the Republic as Italian fascism, at an earlier date, dug into the Monarchy.

This book was written in exile.

A journalist and a parliamentary Deputy, I could not return to France where journalists are muzzled, where Parliament is closed down, where the radio is monopolized, where I could neither speak, nor write, nor guide the French public.

De Gaulle could only fight the Pétainist error in exile; no one could have fought it at Vichy—I can only fight the De Gaullist error in exile, for no one could publish in Paris what I have been able to print in the blessed land of America, on the beloved soil of Canada, on the great victorious continent where men are still free.

To accomplish a useful, necessary, and noble task, I have refused to join the upstarts of the defeat; I have sacrificed my political career; I have renounced all hope of stating my case before my constituents. I have accepted the lengthening of my exile in the autumn of my life, when the years count double. I have put off, perhaps for a long time, the moment when I shall kiss the soil of my fatherland, which I left more than five years ago, to escape the Gestapo. Victor Hugo said after nineteen years of exile: "I have remained an outcast in order to remain erect and defy tyranny. That is well worth while!"

Yes, it is worth while.

It has been painful to write this book. Above all, it has been painful to think of those who might be hurt by it, of the irritation it might cause those sincere people who caught hold of De Gaullism in June, 1940, in a superb revolt of injured honor, in pure and selfless patriotic enthusiasm. While writing this book, I have never forgotten them.

I have kept my attention riveted upon the millions of Frenchmen who heard the appeals of the Unknown Man during the hours of darkness and despair; upon the heroes of the military epic in which De Gaulle never participated; upon the legionaries of Bir Hacheim;

upon the sailors of the *Surcouf;* upon the aviators and parachutists of the London squadrons; upon the titans of the Resistance who fought and died on the defiled soil of France.

How could I have escaped being obsessed by the fear of inflicting shock or injury, when my own son was killed in the De Gaullist ranks, after discovering, it is true, that it was a great political mystification?

But we political men must be able to overcome the most affecting and most highly valued sentiments. We have no right to allow the masses to be plunged into myths, illusions, and lies. We have a sacred task to fulfill, a hard and austere priesthood. Above everything else, we must be the priests of Truth.

France fell very low as a result of the machinations of politicians and demagogues. I have written this book in order not to act as they acted. I have written it in order to be worthy of an epoch of sacrifice, of tears and of blood, the like of which the world has probably never seen before: to be worthy of great America that granted me asylum in my misfortune, while she was rescuing the conscience of mankind: to be worthy of my beloved France, through aiding her by my humble testimony to achieve her liberation.

October, 1945

Index

Lightning Source UK Ltd.
Milton Keynes UK
UKHW021857270521
384511UK00002B/180